Chain letters

Chain letters

Narrating convict lives

edited by Lucy Frost and
Hamish Maxwell-Stewart

MELBOURNE UNIVERSITY PRESS

Melbourne University Press
PO Box 278, Carlton South, Victoria 3053, Australia
mup-info@unimelb.edu.au
www.mup.com.au

First published 2001

Designed and typeset in 9.5 point Slimbach by Melbourne University Press
Printed in Australia by Brown Prior Anderson

National Library of Australia Cataloguing-in-Publication entry

Frost, Lucy, 1941- .
Chain letters: narrating convict lives.
Bibliography.
Includes index.
ISBN 0 522 84977 6.
1. Convicts—Australia—Biography. 2. Australia—History—1788–1851. I. Maxwell-Stewart, Hamish. II. Title.

994.020922

Dedicated to the transported men and women, girls and boys, whose names and stories have vanished from cultural memory

and to these convicts whose lives have been the subject of our narrating:

Alexander Anderson
Richard Bankin
George Barrow
Thomas Brain
James Brown
Simon Brown
Rebecca Bull
Jack Bushman/Thomas Brooks
Margaret Catchpole
Eliza Churchill
Margaret Connor
George Cooley
Ellen Cornwall
Ann Davis
James Davison
Michael Duggan
Thomas Francis
Sophia Frayer
James Gemmell
John Goff/Gough
John Hawes
George James
Warren Kerr
Mark Kirk
Theodore Krakouer
Lewis Lazurus
Bridget Magahan
Maria
Henry Marson
Margaret Martin
John Masters
William Mollett
George Molyson
John Frederick Mortlock
Mary Odeland
Catharine Owens
Elizabeth Phillips
James Porter
John Sanderson
Ellen Scott
Alexander Simpson
Stephen Smith
Elizabeth Studham
Richard Taylor
Adelaide de la Thoreza
James Hardy Vaux

Contents

Illustrations

The illustrations on pages 20, 24, 52, 84, 139, 140 and 186 are by Simon Barnard.

Acknowledgements

Research for this book was undertaken with the assistance of the Australian Research Council. We are grateful to the many library and archival staff who have helped the contributors, and would like to extend special thanks to the staff of the Archives Office of Tasmania who have put up with persistent questions from many of the contributors attempting to navigate through the voluminous records of colonial Van Diemen's Land.

During the process of turning an idea into a book, nothing is more important than working with a sympathetic editorial and production team. From our first contact with Melbourne University Press, we have been confident that Teresa Pitt as the commissioning editor understood our project, and we thank her for her support. Gabby Lhuede has been unfailingly helpful as she steered us through the production process. We owe special debts of gratitude to Ev Beissbarth, who edited the manuscript, and to Kerry Biram for the index.

Raymond Evans and William Thorpe acknowledge the assistance of Denis Cryle, Jacqui Donegan, Rod Fisher, and Jennifer Harrison in the preparation of chapter 2. Susan Ballyn and Lucy Frost (chapter 6) acknowledge the generosity of Joan Smith and Jean Waugh who shared with them their research into the families of Adelaide de la Thoreza and J. B. L. d'Arrieta. Eleanor Conlin Casella and Lucy Frost thank Irene J. Hyde for permission to publish Ellen Cornwall's letter in chapter 7, and express their deep gratitude to Carol Richardson-Bunbury, Honorary Secretary, The Friends of Lawrence House Museum, Launceston, Cornwall, who organised a network of researchers to look for Ellen and Frederick Cornwall.

Tina Picton Phillipps (chapter 9) records her thanks to Sandra Connelly, who generously shared her research into the Bankin family's history. Bruce Hindmarsh acknowledges gratefully the assistance of Bernadette Trotter, Hobart College, Tasmania, who drew to his attention the letters forming the basis of chapter 11. He thanks Bruce Jackson, County Archivist, Lancashire Record Office, for permission to publish extracts from the letters, and extends his appreciation as well to Todd Crawford, Archives Office of Tasmania, and to the staff of the Lancashire Record Office; the City Reference Library, Preston; and the York Library, Reference Section, York.

The editors would like to thank Simon Barnard for his meticulous and thoughtful map-making, Tony Stagg for his impeccable proofreading, and above all, extend their appreciation to Fiona Polack, who kept chaos at bay.

Contributors

SUSAN BALLYN is a Senior Lecturer at Barcelona University and Executive Director of the Australian Studies Centre there. Her recent publications include *Douglas Stewart: A Bibliography* (with Jeff Doyle) and *Imagining Australia: A Handbook for European Students* (with John Barnes).

JAMES BRADLEY is a Research Fellow at the Wellcome Unit for the History of Medicine at the University of Glasgow. He contributed to *Convict Love Tokens*, and is the co-editor with Ian Duffield of *Representing Convicts*.

ELEANOR CONLIN CASELLA is a Lecturer in Colonial Archaeology at the University of Manchester. She contributed to B. Voss and R. Schmidt, *Archaeologies of Sexuality*; co-edited *Archaeology and Cultural Landscapes of Confinement*, a special issue of *Australasian Historical Archaeology*, and published *Archaeology of the Ross Female Factory*.

PAUL DONNELLY is a Curator of Decorative Arts and Design at the Powerhouse Museum, Sydney. He curated the highly successful exhibition 'Convict Love Tokens' mounted at Hyde Park Barracks in 1997, and is a contributor to *Convict Love Tokens*.

IAN DUFFIELD is a member of the History Department at the University of Edinburgh, and former President of the British Australian Studies Association. He has published extensively on convict history, and with James Bradley edited *Representing Convicts*.

RAYMOND EVANS is a Reader in History at the University of Queensland. He has published widely on Australian social history, war and society, race and ethnic relations, gender relations, convict historiography, and popular culture. His latest publications are *Fighting Words: Writing about Race* and *Pursuing the Popular*, a special all-Australian issue of the *Journal of Popular Culture* (US), edited with Clive Moore.

LUCY FROST is Professor of English at the University of Tasmania, and has published extensively in the area of Australian literature. Her books include *No Place for a Nervous Lady, A Face in the Glass, The Journal of Annie Baxter Dawbin 1858–1868, Those Women Who Go To Hotels* (with Marion Halligan), and *Wilde Eve: Eve Langley's Story.*

BRUCE HINDMARSH is a PhD candidate at the University of Edinburgh, where he teaches history. His thesis is concerned with assigned convict rural labour in Van Diemen's Land.

HAMISH MAXWELL-STEWART is a Lecturer in History at the University of Tasmania. A graduate of the University of Edinburgh, he edited and contributed to *Exiles of Empire*, a special issue of *Tasmanian Historical Studies*, and was a contributor to *Convict Love Tokens* and *Representing Convicts*.

TIMOTHY MILLETT is a former director of the international firm of numismatists A. H. Baldwin and Sons Ltd. His private collection of convict love tokens was the subject of a recent exhibition which was mounted at Hyde Park Barracks, Sydney, before travelling to various locations including the British Museum. He was both a contributor to and an editor of *Convict Love Tokens*.

TAMSIN O'CONNOR is a PhD candidate at the University of Edinburgh. She has published several articles on the penal stations of Newcastle and Moreton Bay and is a contributor to *Representing Convicts*.

TINA PICTON PHILLIPPS is a PhD candidate at the University of Edinburgh, where she teaches history. She is a contributor to *Representing Convicts*.

CASSANDRA PYBUS is a Senior Fellow of the Australian Research Council, appointed jointly in History and English at the University of Tasmania. She is the founding editor of the e-journal *Australian Humanities Review*, and the author of seven books. Her most recent, *The Devil and James McAuley*, won the 2000 Adelaide Festival Award for Non-Fiction.

WILLIAM THORPE teaches at the University of South Australia. He has published in the areas of industrial sociology, the State in Australia, oral history, Aboriginal history, Queensland historiography and environmental history, and is the author of *Colonial Queensland: Perspectives on a Frontier Society*.

TERRI-ANN WHITE runs the Institute of Advanced Studies at the University of Western Australia. For many years she was an independent bookseller. She is the author of *Night and Day*, a collection of short fiction, and of a novel, *Finding Theodore and Brina*.

Introduction

Lucy Frost and Hamish Maxwell-Stewart

This is a book about narrating convict lives. Its stories are of loss and hope, escapes and acts of fraud, love and betrayal, power, wit and imagination. Our aim has been to find out what happened to some of the many thousands of men and women sentenced by British courts to be separated from their family and friends and sent to a penal existence on the other side of the globe. We began with accounts of incarceration written and told by ex-convicts, thinking that about a hundred such tales, all authored by men, had survived the ravages of time. For 'convict accounts' we were unconsciously assuming 'convict narrative', a sub-genre of autobiography and fiction. We were academics, trained within disciplines, and thinking within our institutional frames. 'Convict narrative' meant 'document' to an historian, and 'text' to a literary critic. And then, we made a simple decision: change 'convict narrative' to 'narrating convict lives'.

The effect of this change was instantaneous. Lists of convict names transformed themselves into a vast crowd of characters, each with a story. Pick a name, follow its thread through the archives, and weave a tale. Now women and children could join the narrating men, and the literate who wrote join the illiterate who could not. But how to put faces to individuals in the crowd without losing sight of the crowd itself? Remembering Chaucer's *Canterbury Tales* was a help. The fourteenth-century poet evoked vividly the motley crowd on its yearly pilgrimage from London to Canterbury, and yet the tales were attributed to individuals: a knight, prioress, clerk, miller, nun, pardoner, merchant, parson, the wife of Bath. *Chain Letters* too offers individual stories of often idiosyncratic figures who shared a collective experience—transportation. Many of them, as might be expected, began their lives in England, Ireland, Scotland, and Wales. Some came from places which surprised us: the Bay of Honduras (Belize), the Congo, British Honduras, Jamaica, Demerara (Guiana). We have an American from upstate New York, a Spanish woman born in Madrid, a Jew from Poland. Even convicts born and bred within the United Kingdom and speaking English would have sounded foreign to each other: the Irish farm-worker from County Mayo (whose mother tongue was probably the Gaelic) would have been barely comprehensible to a handloom-weaver from England's industrial midlands, a nursemaid from Glasgow, or a law clerk from London. When the convicts whose lives we narrate arrived at their place of exile, they were required to identify themselves as workers. According to the records, our transportees included cabinetmakers and cooks, lots of farm hands and household servants (both women and men), a solicitor, a law clerk, a fly-boat driver. There were handloom-weavers, milliners, needlewomen, and dressmakers; industrial labourers and blacksmiths, brick-makers, caulkers, and carpenters; a tailor, shopman, painter; sailors and soldiers, and a beer machine maker.

The crimes for which they were transported span a similar range of the expected and unlikely. Many had been convicted of stealing fairly small personal items: an umbrella, sheets and blankets, a glass decanter, handkerchiefs (sometimes silk), and things to wear—boots, shoes, gowns, apron, petticoats, nightgown, shift, frill. One man more ambitious than most had gone for eight diamond rings, another for a gig and harness, another for three swords and a gun. As well as money, women had stolen seals, watches and a watch-key 'from the persons' of men who in some cases were probably clients, although prostitution was not itself illegal, and the sweeping assumption that all convict women were prostitutes is prejudice, not fact. Some convicts had been done for receiving stolen goods, uttering base coin (counterfeiting), forgery, fraud. These crimes were ordinary, run of the mill. A few charges stand out: the black woman in her teens transported for murder, the soldiers court-martialled for desertion from posts across the empire, four men convicted of piracy on the high seas, one of inciting slaves to rebellion, several with invading Canada. Once in Australia, there would be further convictions for bushranging, and the harbouring of bushrangers. Our project in *Chain Letters* is not to argue for these convicts as innocents or victims, but rather to follow women and men compelled to live within the social world created artificially through transportation.

We begin by dedicating our book to the convict cavalcade. The list of men, women, and children in the dedication initially will mean no more to most readers than to any of us who have peered into microfilm readers, casting our eyes down the columns of a ship's indent. There we could read information recorded for each transportee: convict number, name (with alias sometimes added), age, religion, marital status, native place, trade or calling, offence, where and when tried, sentence, height, complexion, colour of hair and eyes, distinguishing marks (including tattoos) and 'how disposed of'. Beneath most names, more numbers have been added in other hands, signposts to further documents in a convict career ending often with a ticket-of-leave and a subsequent certificate of freedom. Trace the numbers, and before long the story of a convict life begins to take shape. Names on a ship's indent become faces recognisable in the crowd. Names on the dedication's list will similarly, we hope, attach themselves to memorable characters within the narrated lives of *Chain Letters*.

We have searched high and low for pieces of their stories. Thanks to imperial Britain's penchant for record-keeping, caches of convict words survive. We have found words penned by men who thought that they were going to die—last words scrawled before the trap swung open and the jerk of the noose choked the final breath of air as it broke the prisoner's neck. In files of petitions to government departments, we have come upon words from men desperate to escape the choking noose—artful words designed to sway public and legal opinion. We have read words recorded during an official enquiry into the female factories, words from women who seized the unexpected opportunity of early release in exchange for their convict narratives. Letters have surfaced in England from convicts writing home, from transported step-brothers to their father, a penitent wife to the husband who had already taken her back more than once. Some literate convicts after they were freed wrote of the perils and humiliations of bondage, and published their accounts from home. Some of the autobiographical narratives remain unpublished in the manuscript collections of state libraries and archives. Others were reconfigured by prison reformers who, like their contemporaries in the movement to abolish slavery, were alert to the power of first-person witnessing. Stories told by ex-convicts were retold by those who listened, sometimes spiced up and published as ripping yarns with physical violence aplenty and the suspense of daring escape. Some of these stories made their way into fiction—one turns up often word for word in Marcus Clarke's convict saga, *For the Term of his Natural Life*. Every narrative or snippet of life we retrieve is constrained within technologies of penal power and inflected by the colonial politics of the period within which the words were written. And then there is the politics of survival. Records were kept, yes, but many were later destroyed, either wilfully or through neglect. Some narratives are retrievable because they were published in newspapers, but under what circumstances? How did the journalists make contact with the story-tellers? Who did the editing, and what assumptions were made about readers as the convict words were shaped for print? Thousands of letters were written by literate convicts for themselves or for those who could not write, precious letters posted from British gaols and hulks as well as from distant Australia—reminders that loved ones were not dead, that they had not slipped over the horizon into the abyss. A few of these letters were passed down the generations, sometimes losing the story of who the convict was and how the letter came into a family's possession. And then there are fragments of story never committed to paper. Convicts awaiting transportation to the other side of the world sent messages carved into coins as symbols and words, and enclosed these love tokens with letters or pressed them into palms of those bidding them farewell. Many prisoners wore bits of story on their own bodies as tattoos punctured into the skin with soot and gun powder, and recorded for posterity as identifying marks useful to those administering the penal system.

And what are we to make of the convict words and snippets of story we track down early in the twenty-first century? The intellectual challenge faced by anyone who wants to narrate convict lives is epistomological: what meanings can we legitimately attach to the documents (textual or material) which are the source for knowing the past? How can we narrate the lives of people long dead? As a conceptual problem, the issue is highly complex and theoretical, and often in chapters we make reference to the current intellectual debates within which we read and write. In *Chain Letters*, the theories enter the prose as methodology employed to address particular and practical problems, including authorship, authenticity, the conditions of textual production and their implications for meaning, the use of general data to elucidate particular instances or to account for gaps in the records. For our academic readers, the theoretical issues embedded within the specifics of narrating are signalled in the notes. We have tried to keep specialised language out of our prose, because we have enjoyed the detective work involved in research, and we want to share the pleasures of the chase.

These are pleasures we have increasingly come to share with each other, moving from the model of the single researcher to that of a collaborative venture. With this shift, the borders pushing research into the institutionally constructed disciplines of academe become much easier to cross, as do the boundaries separating academics from their colleagues working outside the university. Professionally, the contributors to *Chain Letters* are demarcated as historians, literary scholars, a curator, an archaeologist, a numismatist, and a novelist. Like the transportees of whom they write, their entries under 'native place' include the expected Australia, England, and Scotland, and origins less likely for this project—West Africa, Texas, California. Unlike the convicts coming together in the cramped quarters of a transport ship, the contributors to *Chain Letters* remain physically apart, living and working across Australia in Adelaide, Brisbane, Hobart, Launceston, Perth, and Sydney; across the United Kingdom in Edinburgh, Glasgow, London, Manchester, and North Wales; and—for the requisite unexpected—one of us is in Barcelona.

The vast physical distances separating us do pose obstacles which cannot be overcome by e-mail. Nothing replaces talking together in person, and that is one reason why conferences are invaluable. *Chain Letters* began at a conference, 'Colonial Eye', hosted by the University of Tasmania. At the same conference, the International Centre for Convict Studies was formed, a virtual centre with its website at http://iccs.arts.utas.edu.au/. The website includes some of the narratives mentioned in *Chain Letters*, and we would welcome from our readers any convict letters or other texts held in their private collections. The convict experience was just one stage in a life, and to follow the transportees from birth to death is to criss-cross the continents of North and South America, Europe, Africa, and Asia. Pieces of the puzzle are scattered across the globe, and in our research we have often depended upon the detective work of others. Family historians with the patience and determination to scroll through microfilm for hours have been invaluable to many of us, and we are grateful for the generosity with which they have shared their research.

There are at least as many stories told by convicts as there were transportees shipped to an antipodean exile. We say 'at least' because many convicts told their stories more than once, depending on their circumstances. This is a polite way of saying that at times they lied or were economical with the truth. This does not mean that such accounts should be put to one side as being of little historical worth—all autobiography is shaped to suit the purposes of its subjects. Our aim has been to uncover some of those purposes by exploring the conditions under which the transported laboured, and the strategies they employed to lessen physical and psychological loads. In short, *Chain Letters* is about that most crucial element in any detective work, the search for motive. We begin the search by examining what, for want of a better phrase, might be called conventional narratives, a mixture of published and manuscript stories varying in length from nine thousand to many tens of thousands of words. The chapters move to less stable texts, to tiny micro-narratives—a few words provided to the muster master, or scratched on a precious object of memory, or inked under the skin. Each story poses its own challenge as, from the First Fleet to the last, the condemned speak.

Prologue

Run-a-way Theodore: a fictional quest for roots

Terri-ann White

I am ghost-trading. Theodore's body in the dormitory dreaming of other times, dreaming of his life. A sleeping body, a mound on a mattress under a regulation blanket. There isn't much body left, only a skinny thing; not so much emaciated as worn down. The volume of the mound is child-size, but the length of his body is still there, five feet eight. He is going mad here and that is why he is hiding.

He stands up and moves away from the bed. His walk is like a dance in slow motion: he needs to find a balance and this he does in an elaborate sway, a complex signal system of four limbs. The head moving too, in counter rhythm to his body. *A straddling walk*. The year is, approximately, 1875.

If, out of respect to the dead and the still living, flesh and blood are banished in this account, and only the paths he took are shown, lines and paths and that is all, how will his journey be shaped? Will he look like a madman or a pioneer, a criminal or a father and grandfather? Ghosts must suffice; disembodied voices that spring from the belly. There are no other mementoes or objects carried down, none that I have found, aside from court notices in newspapers and a certificate of lunacy. His crimes always clever and playful; my memorial is made of the most precarious materials. This is the beginning of my research: the first artefacts are two letters and a certificate.

August 30 1873

To Honourable Colonial Secretary Perth

I have the honour to inform you I have this day, on certificate of Resident Magistrate and of this Medical Practitioner admitted Theodore Krakouer as a patient to the Fremantle Asylum.

I have obtained from his son, and now enclose to you an engagement to pay for the maintenance of patient during the time of his confinement as patient.

HC Barnett

744/160

September 24 1873

To Honourable Colonial Secretary

I have the honour to inform you that I have today in conjunction with the Colonial Inspector examined carefully into the medical condition of Theodore Krakouer, and as we are satisfied of his convalescence we recommend his discharge.

HC Barnett
744/160

LUNATIC'S CERTIFICATE

I, the undersigned, HC Barnett of Fremantle in the Colony of Western Australia, a medical practitioner of the said colony, and now in actual practice, hereby certify that I on the 10th day of October at Fremantle in the said colony personally examined Theodore Krakouer of Fremantle and that the said Theodore Krakouer is a Lunatic and a proper person to be taken charge of and detained under care and treatment, and that I have focused this opinion on the following grounds.

1st Facts indicating insanity and found by myself:

Delusion. Says he hears a voice operating from his belly giving him messages from God Almighty to destroy the world.

2nd Other facts indicating insanity communicated to me by other/s:

Has been drinking since he left the Asylum and is in a state of delusional excitement.

Dated 11 October 1873
HC Barnett

[Handwritten note at top of Certificate: Provided for the information of the Colonial Secretary. Krakouer is in Fremantle Jail by Section 42 of the Lunacy Act cannot be moved without the order of the Colonial Secretary.]

744/164

My life has proceeded viciously. My mind shaped and locked itself against these brutalities until now I am a shell of a man without even a functioning mind. Moments of lucid thought and then I'm gone. There is nothing neutral about life. I recall my parents in Cracow—this English you know is not my native tongue—and in their imagination Cracow was a haven, it was where we would rest at the end of our days. In the shtetl we were our community, autonomous, a complete community.

> *And God saw the wickedness of man was great in the earth, and that every imagination of the thoughts of his heart was only evil continually.*

And then we had to move, always moving, being chased from beloved places when foreign powers meddle in how we will live. In time we go to Berlin. This burden of our race. How I ended my days in this place when I started there—the burden of our race. My midnight breathing, the only time I pause and am not hot. An infernal heat. Bright sun beating down all year. And that fierce ice wind at night through Fremantle town just to remind you between day and night, cold and hot. There is nothing in the middle. The bush like Palestine—covered in Spring by beautiful green of grass and herbs and then soon scorched brown and parched as the heat and drought of summer comes. But always cold at night. Now these are the names of the children of Israel, which came into Fremantle; every man and his household came with Theodore.

Abraham, Phoebe, Rachael, Fanny, Sampson, Rudolph, Philip, Raphael, David. And all of the souls that came out of the loins of Theodore were many souls and they also numbered Samuel back in London, my forgotten son. Seven sons and three daughters I am responsible for.

> *There was a man in the land of Uz, whose name was Job; and that man was perfect and upright, and one that feared God, and eschewed evil. And there was born unto him seven sons and three daughters.*

The Times, London. October 18, 1848

CLERKENWELL—Charles Theodore Krokower, a German Jew, was placed at the bar for final examination, charged by Mr. George Joseph, diamond merchant and jeweller, of No. 19 Woodbridge street Clerkenwell, with stealing eight diamond rings value 47/-.

The prisoner, it may be recollected, called upon the prosecutor and, representing himself as a merchant in partnership with his brother, inspected some diamond rings, eight of which he selected and ordered to be sealed up in a box, and promised to return for them with the money changed for them; but, before he left the house, he dexterously contrived to substitute another box in lieu of the genuine one containing the rings, bearing an exact resemblance, and as he did not return with the money the box was subsequently opened and found to contain nothing but rags and two half-boiled potatoes. The prisoner was traced and apprehended at Bristol, but none of the property was found.

Benjamin Britton, a Bristol officer, produced a coat and cap which were found at the prisoner's lodgings, and were identified as being those worn by him on the day of the robbery. The prisoner, by the advice of Mr. Sidney, reserved his defence, and he was fully committed for trial on this charge.

> The prisoner was then charged by Mr. Robert Cooper Casper, tailor, of St. Mary Axe, with stealing a suit of clothes. The prisoner ordered the clothes, which were taken home by the prosecutor, when he put them on and said he could not pay until he got some French notes cashed, and he requested prosecutor to accompany him to a bullion office in Lombard Street. He walked with him as far as King William street, city, where the prisoner entered a house and escaped with the clothes, and he did not afterwards see him until he was in custody at the bar of this court. The clothes were now produced and identified by Mr. Casper. The prisoner was fully committed for trial on this charge. Other charges of a similar description were preferred against him, but they failed in legal proof; the parties, however, were left to indict at the sessions if they thought proper.

I look at the walls of limestone in this asylum, I sit and stare through long days. Think I have captured every detail, every rivulet, the cadence of a wall. And then after hours, days, months, I suddenly see a new component. Seen entirely for the first time. A pattern in the limestone, its colour at the different times of the day. The same with the symmetry of the windows on the asylum's north-facing wall, all the way up to the tower. The way that they have been placed, the logic of the pattern. I look and look at these things, the things around me, and I do it for my own comfort and to stay in the world. Because when I can notice a perfectly new thing after habituation then I know my mind still works.

I WAS EDUCATED IN THE PUBLIC SCHOOL OF BERLIN. That is what I told them in a loud voice in England in gaol when I was asked everything about myself. They wouldn't know our words for education and schools. But I attended the Yeshiva in Berlin, and I studied the Talmud. My father struggled to support me and I was a devoted student as long as I could be. We started early in the morning with prayers and used all of the day for studying the holy book. We students with the old men gathered around tables in the synagogue to ward off the melancholy of dusk. My study there didn't last long, but those lessons and that dedication to learning I have kept with me for all of these days since.

The voice in his belly was a noisy one: it forced him into places he hadn't before considered going. He heard it clear as day; it wasn't just an abstract thing. It moved up from his guts, his nether regions, and it spoke to him of various horrors. For a short time he thought he had been returned a king: remembering the kings of Israel, remembering how Ehud slashed the guts of Eglon because he was a bad king. He *said I have a message from God for you* and he thrust his sword into the king's *belly so that the hilt followed the blade, and the fat closed upon the hilt; he did not withdraw the sword from the belly, and the contents burst out.*

This voice. The sound of its imperfections. The carriage of a bronchial condition turned into sing-song and sometimes bellowing but always this sound coming up, up from the belly, plonk, right into the cache of what he knows. The sound of imperfection; always there was an echo, a rasping, gasping for air.

Having the voice so intimately attached made him lonely. A profound solitude this was, a ghostly walk through loss. It was an impediment. One day he decided he must counter this voice and become as loud as he could be. Block out everything with his own formidable sound. That was his control. He had become detached from everything ordinary, even the cadence of a voice in conversation.

> Can I get?
> out
> a master insistent pressing down on me every night
> telling me   over and over
> horrible   I never   thought such things   before
> killing and pulling it all apart
> it is the world   and he wants me to do it
> be his servant   do it for him he too meek   or scared
> up on top of this hill   looking down on free-mantle
> on the busy town   full of bastards   my children.
>
> Well well here we are and you aren't safe
> there's a lion in here for the ladies
> a big steel trap for the men   a bucket for the babies
> fires will roar through after   the disease has mangled anyone left
> I will kill   it must be done
>
> blood will flow   and then disaster
> we are finished
> a bad idea   this life.

There were good and bad convicts everywhere and that is probably why the trade in bodies ceased—it was too hard to make judgements and the community always wanted to do the judging. The colonists asked for a certain type of prisoner. They had a list: no men from Irish prisons; no hardened or serious criminals; none who would lower the moral tone of the colony; no men over forty-five years; no females. They had another list: able-bodied; well-conducted; guilty only of minor offences; with at least half a sentence still to serve. The British sent whomsoever they pleased, although the concession at the start was to send minor criminals to let the colony get used to their new demography, and then later to empty their gaols of hard cases and send them out to Western Australia. Change the offence on the convict papers if they needed to. Almost ten thousand men came in a period of eighteen years, along with Pensioner Guards and their families.

Words are wrapped around the picture. Hundreds of new bodies in the colony, rough-looking men. Everyone here can tell they have been locked up for a long time. These reminders of home, of light deprivation, of poor diets, although the food supply available to the average colonist is also not of a high nutritional count. When these men were despatched from the ship anchored out at Gage Roads and landed on firm ground after one hundred days at sea, they looked perplexed. Probably just getting used to the light that was a harsher pitch than the ocean-borne light because it was reflecting off limestone and sand.

For all the colonists, including these new ones who had not had a choice, there must have been a bedrock of common understandings and shared experiences. Even for the first to land in the colony, those founders. The idea of home, of Britain, of green and pleasant lands, of congested cities, of family and enterprise and, now, of immense travel. And probably, for all of them, the puzzling visage of the black man. Never had they seen anything as uncivilised.

Where did Theodore acquire his French currency, and when did he learn English? He was proficient in 1849 but, it is claimed, not the year before. My words are wrapped around a picture of Theodore in London, looking respectable and being the jewellery merchant; the German Jew who appears in court regularly, who travels around England purposefully.

Theodore had no distinguishing features, no tattoos or scars across his face. He was, after all, *a respectable looking German Jew* and a merchant as well. Although in that decade there was an intense debate about the value or otherwise of the science of phrenology, a debate that continued all of the century and into the next, there is no evidence that Theodore's skull was measured and any determination on his intelligence handed down.

This thing that happens, just on the edge of consciousness, usually in the responsible spaces of daily life. A blooming of romance, about the family, transmitted as an involuntary picture from memory, a tic. Appearing, reappearing, on the edge of things. Fleeting. Flashes that can catch you unawares. Driving through the city and, suddenly, after all the recent optimism, what you realise you want to do, split-second, is to keep driving, right down and into the river. Coming out of a dream filled with good advice, entwined with a warm and beloved body, and suddenly, there it is. One thing, a recognition. Sure to be dismaying: so little to learn from.

The inheritances of a past become mute, shamed into silence and stupidity. A childhood and then adulthood without the referents offered through blood. Without sticks and stones, those grand contretemps, noisy tantrums. Any conflict in this family has been patched over and nobody can remember any detail of the reasons for sisters refusing to speak to each other for the rest of their lives, for half a century. Left for dead, or for conjecturing, isolated, curious members of new generations. Like me.

Memory tics offer up outlines of bodies and events, of those stored distresses, a complicated sadness, and, uncannily, some pleasures. Reconstructions of the intricate lives of people you follow in a family. But also more instructional; from this I want to know about how mistakes, bad mistakes that teach you nothing after the first time, can be avoided.

I don't want to forget Theodore Krakouer and Brina Israel even if everybody else in the world already has. There is so little passed down that I have had to become a collector of shards; of memory, what might have been told to me at the end of this long line of tales. I want to catch these shards, these half-lit, often, paste jewels. I don't know how authentic they are, but that doesn't matter. I want to see what can be made anew and built from the remains. To honour the fleeting; the fragment, fractured histories and stories. None of this passed down; it all has to be dredged up.

This is me:
Man with funny whiskers   he's a Russian   a pole   a convict
a Hebrew man   a handsome man because he's so big—tall and
broad   that's good in this country—a big   broad country
Australia   with more opportunities than Krakow
London   Berlin   other places he lived   dealing prospecting
exploring   belonging with money one day a month   making money
wily   possibly not to be trusted—he once was a convict   he stole
clothes in London, England   left a wife and son and got himself a
new woman and had nine children   then he went mad

Lies, damned lies and convict narratives

1

'the d— Yankee quill-driver'

Cassandra Pybus

'I am an American Citizen—I am a British Slave!' wrote a desperate Linus Miller, a convict from New York State, in his retrospective account of penal servitude, *Notes of an Exile to Van Dieman's Land* [*sic*] published in New York in 1846.[1] Were it not a sin, Miller confided to his readers, '. . . I should have put an end to my existence, rather than endure the dreadful reality'.[2] And the reality *was* dreadful for Miller and the other ninety-one political prisoners, collectively known as 'the Patriot exiles', who had been transported to Van Diemen's Land in 1840 after being captured in armed incursions into the colony of Upper Canada. While some of this group had experienced periods of residency in both Canada and the United States, over 90 per cent of them were citizens of the United States. The British Ambassador to Washington hit the nail right on the head when he argued that 'the penalty of transportation is regarded with extreme terror by the Americans'.[3]

Presenting himself to the reader, Miller was very careful to cast himself as a radical republican in the mould of those great American heroes, Washington, Lafayette, Franklin, and John Adams. At the beginning of his narrative he explained how he had given himself over to the Patriot cause for a republican Canada after a visit to Niagara, the site of a major battle of the War of 1812. With the roar of the falls for backdrop he knelt upon the graves of the fallen and prayed for Canada 'that final success might crown the efforts of her sons, to emancipate her from British thraldom; . . . and there upon my knees, I dedicated myself to the cause, for life or for death, as Heaven might will'.[4]

This kind of flourish was typical of Miller, who was given to grandiloquent exaltation of the American republic and to flamboyant self-dramatisation. One suspects he was drawn to the Patriot cause more by his desire for heroic theatre than his grasp of the principles of good government. He wrote the whole business of the invasion of Canada at the Short Hills, and his subsequent capture, as a series of heroic adventures, casting himself as swashbuckling hero who faced down the venal Jacob Beemer, a fellow Patriot invader who had tried to hang a clutch of captured British soldiers. Miller

Upper Canadian State Prisoners in England, *by Edwin C. Gullett (from* The Lives and Times of the Patriots, *Toronto, 1938). Linus Miller is second from the left.*

evaded capture for some time by adopting a series of ingenious disguises—a republican version of the Count of Monte Cristo.

Describing his engagement with the failed Patriot escapade, Miller was not only giving voice to the popular doctrine of Manifest Destiny, he was also explaining the moral necessity for Americans to intervene on the Canadians' behalf, since decades of imperial government had so sapped the will of the Canadians that they lacked the capacity to help themselves.[5] To drive home this point Miller constructed a scene between himself and an Englishman who demanded to know what an American was doing taking up arms in Canada. Miller replied:

> What Right, my dear sir, had Lord Byron to go to Greece? . . . What right had General Evans and his seven thousand followers to go from this country to Spain? . . . Theirs was a parallel case; and yet you blame me for copying an example which your countrymen have ever been found ready to set.[6]

This bold response completely unnerved the poor man who turned deathly pale and bolted from the room, his own son having been killed in Spain. But as Miller was to learn to his cost '. . . Englishmen at once detect the mote in the eye of a brother while unconscious of a beam in their own'.[7]

All his vainglorious appeals to be considered another Lord Byron did him little good, although he was lucky enough to be chosen as a test case for a writ of *habeas corpus* taken by English radical reformers Joseph Hume and John Roebuck, before the Queen's Bench.[8] Even though the case failed, Miller's radical friends still held out hope that he would receive a free pardon. Not so, Miller bitterly recounted, regretting his faith in the British system of justice: 'We might as well have believed that his Satanic Majesty would engage in the Bible trade, as that the British Government would do an act of either justice or mercy . . .'.[9]

Separated from the main body of his compatriots, Miller had to endure the degradation of the Portsmouth hulks. Fellow Patriot Benjamin Wait, who had passed through the *York* hulk three months earlier, described how the system was designed to reduce a man to *thing*: stripped, shorn, and clothed in the hulk uniform, every article of which was marked with the broad arrow as 'a particular badge of disgrace', while the iron manacles were 'a token of unmitigated slavery'. Wait understood that the intention was 'to assimilate us, as much as possible to the condition, character and appearance of 'the world's most degraded wretches preparatory to their immersing us in [an] undistinguishable state of debasement'.[10]

For young Linus Miller, used to being treated with respect as a celebrated *habeas corpus* case, the regime of the hulk was a terrible indignity, but one which he was determined to face as a *man*. He may have been chained and in prison garb, but he had the advantage of being six feet tall:

> I observed that the convicts pulled off their hats, and when addressed by either captain or convict clerk, raised the fore finger of the right hand to the head, evincing the most abject obsequiousness . . . When [the captain] approached I stood stiff and erect, and as he was but a short man, looked down upon him with all the dignity and importance I could command. . . . I stared him full in the face, without doffing my hat, or intimating as much as 'your servant sir'.
>
> 'What is your name?', he demanded in a stern voice.
>
> 'My name is Linus Wilson Miller.'
>
> 'That is a long name? Pray what is your trade?'
>
> 'I never learned a trade.'
>
> 'Pray what have you learned that is good?'
>
> 'To respect myself.'
>
> 'Did you ever learn manners?'
>
> 'No! such kind of things come nat'ral in my country—all second nature; don't require to be taught.'
>
> 'Pray what uncivilized part of the earth do you claim as your country?'
>
> 'I am an American.' . . .
>
> 'What is your crime?'
>
> 'A virtue.'[11]

Miller was stripped, shorn and interrogated just like any other felon, in a process 'intended not only to torment the body, but to crush and destroy all those attributes which constitute the man as distinguished from the brute'.[12] He was obviously terrified by the experience. 'Despair, with his grim, ghastly visage, would sometimes haunt my spirit', he wrote, but he had 'too much pride to allow my enemies the satisfaction of crushing and breaking an American's spirit'.[13] And he did have spirit, firing off a number of letters to the captain of the hulk and to Lord John Russell, complaining that he was not being treated as a state prisoner, and instead:

> herded with the offscourings of England, indeed of the earth, compelled . . . to . . . a slavery far worse than has ever fallen to the lot of the Negro race in any age or part of the earth in consequence of the contaminating influences of the most revolting vices.[14]

His complaints drew a private visit from Mr Capper himself, but did not ameliorate his terrifying and humiliating situation.

As a fastidious young man of just twenty, he could well have been especially at risk from 'the most revolting vices'. Homosexual exploitation was the aspect of life on the hulks which most shocked and repelled him, both for its threat to his body and more particularly for the threat to his soul:

> Vice and crime of the most revolting nature, such as called down the vengeance of heaven upon ancient Sodom and Gomorrah, are prevalent to an alarming extent, . . . the natural results of herding depraved men together under such a system—a system which insures not only their entire ruin in this world, but, what is of far more importance, in that which is to come.[15]

Miller hatched a plan to escape. Unhappily, Beemer was on the same hulk trying to delay his departure to Van Diemen's Land. He got wind of the escape plan and promptly informed the authorities. So it was that in September 1840 Miller was put aboard the *Canton* for Van Diemen's Land. Here was even more indignity to be endured:

> . . . to me the prison was a floating hell! The most horrid blasphemy and disgusting obscenity, from daylight in the morning till ten o'clock at night, were, without one moment's cessation, ringing in my ears. The general conversation of these wretched men, related to the crimes of which they professed to have been guilty, and he whose life had been most iniquitous was esteemed the best man. I tried to close my ears and shut my eyes against all, but found this a difficult task. [16]

Miller was in no way inclined to complain about the ship's officers whom he admired for their good manners and who treated him with proper respect. In recognition of his education and good breeding he was made a teacher in the school established for the 'herd of criminals' on the ship, but his illiterate charges just melted away, leaving him with nothing to do but record his high-minded scorn for their antics:

> Loud talk, singing songs, spinning yarns, altercations, and fighting, were the order of the day the moment the wine was served out. I have often counted a dozen men settling their little quarrels at such times. A ring around the belligerent was always formed on these occasions by the 'lookers-on,' and seconds duly appointed to see *fair play*. The practice of fighting, among the lower classes of the English and Irish, is far more common than with my countrymen. Indeed, I do not recollect having seen but three or four instances of this disgraceful practice during my life in my own country.[17]

When he arrived in Van Diemen's Land, Miller's 'initiation into the mysteries of a penal colony' gave him to understand that he was no more than a slave, subject to the petty tyranny of Her Majesty's craven minions.[18] Summoned for an audience with Mr Gunn, Superintendent of Convicts, Miller was collected by a ticket-of-leave convict, who told him to 'Say "*sir,*" when you address *me*' and more to the point, 'When you go in, take off your cap, say *sir* when the clerks speak to you, and be sure and *help* Mr. Gunn.'[19] Affronted, the young law clerk entered the *sanctum sanctorum* of the *Canton* to see Mr Gunn seated at the table; before him was an immense register in which he was writing. Around him sat three clerks at work on an equally imposing set of leather-bound tomes. A barrage of questions commenced about every aspect of Miller's life and sentence. This procedure was designed to catch out those prisoners who gave misleading or false information since Mr Gunn had already been furnished the answers, thus ensuring that the data collected by the Convict Department was accurate. Every last detail was recorded in the leather-bound volumes which were ordered by ship and police number to aid retrieval.

As became clear to him, Miller's induction was meant to intimidate:

> I was ordered to pull off my shoes and stockings, which being done, the 'measuring rod' was applied. 'Stand up straight, no shrinking, no stretching.' My height was declared to be 'jest six feet.' I was then commanded to strip to the waist, and my person was closely scrutinized for any *marks* or *scars* by which I might be identified in case I became wicked and depraved enough to run away. After my head and face had been minutely described, 'that will do,' was pronounced in a condescending tone . . . [20]

Not only was he forced to parade before the gaze of Gunn who, as the tallest man in the colony, was able to look down on him, but he was disrobed by the sweeping of Britain's imperial gaols. The process was an utterly humiliating invasion of privacy which was to have a lasting impact on the young law clerk. When he later wrote about Gunn he imbued him with encyclopaedic powers of recall:

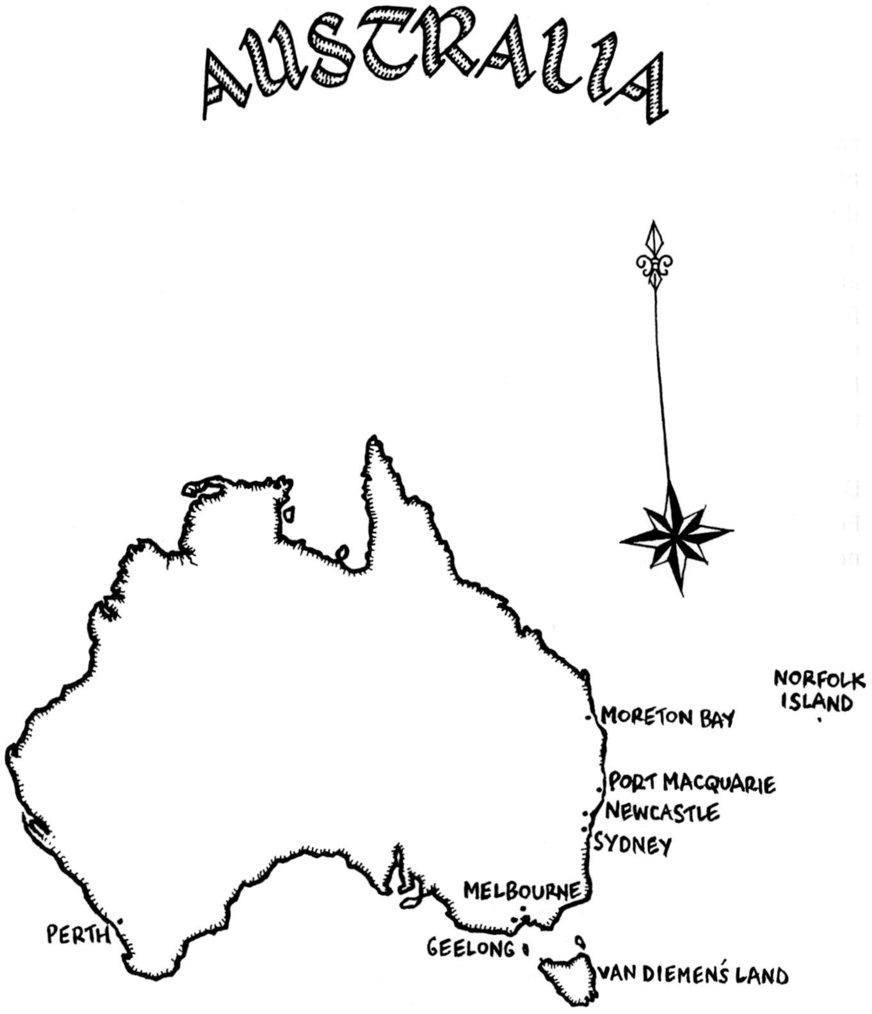
AUSTRALIA
NORFOLK ISLAND
MORETON BAY
PORT MACQUARIE
NEWCASTLE
SYDNEY
MELBOURNE
PERTH
GEELONG
VAN DIEMEN'S LAND

> He has only to see a prisoner once, to be able to detect him in almost any disguise for years afterwards. It is said he can call every prisoner in Van Dieman's Land by name, when he meets them, tell the name of the ship in which they arrived, the year and day, their original sentences, additional sentences received in the colony &c. &c.; in short, that he never forgets any thing. [21]

The description process complete, Gunn had merely to wait for an army of convict informers, policemen, overseers, superintendents, catechists, commandants and magistrates to provide the information which would flesh out the details of each convict life. Every scrap of information would be squirrelled away in the appropriate register to be consulted before any decision was made affecting the fate of a prisoner, whether the prisoner merited relief from suffering or an increased measure of pain. Governor Arthur had once described the operation of the convict system he had devised as a prison without walls. Instead of prison architecture, Miller felt himself to be incarcerated by William Gunn's elephantine memory and his elaborate cross-referenced registers.

But it was not Gunn who sat at the apex of imperial tyranny in Van Diemen's Land. That place was occupied by Lieutenant-Governor Sir John Franklin. Miller was merciless in his description of Franklin's address to the new intake of convicts from the *Canton*:

> Clad in his official garb, adorned with his star, and covered with his cocked cap and feather, no nabob of India could affect more dignity and importance . . . His height was, I should judge, about five feet nine inches; his circumference quite out of proportion, and clearly indicating, that however starved he might have been as 'Captain Franklin,' in his northern expedition, he had never been more fortunate in the south as governor of the land of Nod, . . . A short, thick neck, supporting a head of no ordinary size, really set off his broad shoulders to advantage; complexion dark; forehead broad, low, and standing back like an idiot's; eyes hazel, very large and dull; nose enormous; mouth very wide; chin prominent; these were the leading features of his Excellency. His countenance, altogether, was rather open, frank and honest; and I was not long in arriving at the conclusion that he was an imbecile old man; a paragon of good nature; with an excellent opinion of himself, and little wit to uphold it.

After many hums and haws, Franklin treated the *Canton*'s convict cargo to an absurd series of homilies, interrupted with much huffing and puffing:

> . . . his eyes were rolling in their sockets like those of a person undergoing the most excruciating agony. I did not wonder, for such a speech must naturally cost a great effort. . . . He then came and took up his

> position in front of myself . . . I remembered the justice of our cause, and I felt my American blood thrill through every vein of my system, as my eye caught his and steadily fixed his gaze. I know not how I looked at the time, but I felt that I myself was also a *man*; and that he who stood before me was no more! My soul was *upright* and my body stood *erect*. I had borne the past, I could bear the future.

Miller found himself the object of an unwelcome special interest by the governor once it was made clear that this convict was an American citizen:

> 'What! attempt to set up *your* institutions in Canada! Stir up *treason* and *rebellion* in her Majesty's dominions! Invade a country at peace with your own!—violate not only the laws of your own country, but those of England! *You* are an *extremely* bad man . . .' Here his Excellency appeared to be quite exhausted with the mighty effort he had made; . . . 'Be careful, sir, to restrain your evil propensities here. Your notions of liberty and equality must be kept within your own breast. Van Dieman's Land is not America.'[22]

Miller dwelt on Franklin's absurd manner of speaking for several more paragraphs before he delivered his own classification of Governor Franklin as 'an *old woman*'(his emphasis). Henceforth in the narrative Franklin was always referred to as 'the old granny'. Franklin was such a fool, Miller magnanimously conceded, that his feelings of anger were displaced by those of contemptuous pity. Nevertheless he could not disguise the fact that he was completely in Franklin's power and that being singled out by the Governor was a source of real fear. On the occasion of Franklin's visit to the hell-hole of Port Arthur, where Miller had been sent for absconding, Miller's portrait of Franklin was still comic, but the terror of what Franklin could do to him was palpable:

> [My] appearance was such as should have moved the heart of the most brutal savage to pity. . . . pale and haggard, and the heavy logs, under which I had often been crushed to the earth, had so injured my chest that I was compelled to lean my head forward several inches; as standing upright, in a natural position, occasioned dreadful torture to my breast. My waistcoat and jacket, about the shoulders, were red and stiff with the congealed blood, from the wounds underneath, and my whole appearance indicated that I had suffered to the very extreme of which human nature was capable, and that my days on earth were few, unless my condition was speedily ameliorated. It was not until Franklin's eyes were fixed upon me, in which I at once saw rage, malice, and, I think I may add, *murder*, fearfully gleaming, that I suspected his motive for calling me from the ranks . . .

> 'O! you are a bad man. How I rejoice that I have got you here. I'll break your *American spirit!* I'll teach a young stripling law student, full of Yankee conceit and impertinence, a lesson. I'll break your low republican independence. I'll cure your fighting for the Canadians. You young *American puppy!* I'll give orders to have you treated your whole life, with greater severity than you now are.' Turning to the 1300 convicts present, the refuse and scum of mankind, the dregs of Van Dieman's Land, and stretching forth his hand toward them, he concluded as follows: 'Now, *my good men*, I caution you all to *shun* this man. Don't let him lead you *astray*. Don't let him get up a rebellion here, which he is sure to do, if you listen to him. BEWARE OF HIM! *shun* him as you would a *viper!!*'[23]

Nothing could be better calculated to demean Miller than an invitation for the refuse of Port Arthur—that Sodom and sink of infamy—to shun him as worse than themselves. Contrary to intention, it had the effect of hugely raising Miller's stakes among the prisoners who became 'anxious to form an acquaintance with one declared to be *such a devil*'.[24] But Miller wanted nothing to do with the friendship of felons. 'I now gave myself up for lost', he wrote, for once at a loss for fancy descriptions.[25]

Though Miller did not expire under the rigours of penal labour, he was brought to death's door by the intolerable demands of forced labour on the gangs. One curious interpretation Miller put on this harsh experience was to insist that he and his American comrades were *tricked* into the labour gangs by first being invited to take some voluntary labour for fresh air and exercise. It is unclear how he hit upon this explanation for being compelled to undertake brutally hard labour—carting rocks and trees like a beast of burden under the threat of the whip and treadmill—but he told his readers that he had it 'from an unquestionable authority' that Governor Franklin expected the Americans to refuse to do the voluntary 'exercise', and would not have forced them to work *'through fear of consequences'*.[26] Miller's source for this was probably Edward MacDowell, who had been Attorney-General under Franklin and who took Miller into his law office after he got his ticket-of-leave. However, official correspondence indicated no intention on the part of Her Majesty's government to treat the Patriot exiles other than as common felons.

Miller's recollection was that the trickery involved being invited to take some exercise in the convict barracks soon after he arrived. When a convict overseer handed Miller a broom and indicated he should sweep, Miller retorted with contempt: '. . . you must give me some instructions, as I was never bound apprentice to a *sweep*'. Here the fellow turned his back upon me, and muttered, 'the d— Yankee *quill-driver*'.[27]

While he maintained the fiction of voluntary work, Miller found himself with a broom put in his hand every day, including the Sabbath. At this he

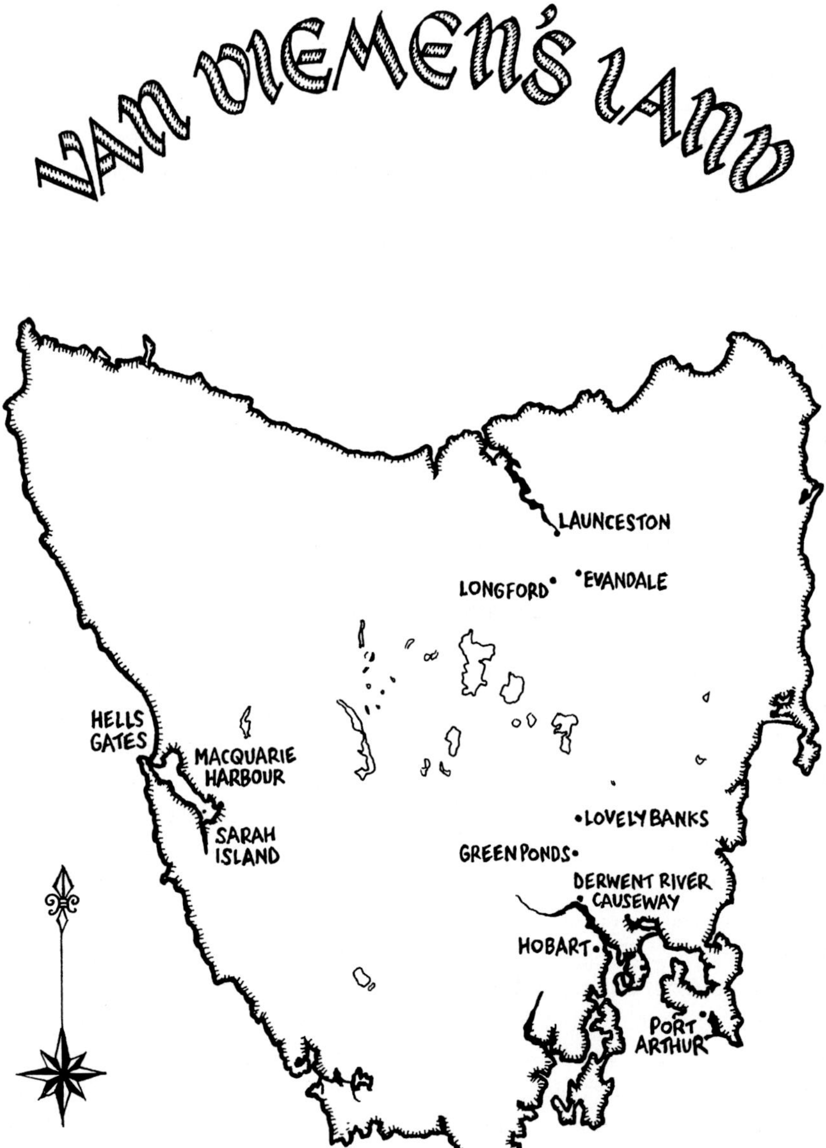
VAN DIEMEN'S LAND
LAUNCESTON
LONGFORD
EVANDALE
HELLS GATES
MACQUARIE HARBOUR
SARAH ISLAND
LOVELY BANKS
GREEN PONDS
DERWENT RIVER
CAUSEWAY
HOBART
PORT ARTHUR

rebelled. When the threat of flogging failed to move him, the convict overseer pleaded that Miller should sweep or else he would lose favour:

> 'You will offend Mr. Gunn, who is your friend, if you don't.'
> 'I shall offend my God, who is greater than Mr. Gunn, if I do.'
> 'God Almighty is nothing here compared with Mr. Gunn.' . . . shouted the overseer.[28]

The exchanges with this 'depraved, debased . . . hardened wretch in whom every ennobling quality was forever annihilated', makes it very apparent why things might not have gone too well for Miller, who soon found himself in solitary confinement for shirking his 'voluntary' work.[29] Still, it does seem that Gunn kept an eye out for Miller and sheltered him from the extreme brutalities of the probation system. When a further seventy-eight Patriots were landed on the *Buffalo* two months later and sent to a probation station at Sandy Bay, Miller immediately sought to join them. Mr Gunn cautioned against it, warning that things would go much worse for those at Sandy Bay. To which Miller gave a characteristic reply:

> 'I shall esteem it a privilege to share their fate, and would rather spend my whole life in slavery with them, than two years comparative ease among such wretches as the English prisoners.'
> . . . They were all strangers, but they were MEN.[30]

Miller was adamant that while the British were trying hypocritically to suppress the African slave trade, they operated a slave system of their own, brutally exploiting their own underclass. Apart from the widespread use of bonded labour, it was the ubiquitous use of the lash that most convinced Miller that this was indeed slavery. He was genuinely horrified by being forced to watch floggings, rightly perceiving that beyond the infliction of pain, flogging was used to strip every vestige of manhood. No matter how much the offender offered initial verbal resistance to the scourge, he was always reduced to a slumped, insensible, barely human mess of battered flesh by the time the surgeon determined that he could take no more. Miller was utterly revolted by the spectre of flogging: the exposed backbone under a jelly of bruised flesh and congealed blood; the hunks of raw flesh and spatter of blood which flew from the flagellator's whip. Under the circumstances of a public spectacle of such complete disempowerment and emasculation he felt that no real man could wish to live:

> I felt that I could endure any thing but a flogging; and even the torture of the lash I cared but little for, but the *degradation* I could not bear; and resolved that I *would not*. There was an alternative in case I was

> sentenced to this punishment, which was to perish first by my own hand.[31]

Miller claimed the Americans were often threatened with a flogging; but gave the authorities to understand if any attempt was made to flog one of them, the remainder would openly rebel. Certainly their ability to avoid the lash provides a good case for safety in numbers. However, when Miller and Joseph Stewart were sent to Port Arthur for attempted escape—foiled on this occasion by a cowardly mason in Hobart—they found themselves at the overseer's mercy. Stewart was the first to be ordered a flogging. According to Miller he pitifully begged the Commandant to spare him the degradation of the lash: 'Starve me to death in the cells; load me with irons; extend my term of sentence; any thing but a flogging.'[32] To the bemusement of the old lags, Stewart was deeply grateful to receive three days in solitary instead of his puny twenty-five lashes. When Miller's turn for a flogging inevitably came, his account was less histrionic, laying emphasis on the moral argument, rather than naked terror, although Miller was beside himself at the prospect. Addressing the commandant, Miller claimed to have said, 'I could bear the pain of the lash; but, sir, I have the feelings of a man, and cannot endure the degradation.'[33] He was never flogged.

By late 1844 the Patriots' free pardons began arriving in Van Diemen's Land. Governor Eardley-Wilmot, who replaced the disgraced Franklin, took the view that he should exercise his own discretion by giving out the pardons in stages and withholding any pardons for convicts who had bucked the system. On this matter Miller was characteristically forthright, demanding an audience with Eardley-Wilmot and telling him that he had been subjected to '. . . as gross an outrage upon our rights as was ever perpetrated against the African race', and had been persecuted because he had dared to rebel against it.[34] After 'suffering years of horrible slavery', Miller insisted that it was both 'unjust and cruel in the extreme' to withhold his pardon.[35] When told that he had his pardon withheld for absconding, Miller exploded in indignation that this punishment was for being 'an American, in spirit and in heart, for not meekly wearing the yoke and kissing the burden upon my shoulders; for daring to evince the spirits and feelings of a man in the presence of my tyrants'.[36] Miller got his pardon in July 1845, more than a year after it had been sent from London. His fellow absconder Joseph Stewart had his pardon withheld indefinitely.

Pleased though he was to be pardoned, Miller was far from grateful, declaring: '. . . we had been, *de jure*, *free* men for years, and that the abominable slavery we had endured was not only a wanton violation of the laws of justice and humanity, but even of Van Dieman's Land'.[37] To prove the point he set about organising a legal case for unlawful imprisonment on behalf of all the

American prisoners. In this endeavour he was supported by Edward MacDowell, the former Attorney-General of Van Diemen's Land. MacDowell had long since fallen out with the government, and had informed Miller that he had seen '*not the scratch of a pen to authorize the Governor to receive you upon this Island, much less treat you as convicts*'.[38] The Patriots should have been free men from the moment they arrived, according to MacDowell.

This was not an example of wishful thinking. Miller did have a compelling legal case.[39] Though he was probably not aware of it, there had been great concern expressed by the Law Officers of the Crown and Colonial Office, between July 1838 and May 1839, about the legality of the act under which he was sentenced and the fear that the Crown would be exposed to writs for wrongful imprisonment. With encouragement from MacDowell, Miller arranged to sail to England to institute a legal suit. He departed carrying a letter from the American consul in Van Diemen's Land to the American Ambassador in London requesting assistance in proceedings against the British government for damages. En route to England, however, Miller's ship encountered an American passenger ship destined for Philadelphia. The lure of home was too great. He cast his role as republican hero to the winds, negotiated a deal for his passage with the American captain and headed for home.

Reunited with his anxious parents, who had scarcely heard from their son since his quixotic departure eight years earlier, Miller finished his story with an image of himself with family and friends around a pleasant fireside. 'I still am blessed with a strong arm and a willing heart to wield a sword in the sacred cause of LIBERTY, either in the defence of my own country, or the rights of an oppressed people', he wrote, but his immediate need was to put his life together again.[40]

With his dreadful experience behind him, probably the last thing Miller might have been expected to do was write a detailed account of his travails in Van Diemen's Land. Yet as an educated man, now a lawyer, Miller understood the extent to which he was still captive to the legal apparatus of the penal colony, having been written into those leather-bound ledgers which had imprisoned him as surely as the walls of Port Arthur. He needed to invoke the power of the written word to liberate himself from the system of notation which had categorised him along with the debased 'offscourings of England'.

By the time he returned to New York in 1846, an effective mode for his counter-response was readily apparent in the burgeoning genre of slave narratives, which were the Yankee abolitionists' most effective weapon in the fiercely combative debate over slavery. Like the slave narratives, the purpose of Miller's *Notes of an Exile to Van Dieman's Land* was didactic and political: it aimed to instruct the reader in the hideous barbarism of the British penal system in order to strengthen opposition to the imperial presence in North America. 'Wilt thou look upon the dark picture of Van Dieman's Land, and learn wisdom?', Miller demanded in his introduction to the penal colony, having opened his narrative with a passionate exhortation against those who 'would sell their country for a smile from the British aristocracy'.[41]

But where the emphasis of the slave narrative was a catalogue of horror inflicted upon the passive body of the African, violently torn from his childlike state of nature, the role of brutalised victim would not do for a white, middle-class Yankee such as Miller. No white American male could be positioned in the public perception as the abject victim of imperialist taskmasters, cruelly enduring the indignity of being treated like a dog. Consequently there was a crucial tension in Miller's narrative between his vivid recreation of the systematic degradation and brutality of convict life and his claim to superior American manliness and republican virtue. Rather than present himself as cowed or victimised by the weight of the systematic dehumanisation of the penal system, Miller cast himself as the dramatic hero who courageously challenged the imperialist sycophants who controlled his fate. At every opportunity he sought to escape from their tyranny, only to be cruelly foiled by the venal Jacob Beemer. Like Simon Legree in *Uncle Tom's Cabin*, Beemer is the quintessential villain of Miller's narrative, perpetually the agent of his abjection and his loss of heroic virtue and republican honour. At each heroic step in his drama, Miller revealed himself cruelly undone by Beemer, who accompanied him in every stage of invasion, arrest, trial and exile. According to Miller it was 'the *Prince of Traitors*, JACOB BEEMER' who betrayed his first attempt to cross into Canada to mount a daring rescue of imprisoned rebels, and it was Beemer who turned the raid at the Short Hills into a tragic and criminal fiasco.[42] His transportation to Van Diemen's Land was an *illegal* sentence, he insisted, handed down to answer for Beemer's acts of criminal irresponsibility.

Leaving the shores of America was insupportable. Of course his readers would ask how any self-respecting Patriot could permit himself to be torn away from the glorious radiance of the American republic. He would have to resist. So, as Miller told it, the Patriots planned to seize the ship taking them to the hulks in England and sail to New York. On the day of the mutiny they found the hatches bolted down and the Captain, acting on information from Beemer, had each chained pair of men interrogated and threatened them with the cat. Curiously the story of the closed hatches was given a different twist in the account of fellow Patriot Benjamin Wait, who was astonished at the Captain's ludicrous supposition that a ship could be taken by a group of unarmed and manacled men. His explanation was that Beemer, attempting to ingratiate himself in the hope of a pardon, had manufactured the whole business. As for the role of Miller, according to Wait, the poor lad was so debilitated with seasickness he was too weak to stand.[43]

When faced with the terrifying degradation of the hulks, Miller reported that he again sought to escape, only to have his plans betrayed by Beemer once more. In this case we have only Miller's word. His bold plan was probably another retrospective wish-fulfilment to confirm his status as a true American; a *man* who would never *willingly* submit to degradation, slavery and even worse. It is much more likely that Miller, so young and terribly vulnerable, was scared out of his wits.

Beemer fitted the role of villain, even though he was a fellow Patriot and a republican rebel, because he was not born an American. As Miller explained at the beginning of his tale, 'Beemer, the chief agent in the tragedy, was a British subject, of their own raising; and not one of my countrymen . . . .'[44] So pervasive and virulent was the corruption of British imperialism that it infected even its own rebellious sons. British subjects were bred to infamy and deceit; they could not help themselves.

Americans, in Miller's view were *men*, as opposed to old grannies, degraded wretches, snivelling sycophants or compulsive traitors. His narrative pits the masculine virtues of Americans against a system which derived its authority from a woman, in a colony whose imbecilic governor was so unmanned that he took orders from his wife. That the Americans were the perpetual losers in this contest was only because of treachery, deceit and the sheer weight of state-sanctioned brutality. Miller sought to disempower the apparatus of the imperial state by rendering ridiculous those at its apex, like Governor Franklin, as if by rhetoric he could somehow turn the tables on the system which had described, classified and dehumanised him from the moment his unsteady feet touched the ground in Van Diemen's Land. His other weapon was the written body of the law.

A lawyer at the time he wrote, and a law clerk when sentenced, Miller devotes a major part of his narrative to arcane legal argument, and to melodramatic dramatisation of his various trials and appeals. Consistently he asserts his command of English law and shows how it was abused by the courts in which he appeared. At his indictment he refused to plead, telling his interrogators—no less than the Chief Justice and the Solicitor General—'I understand your wishes and my own interest too well'.[45] To his sentence of death he responds with four pages of passionate protest. Nearly one hundred pages are devoted to the *habeas corpus* action before the Queen's Bench in England, yet his trial in Canada merited no more than a passing glance, a line or two that his defence was a ruse, forced upon him in the face of a corrupt court.

The evidence of the trial records tells a rather different story. When required to plead at his indictment, Miller entered a plea of not guilty on the grounds of insanity. In contrast to the swashbuckling hero and legal expert of his own account, the testimony of his companions-in-arms at the Short Hills pictures a loner, rather fanciful if not downright odd. Various witnesses swore that it was not Miller but two other Americans who had made a stand against Beemer. The young law clerk took little part in the action and was 'curious in his manners' and 'frequently off by himself', they reported; he 'would fly from one subject to another', and 'would never give a sensible answer'.[46] One witness said further that he had seen Miller 'demean himself in a singular way'.[47] His brother explained that before Miller had suddenly left home in New York State, without telling his family of his intentions, he had not always been in his right mind and 'often changeable in his conversation'.[48] Miller's family believed he was unlikely to succeed at law, 'since his mind appeared filled with speculation and other flighty things'.[49]

The disparities between Miller's picture of himself and the court record points to the reason why Miller was so quick to negotiate a passage to Philadelphia rather than go to England to pursue a case for illegal imprisonment. Rhetoric aside, he had no faith in his capacity to win the legal argument in a court of law, as opposed to the pages of a book, any more than he did when he chose to plead insanity in 1838. He had already been through the British legal system, from top to bottom, and failed, with resulting mortification and misery. It should be no surprise that he could not face the prospect of going through it again, even though his law suit would benefit hugely his American comrades, especially the forty or so who still remained in penal servitude when he departed from Van Diemen's Land. At some level Miller knew he was abandoning these less fortunate comrades, which is no doubt why he makes no reference to their fate in the body of his narrative and simply lists their names in an appendix. True, when he arrived back in the United States he wrote a letter to a New York newspaper to plead for intervention on behalf of those Americans still in Van Diemen's Land, but he took no further part in processes to secure their freedom.[50]

Miller's book was published in 1846. By 1850 he was married and settled in a law practice in New York. What did he think when he heard about Lady Jane Franklin's appeal to the United States Congress for help in finding her husband, lost in the frozen Arctic wastes? Or when he learned that a New York businessman had outfitted a ship to search for 'the old granny'? Did Miller spare a thought for his companion-in-arms George Cooley, who in 1850 was sentenced to three days in solitary confinement in Van Diemen's Land?

Cooley was no quill driver. In Miller's narrative he appears as 'a mere lad, and extremely ignorant . . .'.[51] He is always 'the boy Cooley', although two years older than the self-important Miller. But then Cooley had joined the Short Hills invasion impelled less by heroic ideals of republican virtue than by dire need. He was one of several unemployed farm labourers enticed into the Patriot force with the promise of $100 a day and a grant of land.[52] While he may have believed Linus Miller's rhetoric about Canadians groaning under the tyranny of the British Crown and needing their magnanimous neighbours to spark the fire of rebellion, American agriculture was in a depressed state, and Cooley had not worked for some time.

Illiterate and without family at home to intercede for him, Cooley was simply left off the list of Americans to be pardoned. He had not a mark against him on his convict conduct record until his attempt to escape on a whaling ship in 1846, obviously desperate that he was not going to get a pardon. In 1850, when he entered that solitary confinement cell, he still had no pardon, nor even a ticket-of-leave. Yet, as far as the British Crown and the colonial authorities were concerned, the case of the Patriot exiles was completely closed. George Cooley had become invisible. For all his muscular rhetoric about LIBERTY, Linus Miller had abandoned and forgotten 'the boy Cooley' just as readily as had the snivelling sycophants of the British legal system.

In the reverse of Linus Miller's experience, Cooley seems to have been doubly punished for 'meekly wearing the yoke' and not rebelling against his illegal bondage. In April 1846, understanding that he was in Van Diemen's Land for the term of his natural life, Cooley applied to marry a fellow convict, Catherine McIntosh. Permission was given but no marriage took place and McIntosh later married another man. After that disappointment Cooley's clean record shows a marked change. In June 1850 he was caught out after hours, which cost him four days in the appalling solitary cell and the loss of his imminent pardon.[53] Late in 1851 he finally received a conditional pardon, which did not permit him to leave the Australian colonies. It is not known what happened to him, but it is a sure bet that the comfort of an American fireside with family and friends was never to be his.

2

In search of 'Jack Bushman'

Raymond Evans and William Thorpe

> I trust that you will not apply the test of veracity too particularly to my story, as I might be found wanting in names and dates, and taking a trifling liberty with conversations.
>
> 'Jack Bushman', *The Lash*[1]

In April 1859, just two months before Queensland separated officially from New South Wales, a series of chapters appeared in the *Moreton Bay Courier* about the life of a former convict who had served the bulk of his penal servitude at Moreton Bay between 1826 and 1839, gaining his ticket-of-leave in 1843 and conditional pardon in 1852. These chapters, entitled 'Passages from the life of a "Lifer"', were written under the pseudonym 'Jack Bushman'. 'Passages' was not Bushman's first or only literary effort, however; from November 1858 to February 1860 he had published nine other short stories in the *Courier*, five of which were printed before 'Passages' appeared.[2] The 'real' 'Jack Bushman' has been especially difficult to uncover. However, two major propositions in what follows are that 'Jack Bushman' was a real person, interpolating the career of the convict and ex-convict, Thomas Brooks/Brookes; and that 'Passages' provides a reliable guide to Brooks's life in the colony. Both 'Passages' and the short stories combine to represent first, a valuable convict narrative (albeit overdetermined by another authorial presence), and secondly an example, among other productions, of a burgeoning colonial writing culture—one which figured the politics of Separation and race.

This chapter deals with five connected matters: the life and times of Thomas Brooks; the veracity or otherwise of 'Passages' as a source in reconstructing this life; an attempt to find who the author of 'Passages' was (or at the very least who he wasn't); and the contexts for the public emergence of this 'convict voice' in the 1850s. Finally there is the question of analysing such a narrative, as 'distinct from the empirical quarrying' of it.

Penal passages: Thomas Brooks in colonial Australia

Recent work has begun to redress the implicit, unproblematised 'whiteness' in mainstream historiography, and to resituate Australian history more firmly within nineteenth- and twentieth-century imperial frames. This chapter is committed to this project; and to furthering the proposition that colonial Australia was composed of interacting, sometimes colliding, sometimes colluding cultures 'from the jump', while recognising that very different discourses to contemporary 'multiculturalism' were evident about the diverse peoples who made up its history in the penal and post-penal period.

The biography of English convict Thomas Brooks illustrates such socio-cultural complexity. Born in 1791 into a large working-class family in the north of England, Brooks was a child labourer from eight years of age and a handloom-weaver in the cotton industry at thirteen, continuing at this until he married. His wife died a few years afterwards and he, inconsolable, lost interest in his work. He remarried but had little affection (apart from strong sexual attraction) for his new wife. He started drinking and began to steal. Economic depression had hit the textile trade, and Brooks entered that ambiguous zone in which people were increasingly oscillating between 'workers' and 'convicts'. Ultimately, he joined the convict workers destined to land on Australia's 'fatal shores'.

Convicted in August 1818 after two episodes of theft, Brooks was transported aboard the *Grenada* to New South Wales, arriving in Sydney in October 1819. For two years Brooks worked at the state quarries that supplied the stone for Governor Macquarie's grandiose infrastructure program. On Macquarie's departure in 1821, he was assigned to less congenial private service, from which he absconded. As punishment he was sent in early 1822 to Newcastle to hew coal. A couple of years later (after absconding twice more and receiving his first flogging), he was at another punishment centre, Port Macquarie. This establishment in the 1820s 'witnessed experimental plantation production of sugar and tobacco'—somewhat akin to plantation colonies elsewhere. Here he met 'Black' John Goff, a transportee of West Indian and/or African background. In June 1825 Goff escaped and organised twenty-two others into a bushranging gang which included Thomas Brooks and John (or Jack) Banks.[3]

Goff, Brooks and Banks were captured later in 1825 and tried at the Sydney Supreme Court on 2 December. Clemency, however, was extended due to Ralph Darling's arrival as incoming governor and Brooks's and Banks's death sentences were commuted on 7 December to retransportation to Moreton Bay. Brooks and Banks travelled on the *Amity*, the same vessel that carried the newly appointed commandant, Patrick Logan, on 17 March 1826. 'I thought we had come to a wild country', Brooks's narrative avers, 'where cruelty might be practiced [*sic*], or a man be "put out of the way" without much inquiry as to the circumstances'.[4]

Brooks endured heavy penal servitude at Moreton Bay from 1826 until 1836 before Commandant Foster Fyans reviewed his case in October and decided to remove his heavy irons and place him on probation for a ticket-of-leave. Brooks's first duty in 1826 at Moreton Bay—together with a number of other felons, notably John (Jack) Banks, his ally—was as part of a heavily ironed chain gang clearing the land. He continued thus until early December 1827 when he escaped again. His other jobs included transporting cedar by boat to the settlement—during Logan's term from 1826 to 1830—and later, after his numerous abscondings had been met by increasingly heavy floggings, taking laundry by bullock dray to and from the female factory at Eagle Farm. Most of the time he appears to have laboured outdoors, mostly in heavy irons.[5]

Altogether, Brooks absconded from Moreton Bay possibly five times by 1835, actually reaching Sydney on his second-last attempt and almost succeeding in escaping by boat from New South Wales before his 'weather-beaten face' was recognised and he was retaken. The secondary penal outposts punished runaways severely: Brooks was flogged several times—once with 300 lashes—and the weight of his leg irons was increased. In most bids for freedom, whether by himself or with others, Brooks had Aboriginal help—encounters which underscored his awareness of, and reliance on Aboriginal people. As discussed below, these experiences had further import when Brooks was finally freed and began to work for himself.[6]

On his release, Brooks hoped he could return to England but the authorities prohibited this. Resigned to staying at 'Moreton Bay', he 'took to the bush', and earned enough to buy a bullock team. However, he remained lonely and isolated. He started drinking heavily to deal with the 'solitude', appearing before the Small Debts Court in 1850 and 1851, losing his bullock team and savings in the process. He was thus forced into the ranks of the rural proletariat, the 'nomad tribe' of itinerant men getting their living by clearing, fencing, sawing and splitting timber.[7]

By the early 1850s Brooks returned to Brisbane and established himself with a mate several miles from Fortitude Valley, to the north of the township where the first significant influx of free settlers, the 'Lang immigrants' had settled from 1849. This location lay adjacent to the Turrbal Aboriginal camp at Breakfast Creek. In June 1852, a serious racial affray occurred when colonial vigilantes accompanied by mounted constables fired into the camp, killing and wounding several Aborigines, including a baby, after an Aboriginal man had stolen a few sweets from a Fortitude Valley shop. Outraged, a large body of about 300 Aborigines, organised by Aboriginal resisters, Billy Barlow, Make-I-Light and Dundalli, went looking for the perpetrators, seeking revenge. Two Aboriginal women, 'Susey' and 'Mary', came to warn Brooks and his mate

Prisoner being flogged at Moreton Bay *(from William Ross,* The Fell Tyrant, *London, 1836).*

The chain gang mustered after the day's work, *by Frederick Mackie.*

that they were in danger and should return home to protect themselves. The Aborigines approached Brooks's hut, but seeing that the two men were armed, continued on and attacked two other whites later that day at Darby McGrath's farm, 'The Gap', situated fifteen miles away. Michael Halloran was killed and Edward Power injured.[8]

This last encounter between Brooks and the Aborigines was decisive. Susey and Mary had saved Brooks from death—the most dramatic demonstration of Aboriginal co-operation he had experienced. Although their warning to Brooks and his companion was not unusual, the concern Susey had for Brooks suggests that she knew him beforehand and judged him trustworthy. Brooks's reliance on Aboriginal people, during his escapes particularly, probably made him less racially antagonistic than other colonials. Indeed, Brooks himself reported that 'the blacks' told him about the fate of his convict companion, Jack Banks, because of the 'confidence reposed in me by them'.

Jack Banks, described on his convict indent as a 'Farmer's Man', had achieved the exceptional height of six feet and one inch, and as such had earned for himself the soubrette of 'Tallboy'. After escaping from the Penal Settlement in the late 1820s, he was accepted into Kabi Kabi society, where he took an Aboriginal wife and immersed himself fully into its ceremonial and communal life. Survivors of the wreck of the *Stirling Castle* in 1836—John Baxter, Robert Darge and even Mrs Fraser herself—all testified later to meetings with 'Tallboy' Banks. Tanned almost black by the sub-tropical sun, his skin scarified and daubed with yellow and white ochre and his long dark hair tied into a bundle on the top of his head, 'Tallboy' spoke excitedly to Baxter of the upcoming Bunya festivities and the prospect of sweet rewards in the mountains, foraging for 'sugar bag' honey in the high trees. As 'Passages' records, Aboriginal informants later conveyed to his companion Brooks the tragic news that Banks had been mistaken for an Aborigine while climbing a tree in search of 'sugar bag', and peremptorily shot by settlers 'out after the blacks'.[9]

Banks's immersion in Aboriginal society was thus a total experience, even to the manner of his violent death. Brooks's own incorporation was simpler, partial and less dramatic—though no less noteworthy. Approaching his seventieth year, after decades of white brutalisation, his loyalties were finally clear. As he explained, via 'Bushman's' pen:

> Susey . . . saved my life; and I, in return . . . took her, to provide for her comfort, as far as bush life goes, the remaining portion of my days. Susey cooks and washes—has gone with me one hundred miles up the country, and ever proved faithful. She likes a glass of grog, and so do I . . . we jog along very comfortably for bush people . . . All these past six years . . . I have no rent to pay . . . plenty of wood to burn, and good water to drink. Mine is not one of the most envious positions . . . , but

> I tell you what, if you had suffered twenty-one years as a slave, and six years as a ticket-of-leave man, had been obliged to live on 'hominy' for months . . . and had your back torn by those hellish thongs . . . , I guess that contrast would take a favourite side for my picture . . . I have plenty of work, . . . plenty of blackfellows who are pleased to serve me because I always perform what I promise them; and for aught I know, my life will conclude in the same society . . . [10]

Notwithstanding his use of the term 'blackfellows', Brooks's affectionate regard for Susey and his easy commitment to the shrinking corpus of Turrbal people was an exceptional position for a white colonial to hold. It marks an arrival, virtually, at the other side of the frontier—a frontier which the perpetual convict escapee had transgressed time and again; as well as a marginal vantage point where colonial views were arguably more balanced, worldly-wise and, perhaps, even truer. For although the central, official voice is invariably taken as authoritative (and thus far less scrutinised), the voice from the so-called margins is equally one from the centres of struggle and should be attended at least as considerately.

'Passages' as a source, a narrative, and a history

How reliable or relevant is 'Passages' as a source of Brooks's experiences? Here we examine its features as writing *qua* writing, and the timing and reasons for its publication. In these reflections, we need to deal with the problematic aspects of this text (and by implication others in this genre) that purport to reveal the 'convict voice'. First, however, we must verify the real convict who is the subject of this narrative.

Without any doubt, the convict interviewed by 'Jack Bushman' *was* Thomas Brooks. His companion was Jack Banks, tried with him for 'robbing a dwelling house' (T. A. Scott's Prospect Station homestead which 'Bushman' mentions in Chapter 2) and 'putting in bodily fear'. To a large extent, Brooks's rather patchy official record and his detailed experiential narrative move chronologically forward in close tandem, and, in certain respects, the silences of one are answered by the resonances in the other.[11]

Many clues and items of supporting evidence confirm 'Passages' as a remarkably accurate source. After a disclaimer in Chapter 1 about 'memory' playing 'fantastic tricks', 'Bushman' starts the story: 'I was born in a densely populated part of the north of England' and recalls that he was working on his own account at thirteen years of age as a handloom cotton weaver. Lancaster, a coastal town in Lancashire, located some fifty miles north-west of Manchester, was the most important site of cotton manufacture in the early stages of the Industrial Revolution, and employed the largest number of handloom weavers.[12]

Brooks's transportation for life between March and October 1819 marked the unexceptional maiden voyage of the *Grenada*; and he comments: 'I have nothing to complain of on board the ship. . . . the bayonet was my monitor . . . It was a long and rough passage but at that time . . . it was not considered out of the ordinary runs.' All the convicts on board survived the voyage. Sent to the stone quarries upon arrival, Brooks refers perceptively to three aspects of Macquarie's rule: first, that it was 'a good time for the prisoners', insofar as convicts 'who behaved themselves were not used so badly'. Tougher times lay ahead under Brisbane's administration and the policies of Bigge. Secondly, under Macquarie's grand schema, stone quarrying was considered 'as second in importance to the masons who fashioned and laid the sharper stones in the construction of noble edifices'. Thirdly, there was a distinct hierarchy of preference operating. Enterprising emancipists were encouraged above 'free-men' to grow wealthy in the same manner as skilled convicts with 'brains' were advanced beyond the common ruck. 'It was not on such as I that the Governor smiled', Brooks observes. 'I was poor and ignorant, had only strong arms, a working disposition with "a thankee" if ever I obtained a glass of rum'.[13]

Placed under assignment, Brooks is again alive to the lottery of labour management. Although former 'Government men' were used 'body and soul' as 'tools for the agency of what their employers demanded', not all employers were alike. Some treated their charges fairly. However, Brooks's first escape from a settler at Kissing Point led to his re-transportation on the *Elizabeth and Henrietta* to the Newcastle 'gaol gang'. His account of ill-treatment in the coalmines, poor food, and heavy punishment accords closely with Hughes's assessment of this retransportation centre in *The Fatal Shore*. The main preoccupation, as he notes, was escape; and Brooks absconded towards Sydney, only to be retaken in two days and awarded, as both 'Passages' and the official record show, a flogging of seventy-five lashes.[14]

Brooks's time at Port Macquarie and his assignment to work for 'Mr Scott' on 'the Plains' are faithfully recorded as is his eventual escape with 'Black Goff'. In February 1825, the Commandant's Daily Diary at Port Macquarie discloses:

> The prisoners when first discovered were repeatedly called upon to surrender . . . and made towards a deep scrub when the party fired at them killed WILLIAM HODGES and WILLIAM DAVENPORT . . . It is supposed that two others were wounded or killed . . .

At the receiving end of this process, 'Bushman', ghosting for Brooks, writes:

> Our sufferings had made us resolute and . . . we tried to escape when challenged, instead of surrendering . . . Scrambling among bushes, hunted by soldiers . . . Again we ran. Immediately the sharp cracking sound of a number of muskets were heard. I turned my head. Michael Clansey had fallen—dead; another of my companions had been shot in the knee, and he had also fallen . . . [15]

Numerous other examples of authenticity may be cited from Brooks's time at Moreton Bay—his numerous escapes and repeated flagellations; his overall assessment of the settlement as 'a spot where they were not very particular how they kept the spirits in subjection'; his ensuing reclamation under the more humane auspices of Commandant Foster Fyans and so on. Yet whereas the official account simply enumerates a sentence of so many lashes, Brooks describes their impact at length upon both the physical frame and the psyche: 'the very hell of agony' inflicted by the nine cruel thongs, as 'sick in stomach and heart' he internally questioned himself, 'Of what use is life?', and resolved never to allow his flogger any satisfaction by crying out. Brooks was what other convicts admiringly termed 'a brick' or an 'iron man' and even during his final punishment of 300 lashes, delivered in serial fashion over three successive days, he 'did not shriek':

> The third morning they tied me up. My back and sides, my every part, were gnawn by excruciating agony, the bones being bared and the old wounds . . . gaping ghastly . . . they flogged on . . . my tongue was swollen and I gnawed a leaden bullet . . . until eighty-five was given, then I heard the word "cast him off" and the voice of him who had said thus greeted me with 'you b___ you will not holloa' and he spit on the ground savagely.[16]

As we have argued elsewhere, such experiential accounts of this 'calibrated process of administering pain' and imposing submission and debasement are by no means overstated and come closer to a rounded depiction of contingent historical truth than the recording of a number of inflicted strokes.[17]

Brooks's recall of events mainly falters upon precise points such as the accuracy of dates and the correct pronunciation of names. For instance, he has the *Grenada* sailing in 1818 rather than 1819, with 262 rather than 152 convicts, upon a voyage of six rather than almost nine months; and he refers to Commandants Morisset and Fyans as 'Morrison' and 'Fines'.[18] Several observations may be offered about this. It is important to note that convicts, as symbolic of their systematic disempowerment, were not in possession of time. They were given no access to timepieces or calendars. Control over time's deployment was largely a power held by others. Especially for convicts enduring secondary punishment, time was measured by the passage of the sun or seasonal change and related to durations of suffering and endurance; or to fleeting bouts of relief granted by periods of escape or sleep. Similarly, few were allowed access to paper or writing equipment and, in certain circumstances, such possessions could become a flogging matter. The names of others, particularly authority figures, were learnt and memorised orally and thus phonetically.

Brooks had no access to clocks, almanacs or diaries, nor any strong inclination to record the passing details of his ordeal in three secondary punishment centres. Yet, for a man of sixty-eight years who had endured serious privations and the gradual infliction of more than one thousand lashes, the verifiable accuracy of his mental recall is remarkable. As his account acknowledges when detailing the plight of another convict:

> I forget his name, but had I known the free people would ever have taken an interest in reading the suffering of criminals; I might have been more particular in jotting down the incidents which daily came under my notice . . . I wish I could remember distinctly . . . but . . . I am growing old, and did not keep any account of ought save my trials for liberty . . .[19]

Thus, despite some discrepancies, 'Passages' can be used as a reliable source to describe one convict's biography in England and New South Wales to 1859. It is especially pertinent to deconstruct implicitly 'white' historical narratives, and to show how Brooks's life, like those of other forced and free immigrants, was integral in creating the diversity of Empire and its Others in an Indigenous land through a succession of cruel transitions. Furthermore, while 'Bushman' refers to hegemonic patterns of mutual antagonism between Aborigines, convicts and settler-colonials that hung over from Moreton Bay's recent penal past, he has another, more human story to tell about interactions between convicts and Aborigines—relationships that suggest a more nuanced history for 'race relations' where, at least in some cases, genuine conciliation between invaders and indigenes seemed sometimes possible.

Whether 'Passages' represents an unambiguous 'convict voice', notwithstanding its veracity, is a more complicated matter. Part of our discussion acknowledges the misgivings of Ian Duffield about the manner in which we have interpreted this work in another context. As Duffield puts it, Evans and Thorpe 'hail "Passages" as incontestable historical truth *because* it exhibits the "convict voice", thereby exhibiting "innocence" concerning the problematic of convict narratives'.[20] Duffield should be heeded for a number of reasons. The first is that 'Passages' is not first-hand: 'Jack Bushman' was Brooks's ghost-writer. Secondly, it is debatable whether 'Passages' discloses historical truth about convict experiences although, as we argue presently, it does not follow that it does *not* reveal it. The postmodern-inspired charge—

which Derrida, among others have posed—is that historians in their practice still cling to a 'naively representational theory of language'. In other words, this critique claims that the tenor, the timing and the publication of 'Passages' strongly suggests that the narrative was an ideological weapon which the pro-Separation, anti-squatter movement used to further its ideals of an 'imagined colonial community' based on agricultural free settlement.[21]

The fact that another wrote Thomas Brooks's biography, on the face of it, would seem to lessen its authenticity. But even if Brooks were able to write about his life, this does not guarantee authenticity either. Indeed, to rely on direct 'convict' testimony without deconstructing or corroborating it, is to be open to the same charge of naivety regarding all evidence. As Duffield himself notes, other sources, for example convict indents, are not neutral and have their own limitations. One of these is that indents do not tell us much about the life of a convict, and nothing about his or her personal or inner life: we have to resort to 'narratives' for that. This is where 'Passages' has real value, particularly if we wish to say something significant about Brooks and his place in colonial history. We could go further: 'Passages', notwithstanding its undeniably moralistic tone, redolent of tracts like Ullathorne's *The Horrors of Transportation*, is a more complete and illuminating source of male convict experience than a plethora of archivally based, official but truncated documents. This is not to adopt a naïve realist view or to assume that such accounts are 'transparent'. Rather we caution against being overly skeptical about what constitutes 'fact' and how 'facts' are constituted—especially where the 'convict voice' is the one especially singled out for scrutiny.

Duffield rightly questions the limited, representational way historians have deployed narrativity to frame historical writing. However this need not disqualify narrative as a legitimate means of securing past experiences. Indeed, as Somers argues, if narrativity is reframed to recognise that 'social life and human lives are themselves "storied"', and that narrative is intrinsic to human beings epistemologically and ontologically coming to know, understand and make sense of the social world, then 'Bushman's' story assumes fundamental rather than marginal importance as evidence.[22] Moreover, it seems clear (although not conclusively so) that Brooks, given his class position and his penal history thereafter, was functionally illiterate or semi-literate and thus unable to compose a coherent narrative of this nature. It follows that someone else *had* to write his biography. Given the educational standards of the day, this person would have had to have been either another 'educated' or literate author (with or without a convict background), or a person with considerable facility in the English language. 'Passages' is a coherent 15 000-word text whose grammar and spelling are exemplary. This narrows the field of possible authors to journalists and newspaper editors, men of religion, 'men of letters', some politicians, higher government officials, men who attended university, some squatters and certain members of the middle class. The question is, does this disqualify or diminish such authorship as a '*convict* narrative'?

There are numerous cases—biographies are probably the best example—where another author tells the story of the person in question and where in most cases these purport to be 'true'. 'Passages' is a nineteenth-century example of an 'as told to' or, more accurately, 'as told through' biography which corresponds to enough known facts about early nineteenth-century English and colonial history to pass muster as a veridical record of at least one convict's experiences. This is quite a different issue to the discursive and historical contexts which 'Bushman' as *author*, as distinct from 'Bushman' as *convict*, draws on to compose the narrative.

Secondly, aside from the practical matter of a 'second-hand' author being necessary, there is an assumption that a text like 'Passages' cannot, and should not, 'represent' the 'convict voice' because it is more desirable that the convict represent him/herself. At first sight, this seems appealing common sense: but as certain convict- and ex-convict–authored works (for example, 'Alexander Harris' or James Hardy Vaux) attest, these have their own problems as sources for history. Valorising the 'convict voice', to borrow from Spivak, allows the middle-class, educated author to masquerade as the 'absent nonrepresenter' who lets the oppressed 'speak for themselves'. Yet, as she insists, the whole question of 'informants' and the 'subaltern' (which can be transposed in a case like Brooks's) is whether the latter can 'speak' in the first place. Taken together, these conditions are particularly pertinent for this collaboration to make 'Passages' presentable for publication at all: Brooks *may* have been illiterate; he was not inarticulate. Thus, 'Passages' can stand as a reliable 'convict narrative'. The differences between a Brooks-authored text and 'Bushman'-authored one lies in the discursive formations, historical contexts and tendentious agendas which produced 'Passages' as a public statement in Brisbane's major newspaper at the time.[23]

Who was 'Jack Bushman'? The case for James Swan

In 1990, around the time that Evans first came upon 'Passages' in the *Moreton Bay Courier*, John Moran privately published *Jack Bushman's Short Stories* which argued that 'Bushman' could well have been colonial journalist and newspaper editor William Wilkes. Our argument here, however, is that a more likely candidate (perhaps the most likely) was Wilkes's fellow editor, the Scottish liberal humanitarian James Swan. Our case for Swan and, conversely, against Wilkes (or any other author) rests on the internal evidence in the 'Bushman' stories and 'Passages' narrative; the corroborative proofs that derive from what is known about both Wilkes's and Swan's biographies; and the relevant British and colonial contexts in which both men lived.

According to Moran, Wilkes satisfies all, or most, of the criteria. He was a 'liberal journalist' with an 'extensive knowledge of the Moreton Bay district' who supported Separation. He was sympathetic to convicts and Aborigines and was someone who 'enjoyed a drink'. Transported for life for theft, he arrived in Sydney in 1833, joined a surveyor's team in the early 1840s, then came north to Moreton Bay to work for the squatter J. C. Pearce at Helidon Station near Ipswich. In 1848, Wilkes became editor (or, more accurately, joint editor with James Swan) of the *Moreton Bay Courier*, until 1856 when he returned to Sydney. Between 1856 and 1859, Wilkes contributed to a number of Sydney journals, was editor of the *Empire*, and wrote a column for the *Courier*, 'Notes and News by a Sydney Man'. From May to July 1859, the *Courier* serialised Wilkes's 'Bush Life in Australia' under the pen-name 'Charles Wotton', that is *after* 'Passages' had appeared, but with the final four of the 'Bushman' short stories still to come. At the end of this section we return to the significance of this chronology.[24]

Moran's attempt to deal with the problem of Wilkes's geographic location well away from Brisbane (and hence his inaccessibility to Brooks) is not convincing. He simply states that living in Sydney 'can in no way discount the possibility' that Wilkes was 'Bushman'. To elide the issue further, he then asserts that Wilkes gained a reputation for his humorous writings, 'hastily written on a desk composed of a piece of bark . . . "while living in the bush"'. One of these was the poem, 'The Raid', published in the *Queensland Magazine* in 1862 under another of Wilkes's pseudonym, 'Henry Arrowsmith, Cordwainer'.[25]

There is certainly some evidence to indicate that Wilkes may have been 'Bushman'. The latter had to be a journalist and/or a prolific writer and a particularly well-read one at that. Wilkes wrote many articles and editorials. He had written a poem about Aborigines ('The Raid'); was a keen proponent of Separation; was a heavy drinker; had bush experience; and had been in the colony twenty-five years (fifteen at least at Moreton Bay) before the 'Bushman' stories appeared. And, as an ex-convict, one can assume, he would have had a greater empathy with another convict's experience than a freeman colonial journalist like Swan.

Literary references abound in 'Bushman's' stories. These included Swift, Virgil, Donne, Thucydides, Homer, Cicero, Milton, Shakespeare, Gibbon, Macaulay, Burke, Dante, Cervantes, Bulwer-Lytton, Victor Hugo, and Keats. In 'The Raid', Wilkes (writing as 'Arrowsmith') does cite Homer and Milton and uses the comic character, Bardolph, from *Henry V* to describe one of the squatters—all of which show that 'Bushman' and Wilkes were familiar with the Western literary canon. None of this proves, however, that Wilkes was

'Bushman'. It does suggest, as we discuss below, that Swan represents an even more convincing figure than Wilkes on this score.[26]

Wilkes's views of Aborigines require more critical scrutiny in the light of Moran's assessment that some of 'Bushman's' stories, for example, 'My Siesta Disturbed by Justicia', advocate 'the need for justice for Aborigines'. Here we can note significant differences between its tone and content (together with references in 'Passages'), and the tenor of Wilkes's poem, 'The Raid'. Multiple readings are possible, but in our judgement the latter reflects a squatter-colonial perspective of frontier resistance that accords with Wilkes's experience working at Helidon in the early 1840s. Indeed, as Denis Cryle notes, Wilkes himself had taken an active part in this reprisal raid, terming himself 'the Hotspur of the North'.[27] In order to amuse his readers, Wilkes writes in a mock-heroic style which trivialises the seriousness of the bloody encounters actually occurring in south-eastern Queensland during this first, major thrust of pastoral invasion. Furthermore 'The Raid' drew on contemporary tropes that conflated 'savage' people with animals: 'they roll'd in the ashes like kittens at play/or like over-fed hogs on a hot summers day'—metaphors redolent of Thomas Carlyle's white supremacist polemic, *The Nigger Question* (1849), where he described black West Indians in Jamaica as 'sitting yonder with their beautiful muzzles up to the ears in pumpkins'. Furthermore, the poem refers to Aboriginal men as 'rude savages' and Aboriginal women as 'sundry black gins' and 'sable hags'. By contrast, 'Passages' has 'Old Tom' consistently respectful of Aborigines, particularly the women he met; and the 'Bushman' stories that deal with Aborigines never demean them as people.[28]

Instead, in the 'Justicia' story, Bushman quotes 'Ning-a-ning', an Aboriginal warrior from Bribie Island now encamped at Moggill, as saying:

> Many of my tribe have fallen. They have been murdered when offering no resistance. They have been shot down by my side. In the trees when looking for sugar bags have they been killed . . . There has been poison in the flour, and when the spirit of the blackfellow has gone out to meet the friendly feeling of the white, murder has lurked behind the smile.[29]

It seems scarcely conceivable that the man who wrote the insensitive burlesque 'The Raid', or who spoke scornfully of Aborigines as 'cannibals', could also have penned the above. As Cryle notes, 'Wilkes' disdain for the Aborigines and their white protectors . . . was one of the social bonds between squatters and their employees'.[30] This point alone seems sufficient to disqualify Wilkes from serious consideration.

While Moran has explored most of the short stories for clues, he has missed the hints 'Bushman' makes in his final effort, 'The Press Gang', which refers to the power of British journalists. In this autobiographical fragment, 'Bushman' recounts certain aspects of his life as a young man. At fifteen he was galvanised by the 'lamentations of the working orders', Chartism and the campaign to repeal the Corn Laws—movements that emerged after the Napoleonic Wars—and gathered strength into the early 1830s. Later in the narrative, 'Bushman' is editor of a local newspaper in his 'native town'. Some years later, he leaves to push his fortunes in Australia.[31]

This background corresponds more closely to James Swan's biography than to Wilkes's. Swan was born in 1811 in Glasgow, like his older and more historically famous friend, the Reverend John Dunmore Lang. Raised as a Baptist, Swan joined the Glasgow *Scots Times* printing office in the late 1820s. He abetted Lang in his scheme to send nonconformist Scots immigrants to New South Wales and in 1837 came to Australia under Lang's auspices to continue his career on the latter's newspaper, the *Colonist*, for the next three years. He joined the *Sydney Herald* in 1841 and, after two failed farming ventures, became the foundation foreman printer on the *Moreton Bay Courier* under its editor and owner, A. S. Lyons. He took over from Lyons in 1847 and wrote the paper's editorials either singly or alternately with Wilkes, until the beginning of 1856. In 1849 Swan was a leading committee member of the newly established Brisbane School of Arts, remaining an active member throughout the 1850s. During this period he acquired a number of land-holdings and properties, including a bookstore which supplied 'new books' to Brisbane. In 1856, Swan, with James Spence, headed a 'working class operatives movement' and in 1858 resumed management of the *Courier* until late 1859 when he retired, selling the newspaper to Theophilus Pugh.[32]

The significant point of difference between Wilkes and Swan is that the latter is far more likely to have been 'The Press Gang's' writer (and by inference the other stories as well) than Wilkes. As far as we know, Wilkes had no journalistic experience until 1848; Swan did. It now seems that Swan wrote most of the *Courier's* editorials between 1849 and 1856, when he was co-editing the paper with Wilkes, who was rather fond of his 'alcoholidays'.[33] Swan's role in the Brisbane School of Arts, with its 'well-stocked library' and as a bookstore owner, gave him access to books, articles, journals and newspapers that few other colonials in Brisbane or elsewhere could match. In addition, the Scottish Calvinist tradition he grew up with placed great store in education as the vehicle for middle-class social mobility and working-class self-improvement. Both men had convincing credentials insofar as the campaign for Queensland Separation was concerned. Again, however, Swan, as Lang's personal friend and major protagonist (albeit a sometimes critical one) for Lang's vision of a free-settler, Protestant, agricultural and cotton-producing colony, was a more consistent and active advocate for Separation than Wilkes.[34]

On the score of 'bush experience', Wilkes was perhaps ahead of Swan. He was in the colony longer and had experience on survey teams and a squatting property. At the same time, as Henry Lawson's example later showed, it was not essential to have extensive 'bush experience' to write about the 'bush'. Indeed, the idea of the 'Bushman' is a cultural and social construct which artists in various media have valorised throughout Australian history. Here we are dealing with the connections between authorship and representation, and the oscillations between empirical fact and narrative fiction. Like the arguments we made elsewhere about the authenticity or otherwise of 'convict' narratives, it is not necessary for a 'real' bushman to write about the 'bush'. And, as Swan's two failed farming ventures show, he had some experience of bush life. Furthermore, the two locales actually identified in the 'Bushman' narratives—Moggill and Fortitude Valley—were the settling ground for many of the Lang immigrants with whom Swan maintained close connections. Indeed, Swan's associate, William Pettigrew, had originally drawn up the farms at Moggill for Lang's *Lima* migrants, among whom 'Jack Bushman' was depicted as residing.[35]

The 'Bushman' stories allude to his being fond of 'the black bottle in the corner'. Moran has deduced that this could only describe Wilkes, who was probably an alcoholic. As Cryle has observed, such mores were fairly typical of the 'working journalist' habitus; but one quite distinct from the sober, respectable mien of someone like Swan. This is a critical point. Yet Swan was, for a Baptist, an extraordinarily tolerant man, humane towards Aborigines, uncomfortable with religious bigotry and supportive of working-class rights. His behaviour and writings reveal him as both empathetic and imaginative. Constructing a convivial drinking man's persona for 'Bushman' was surely not beyond him.[36]

A final compelling argument against Wilkes is both practical and chronological. While he *could* have sent these stories up from Sydney, as Moran suggests, it would have made him one of the most prolific writers in colonial Australia, given the contributions he was already making to several other newspapers.[37] Furthermore, the internal evidence from 'Passages' indicates that its author *was* in regular personal contact with Brooks and, crucially, that this contact occurred well after Wilkes was living in Sydney. There are three telling statements to this point. To begin with, Brooks relates the story about the clash between Aborigines and colonials at the Breakfast Creek camp in 1852 and dates this episode with some precision as occurring 'about six or seven years ago' before 'Passages' was published in 1859. Secondly, 'Bushman' remarks that he still had 'many stories to tell', which would be delivered 'when opportunity' offered 'for Jack Bushman to yarn with old Tom, the L'f'r' again. Thirdly, at the close of 'Passages', 'Bushman' personally visits Brooks who muses over the narrative as the former reads aloud to him 'page after page'. All these references hint at geographical proximity, not imaginative distance.[38] On the other hand, we know that Swan returned from a trip to

Britain and resumed editorship of the *Courier* in September 1858. The 'Bushman' stories begin strategically in November that year with 'A Romance of Separation'—a dream sequence interrelating life in London and Moggill. They peter out in early 1860, not long after Swan had ceded control of the newspaper to Pugh.[39]

Of course, it is quite likely that someone hitherto unknown may have also been 'Bushman'. Indeed he begins his second story with the observation that the reception of the first 'among his chums' has encouraged him to write again, as though he were a novice author.[40] Yet his literary capabilities and his rich cultural store of allusions point to a seasoned chronicler. Other names already suggested by Evans and Duffield—Thomas Dowse and Pugh—may easily be discounted due either to hostile relations with Aborigines or biographical insufficiencies. All we can assert presently is this: it *looks* rather like the kindly face of James Swan approaching down the track towards Brooks's humpy. Yet we cannot quite make him out.[41]

Thomas Brooks found, 'Jack Bushman' still at large

We should like to be able to state categorically that James Swan *was* 'Jack Bushman'. But we cannot. The evidence remains only circumstantial and there are too many imponderables still involved. What we can affirm with more certainty, however, is the historical reality of Brooks's existence and the substantiality of his convict experience. In saying this, we do not mean to betray undue innocence about the problems of memory-based narratives, whether transmuted by an intercessionary hand or otherwise. On the contrary, we are very much alive to the difficulties involved. Our recent discovery of a body of petitions written by James Hardy Vaux, appealing against retransportation in 1831 to the hell-hole of Moreton Bay, reveals that his famous *Memoirs* of 1819—the Australian colonies' first substantive convict narrative—had been so trammelled by Justice Barron Field as to animate Vaux to disown them. The document was 'erroneously said to be published by myself', Vaux complains, but had only resulted in 'serious injury' to his reputation. He had never intended his memoir for publication in the first place. That had fallen to others after he had composed it for the amusement of Newcastle's Commandant Thompson who had promised Vaux he would only show it 'to a few'.[42] In this case, a document privately prepared by a literate convict about his own 'extraordinary adventures' and never intended for immediate publication was severely reconstructed by a class superior *en route* to a publisher. In certain respects, therefore, the precious record of convict voices might equally be heard to denote as much about their ongoing disempowerment as their answering agency.

'Passages' too can clearly be interrogated for its thread of middle-class moralising which interlaces the narrative and echoes more an agenda-driven 'patron-editor', such as Swan, rather than the unvarnished sentiments of 'a rough convict and working man'.[43] Indeed, at the close of the account, the interventionist narrator shows his hand by wishing that the story's 'perusal be productive of as much good as the Spirit deserves which collates them for the public'.[44] Yet it is doubtful whether Brooks would have been as discontented with this as Vaux was with Barron Field's actions. To begin with, the occasional homily about law and order or the anti-transportationist jibe is relatively muted and unobtrusive. Even where the writer declaims about the moral laxity of the more hardened female convict, he breaks off with the observance: 'I would rather someone else who is more intimately acquainted with these peccadilloes should become their historian'.[45] Secondly, the facts, as we know them, about Brooks's colonial career are remarkably verifiable in this account, apart from the odd glitch in remembering all the dates, names and numbers accurately. 'I have not endeavoured by lying to make myself other than I am', 'Bushman'/Brooks states; and his words encourage confidence in their authenticity, for the official record tends largely and in its stony, authoritative way, to collaborate Brooks's more sanguine, experiential account, time after time.[46]

Thus, the central problem of 'Passages' is not so much one of authenticity as of the mystery of authorship. In its coda, 'Jack Bushman' sits by Thomas Brooks's fire, reading to 'Old Tom, the Lifer' and Susey, his Aboriginal companion, 'page after page' of 'the strange story' for his commentary and approval. Although Duffield prefers to view this simply as 'imagining a scene', we are not so sure. For it is entirely conceivable that someone like James Swan may have left his *Courier* office or his George Street home-cum-bookshop that Saturday evening to visit the old 'Lifer's' humpie near Fortitude Valley and read aloud to him the literary outcome of their various, previous yarns together. It is not inconceivable, therefore, that this is a real 'bush' scene: in the firelight, we can glimpse Brooks's ancient, weatherbeaten face, his 'blue eyes' perhaps still glinting, his once-powerful frame ceding now to time, his back stiffened by its lattice-work of scarification as he bends attentively forward. Yet 'Bushman' himself is in the shadows, his outline illuminated by the firelight's glow, but his back still towards us. We hear his words but we do not know his face.[47]

3

The search for the invisible man

Hamish Maxwell-Stewart

The publication of Stephen Nicholas's *Convict Workers* in 1988 was greeted by a storm of protest. This revisionist history claimed to have turned thirty years of historical writing on its head. The main arguments of the book were that, rather than consisting of the dregs of Britain's industrialising cities, transported convicts were drawn from a cross-section of the British and Irish working classes and that their considerable skills were put to productive use in the Australian colonies. The book challenged the then dominant view of convict Australia as a dumping ground for the refuse of the British gaols, seeking to substitute instead a new vision of early colonial Australia as an efficient unfree labour system.

In an important review article Raymond Evans and William Thorpe attacked *Convict Workers* for its naïve use of official documentation.[1] While Evans and Thorpe welcomed many of the findings of the *Convict Workers* team, they were incensed by Nicholas's claim to have written a history from below. They maintained that an over-reliance on official records (the book was based on an analysis of over 19 000 convict records) had resulted in the creation of a 'statist' history—an account where the lash was largely silent and convicts appeared to be imbued with the Protestant work ethic. Evans and Thorpe suggested an alternative approach to the history of convict Australia which employed prisoners' stories as devices to be pitted against administrative accounts. In particular they called for more work on convict tales of penal station life (penal stations were a particularly neglected topic in *Convict Workers*).

This chapter is a belated attempt to answer that call. It is based on a narrative which was written on the back and front of Commissariat Department order forms and prefaced: 'Memoranda by Convict Davis Servant to Mr Foster, Superintendent of Convicts, Norfolk Island—1843—Relating principally to Macquarie Harbour'.[2] This text has some interesting features. Several sections have been underscored or marked with large crosses. At one point an old,

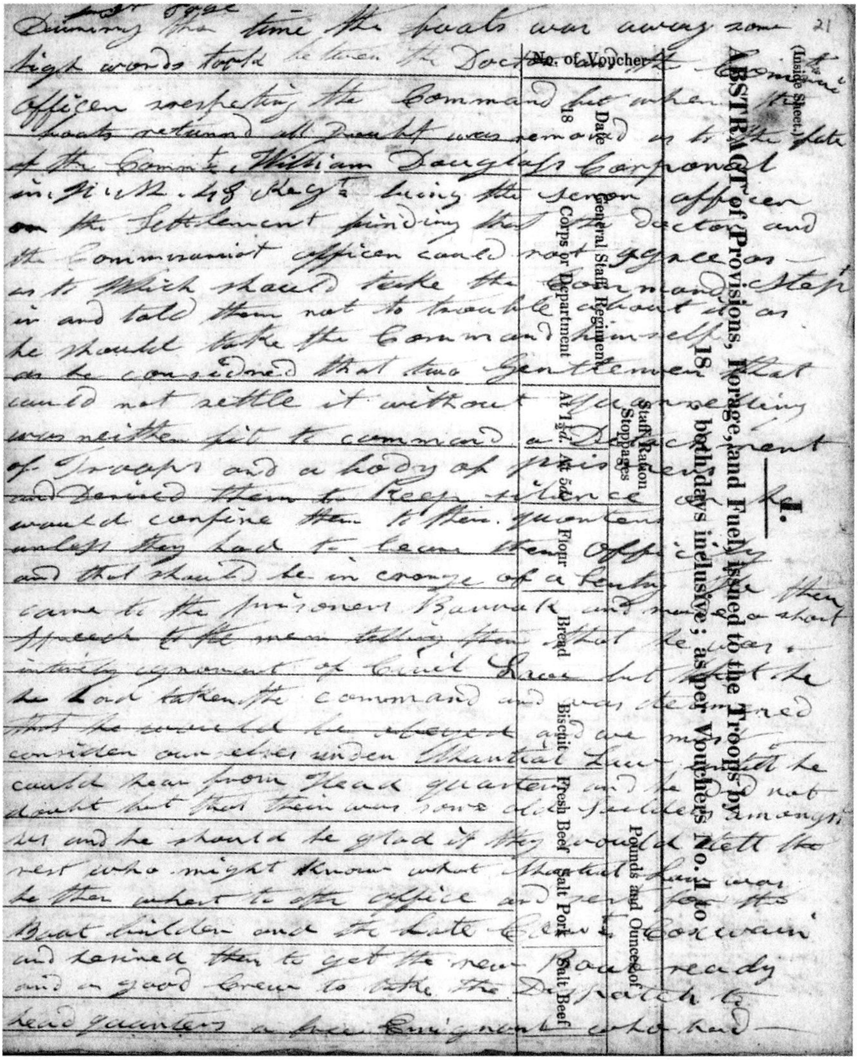

During the time the boats was away some
high words took between the Doctor and the Commissariat
Officer respecting the Command but when the
boats returned all doubt was removed as to the fate
of the Comm^t William Douglass Corporal
in H.M. 48 Regt being the senior officer
on the Settlement finding that the doctor and
the Commissariat officer could not agree as
as to which should take the Command stept
in and told them not to trouble about it as
he should take the Command himself
as he considered that two Gentlemen that
could not settle it without quarrelling
was neither fit to command a Detachment
of Troops and a body of prisoners
and desired them to keep silence or he
would confine them to their quarters
unless they had to leave their Offices
and that should be in charge of a Sentry He then
came to the prisoners Barrack and made a short
speech to the men telling them that he was
intirely ignorant of Civil Law but that he
he had taken the command and was determined
that he would be obeyed and we must
consider ourselves under Martial Law untill he
could hear from Head quarters and he had not
doubt but that there was some old soldiers amongst
us and he should be glad if they would tell the
rest who might know what Martial Law was
he then went to the office and sent for the
Boat builder and the late Crew's Coxswain
and desired them to get the new Boat ready
and a good Crew to take the Despatch to
head quarters a free Emigrant who had

Davis's hand scrawled across a commissariat order form (from Memoranda by Convict Davis Servant to Mr Foster, Superintendent of Convicts, Norfolk Island, 1843).

partially erased, note is just legible beneath Davis's superimposed scrawl. It reads 'Top Hammock For Mr Foster'. At another point, almost as though practising a signature, someone has inscribed in the margin: 'Mr Wm Foster, Mr Wm Foster, Mr Wm Foster, Mr Wm Foster, Mr Da M Wm Foster, Foster, Mr Shone'. The narrative also has an interesting flavour. To quote a section from near the beginning:

> John Cuthbertson of the 48th Regt was the officer—appointed to form the Settlement—and I think the most inhuman Tyrant the world ever produced since the Reign of Nero—I have seen several Commandants on Norfolk Island but the worst was a feeling one compared to him Oppression and tyrany was his Motto he had neither justice nor Compassion for the naked starved and wretched—Humanity was a virtue he did not acknowledge a man taken before him was allowed no apeal he was in a manner tried before he was taken to the office . . . The following is a true copy—

Who was Davis? After an exhaustive examination of convict musters, colonial shipping indents and correspondence files it has proved possible to piece together the records of most of the 1152 convicts who served time at Macquarie Harbour. The list includes five men called Davis or Davies. George Davis was drowned on 28 March 1822 shortly after the settlement had opened.[3] John Davis, a Jewish shopkeeper from Woolwich who had been transported on the *Elizabeth*, absconded from the settlement in January 1823 and is recorded in the official return of runaways as having 'perished in the woods'.[4] A similar fate is thought to have beset Thomas Davis, who made his bid for freedom in mid-1825, never to be seen again.[5] John Davies, who worked at Macquarie Harbour as an assigned servant to the Commissariat Officer Thomas Lempriere, did not arrive at the settlement until 1827, long after the events described in the narrative, thus making him an unlikely author.[6] This leaves William Davis as the only remaining candidate. He was ordered to Sarah Island with his wife Jane in 1824 after they had been caught up in a sheep-stealing scandal. They were both transferred to Maria Island in 1829 and then subsequently freed. No link can be found between them and Norfolk Island and, even if William had been sent there, he would have been in his seventies in the mid-1840s. There are other problems as well. The author of the narrative makes no mention of being sent to Macquarie Harbour with his wife. The historical William Davis was employed as overseer of shoemakers and had his own separate quarters, again details which are missing from the narrative. Finally, the key events covered in the text occurred between September 1822 and April 1824, yet William and Jane Davis did not arrive at Sarah Island until 9 August 1824.[7]

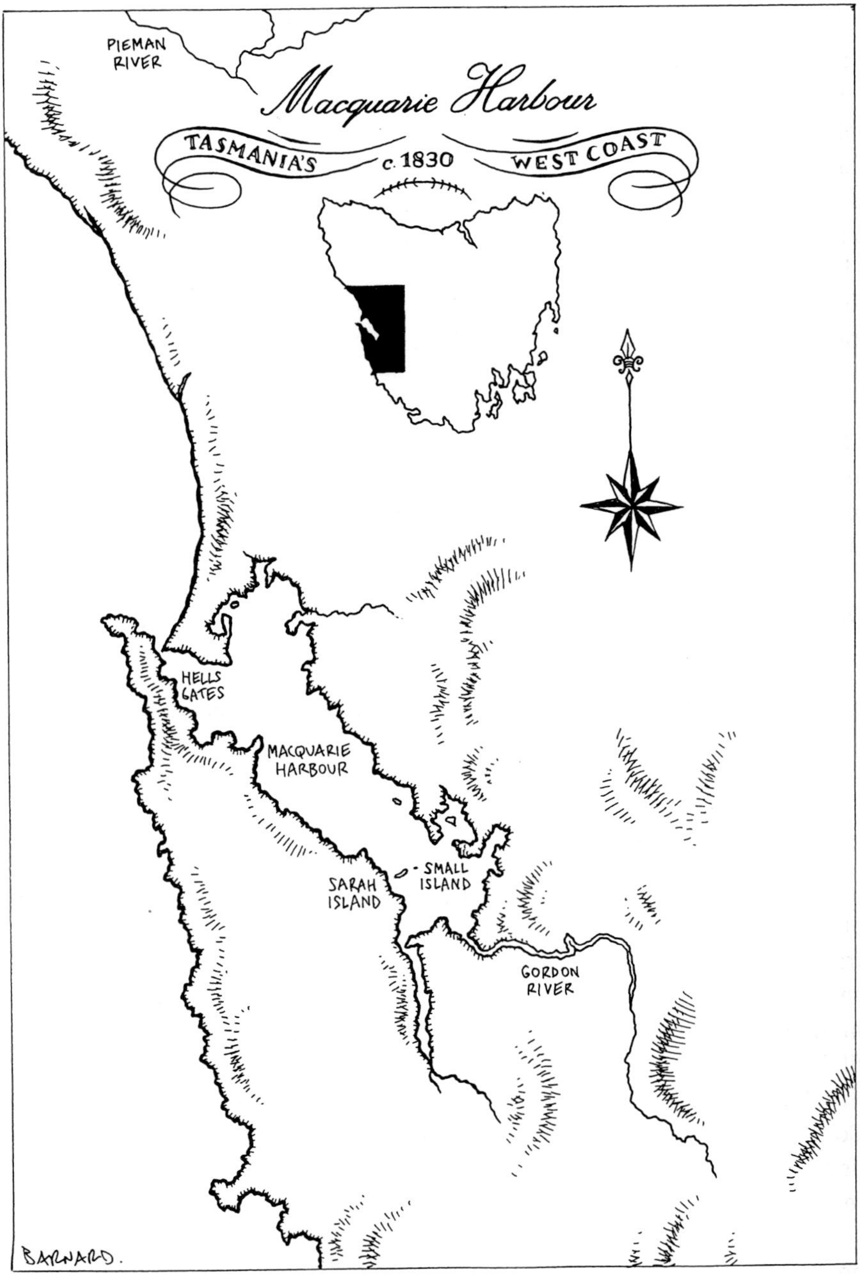

PIEMAN RIVER
Macquarie Harbour
TASMANIA'S c.1830 WEST COAST
HELLS GATES
MACQUARIE HARBOUR
SMALL ISLAND
SARAH ISLAND
GORDON RIVER
BARNARD.

It is perhaps not very surprising that it should prove difficult to find a 'Davis' to fit 'Davis's narrative'. It is not unusual for the authors of working-class tales to assume invented identities, a famous example being the memoirs of 'Jack Nastyface'.[8] The convict identity behind *Passages from the Life of a Lifer* remained concealed behind the pseudonym of 'Jack Bushman' before Evans and Thorpe demonstrated that the tale was based on the life of the convict Thomas Brooks—a discovery made by aligning a section of the narrative with the historical record. It was in fact 'Bushman's' account of his escape from a property at Jerry Plains near Port Macquarie and the subsequent bushranging campaign that he fought with 'Black' John Goff and two other runaways that provided the vital clues. [9]

Is it possible to use the same technique to track down the identity behind Davis's narrative? In what must be one of colonial Australia's great coincidences, Davis also relates an episode when he absconded with a prisoner named 'Black' Gough—clearly the same man who featured in 'Jack Bushman's' account of the escape from Jerry Plains, albeit 'Jack Bushman' spells the name 'Goff'. In Davis's narrative this other escape takes place on the coast of western Van Diemen's Land:

> my third attempt was with a man of desparate character . . . Black Gough and 2 others we took 3 soilders by surprise at their fire in the dusk and took their provisions and Arms they made their way to the Settlement and the commadant dispatched a party in a Whale Boat 75 miles on the main Beach it intercepted us at the Pyemans River they succeeded in taking 3 and that one dead—

John Gough, a black sailor born on the Isle of Wight, did indeed serve time at Macquarie Harbour. He was transferred there as punishment for escaping from Port Macquarie.[10] Gough arrived at Macquarie Harbour along with seventeen other transportees from New South Wales in September 1822. Eight months later he made a renewed bid for freedom. The short entry on Gough's file is remarkably similar to Davis's account and there can be little doubt but that both refer to the same event. On 1 May 1823 he was arraigned before Commandant Cuthbertson for 'Absconding into the woods & assisting in depriving 2 soldiers of their flintlocks'. For this offence he was sentenced to receive 100 lashes and labour twelve months in irons.[11]

The Macquarie Harbour offence registers reveal that Gough was not the only convict to receive a flogging for this daring escape attempt. In all there were six other absconders. Daniel McGee was recaptured on 28 April while the remainder were taken with Gough a few days later. They were: Thomas Knox, a whitesmith tried on the Isle of Man but born in Belfast; James Robert, a goldsmith, and Thomas Yates, a butcher, both from London; Peter Keefe, a shoemaker, from Queens County; and John Sharp, a weaver, from County

Tyrone.[12] Unfortunately, however, none of the six prisoners who absconded with Gough led lives which remotely fit the events described in Davis's narrative. Davis's narrative thus fails the Evans and Thorpe accuracy test.

One of the curious things about the narrative is that it is quite specific about dates. For example, the author claims that he was sentenced to transportation to Macquarie Harbour on 27 December 1823. This use of detail may merely be part of a wider attempt to impose an illusion of accuracy on the mind of the reader—a point made by Rawlings in his discussion of eighteenth-century criminal biographies.[13] Yet, while no convict was sentenced to transportation to Macquarie Harbour on this exact date, Thomas Brain and William Yates, two prisoners assigned to Mr Wade, were tried before a bench for stealing wheat the property of their master a year earlier—on 28 December 1822. Both were sentenced to receive 100 lashes and afterwards to be transported for three years, the exact punishment Davis claims to have received in his narrative. Did Davis make a slip in recollecting the date of his conviction? This seems likely, as the narrative recalls many events which occurred before December 1823. Furthermore, William Yates is referred to by the author of Davis's narrative as 'my Companion'—strong evidence that the elusive author was Thomas Brain (also spelt Brein or Bryan).[14]

If a clinching argument is required then it is supplied by Brain's subsequent history. After his release from Macquarie Harbour Brain was again arrested for stealing three jackets and eight waistcoats, tried before the Supreme Court in Hobart in May 1826, found guilty, and sentenced to death. Although his partner in crime, Rowles, was executed, Brain's sentence was commuted to life transportation. In December 1826 he was embarked for Norfolk Island, thus placing him in the same location as the author of the 'Davis' manuscript.[15]

If only life were so simple. The August 1844 muster of convicts incarcerated on Norfolk Island, the year after the narrative was supposed to have been written, contains no reference to Thomas Brain. This is perhaps not surprising—eighteen years would have been a peculiarly long stretch to serve in this lowest deep of the penal 'system'. The muster, however, does include a further surprise. One of the prisoners listed is John Davis, a Jewish shopman from Woolwich who had originally been transported on the *Elizabeth*. Was this Davis the author of Davis's narrative? If so then the story would appear to have been ghost-written since, according to the official record, John Davis absconded from Macquarie Harbour just twenty-four days after arriving at the settlement in January 1823.[16]

Davis resurfaced seventeen years later at the Campbelltown Quarter Sessions (New South Wales) where, on 18 January 1840, he was charged with 'being at large with fire arms' and sentenced to retransportation for life for a third time.[17] If confirmation is required that the man who arrived on Norfolk

S. W. View of Macquarie Harbour, *by an unknown artist, shows the penal settlement on Sarah Island.*

Island in 1840 was the same individual who in 1823 had slipped into the wilderness of western Van Diemen's Land, then it can be found on the indent of the *Elizabeth*. This was the transport that had originally brought Davis to Australia in 1816. Against his entry an administrative hand has scrawled in pencil the words 'On Norfolk Island'.

In other respects, however, John Davis is an unlikely author. Unlike Brain, Davis could not have been an eyewitness to the events described at some length in the narrative, for he only spent three weeks at Macquarie Harbour before absconding. John Davis's convict record is also a poor match for the manuscript's account of penal servitude. While the author of the narrative claims to have been sentenced to Macquarie Harbour by a magistrates bench in Van Diemen's Land, John Davis was transferred from New South Wales after attempting to escape from Port Macquarie.[18] Yet, the coincidence remains striking—John Davis miraculously reappears on Norfolk Island and is resident there at the time the Davis narrative is written.

The problem of authorship is symptomatic of a wider issue. Whereas there are many details in the text which can be 'corroborated', to use Evans and Thorpe's term, the text also contains narrative flaws which defy logic. Thus, 'Davis', whoever he was, describes one overseer as a 'Sweed' and 'as great a brute as ever existed in the shape of a human'. This was the man who charged the prisoner James Crawford with refusing to work and disobedience of orders when Crawford, who was suffering from dysentery and malnutrition, collapsed under the weight of the load he was carrying. There was a Swede at Macquarie Harbour; farmer's man Hans Olsen gave his place of birth as Norway (remember that in 1815 Norway and Sweden were united in a union only dissolved in 1905).[19] James Crawford was a prisoner at Macquarie Harbour. He served two stints at the settlement in the early 1820s. As Davis correctly recollects, Crawford was a sailor by calling and his punishment record reveals that on 2 November 1822 he was sentenced to '100 lashes and to work in irons until further orders' for 'insubordinate conduct towards his overseer and refusing to work'. There are, however, also substantial discrepancies between the official record and Davis's version of events. Problems arise in placing Olsen and Crawford in the same place at the same time. Crawford was executed in 1824. Olsen, on the other hand, did not arrive at the settlement until February 1825.[20]

Similar problems arise with Davis's description of the cannibal Alexander Pearce. As he relates:

> I believe that his skeleton was sent home to the R[oyal] C[ollege]s of Surgeons London for what reason I cannot tell as he had nothing peculiar about him at least outward appearance he was a man about 5 feet 7 inches in height dark brown hair heavy eyebrows rather stout

> made and stood much after appearance of a Farmers Servant but if I mistake not he was a Seaman Yorkshire was his Native place.

Again, there is a curious mixture of 'fact' and 'fiction'. Pearce's skull was handed over to the phrenologists, and indeed now resides in the Academy of Natural Sciences, Philadelphia.[21] Yet, it seems strange that Davis should get this detail right (a non-Macquarie Harbour event) and the description of Pearce so wrong. For Pearce's convict record states that he stood just 5 foot 3¼ inches tall, and was a native of County Monaghan, Ireland, not Yorkshire. While his hair was recorded as brown, neither of the two surviving descriptions taken of Pearce describe him as 'stout made', although this was an epithet frequently ascribed to convicts.[22]

Mistakes of this nature are worrying. They cast a shadow of suspicion over the authenticity of the entire manuscript. Unless, that is, in our attempts to track down the elusive author we have asked the wrong set of questions. There is a danger that in attempting to authenticate Davis's narrative, we have missed the point of this remarkable below-decks text. Instead of wasting time searching for the hand that signed the paper, a more profitable task might be to search for Davis's readers.

In the passage describing his supposed escape with the notorious 'Black' John Gough, Davis reminds his readers that Gough 'was ultimately sent to this Island and Executed for Murder at the first Mutiney'. This is, in fact, one of the many instances where Davis's text can be 'corroborated'. In 1824 John Gough attempted his third escape from Macquarie Harbour. This time he managed to get clear of the settlement and when he was finally apprehended he was lodged in the gaol in Hobart. From here he was shipped to New South Wales with a recommendation that he should be sent to Moreton Bay penal station. In the event, however, Gough was returned to Port Macquarie where he was involved in yet another armed break-out—the one described in 'Jack Bushman's' narrative. Sentenced to death, Gough was reprieved on condition of transportation for life to Norfolk Island. There he led an attack on the military barracks. The rebels managed to first shoot and then bayonet a corporal to death but lost the element of surprise before they could seize the barracks. Weighing up the situation, Gough and fifty other mutineers decided that discretion was the better part of valour and retreated to the neighbouring Phillip's Island. In the morning the military launched a dawn raid on the island stronghold. A desperate fire fight ensued as the rebels tried to pin the invading soldiers on the beach. The convict insurgents kept up a hail of fire for an hour and then their powder ran out. Fourteen of the insurgents were taken prisoner and two committed suicide by jumping into the sea. Gough and the remainder headed for the interior where they were eventually starved out. At the subsequent Supreme Court proceedings Gough was capitally convicted. Like Alexander Pearce, his remains were delivered to a surgeon for dissection after his execution.

In that little aside Gough 'was ultimately sent to *this* Island and Executed for Murder at the first Mutiney' (author's emphasis), Davis identifies both his intended audience and his message. The story was self-evidently composed, not for a middle-class readership, as is the case with practically every other surviving convict narrative, but for his fellow convicts. Davis's audience was literally captive. This explains why the narrative makes direct comparisons between conditions at Norfolk Island and Macquarie Harbour. Thus, when describing the 'cats' employed on Sarah Island Davis ends with the following passage: '100 lashes may appear a trifle after the talk of their 300 on Norfolk but I do say that they [*sic*] man never was borne that could take 300 at Macquarie'.

As with the Gough episode, the purpose of this passage is twofold. Not only does it serve to place the unfolding narrative within the context of the Norfolk Island experience but it locates the storyteller at the centre of the unfolding drama. Davis claims that he received 100 lashes several times on Sarah Island. If this was not enough to gain the respect of his audience, then the narrator also claims to have suffered with John Gough and to have gazed upon the face of cannibal Pearce. It is for this reason that the narrative rattles off a description of Pearce which has all the appearance of a convict department record.

There is more to this narrative, however, than at first meets the eye. The account of Pearce's initial escape is illustrative of the complexities of the text. The story of the escape and subsequent resort to cannibalism at first appears to be little different from any of the many accounts of this episode in circulation in the early nineteenth century. This, for example, is how Davis recounts the story of the first murder:

> a man was then appointed the Wretch that God may forgive him to do the deed taking up the axe he without the slightest notice struck the unfortunate man a blow on the Temple he then took his knife and stuck him in the neck as a Butcher would a sheep and caught his Blood in a tin dish of which he took a harty drink they then cut some of the Body for their supper the Murderer then cut out the Heart and broiled it on the fire with the greatest Indifference.

The difference with Davis's account is the twist at the end: the gruesome story of Pearce's first escape is used to set up an attack on Lieutenant Cuthbertson's regime as commandant at Macquarie Harbour in the early 1820s. According to the narrative, it was Cuthbertson's misrule which caused the escape. It was because of his cruel tyranny that Pearce and his hapless confederates went to such desperate lengths to escape the settlement. In order to reinforce the point the description of Pearce the cannibal's blood-soaked adventures in the woods is followed by an account of bloody pursuits of an official nature.

> William Holliday I believe was the name of the man was in a weak sickly state and after going in the morning to hospital one day he was brought before the court for endeavouring to impose on Doctor found guilty and sentenced to 50 Lashes he was taken to the point to receive them he pleaded very hard to be forgiven on the score of illness but it was all to no purpose he was tied up and punishment whent on admist the most Heart rendering screams and cries for Mercy but his appeals was made to men that never forgave a Lash—after 30 Lashes he never spoke when he had received 5 more, the sup[t] of convicts returned submisively to observe that he thought the man had fainted the Doctor then stept of the gangway and found that he was quite dead no one new the murmers among the men say that he received 5 lashes after his Death but the affair ended without A question being asked in fact I do not think it was ever known at head quarters afficially.

William Holliday's name occurs in Lempriere's account of life at Macquarie Harbour. He was supposed to be the first person interred on the 'isle of the dead', later renamed Holiday Island in his honour.[23] The Macquarie Harbour death register, however, is at odds with this account. It names the first convict to be buried at the settlement as John Ollery—there must be a suspicion that the confusion has arisen from some kind of convict joke about 'Ollery's holiday'. Ollery died on 2 May 1823 in hospital—another case of Davis getting it wrong. Well, not quite. A shoemaker from Lincoln, Ollery was tried just once at Macquarie Harbour. On 27 April 1823 he was sentenced to receive twenty-five lashes for 'disobedience of orders and refusing to work'. According to Ollery's record he only received ten strokes, the 'Assistant Surgeon being of the opinion that he could not bear the remainder'. Five days later he was dead. Nowhere but in Davis's account is Ollery's death linked to this flogging. There appears to have been no official report and all three accounts of the penal settlement authored by free administrative officials are silent on the issue.[24] The message is inescapable—this is an account about two murderers, Cuthbertson and Pearce, and it is the first who should take the responsibility for the second.

Like Captain Logan at Moreton Bay, Cuthbertson received his just deserts—he was drowned when a whaleboat overturned in December 1823. Davis gives this episode the full treatment. Again his version follows the general drift of the account found in the history of Macquarie Harbour by the Commissariat Officer Thomas Lempriere. Davis, however, adds little touches of his own. According to him it was Cuthbertson's vanity which was responsible for the accident. Disaster struck when in a storm the newly finished schooner the *Governor Sorell* broke her moorings. This was the first ship to be built at Sarah Island and Cuthbertson, naturally anxious to save her, ordered a boat out. In attempting to get a line on board, however, the would-be rescuers were smashed against the schooner in the swell and the crew forced to clamber on board the larger vessel. There was now some urgency as the *Sorell* was rapidly approaching a lee shore. Cuthbertson ordered another boat crew out and then, growing impatient, called for his own vessel to be manned. In Davis's account the sequence of events is dominated by two contrasting characters. On the one hand there is the vain Cuthbertson, on the other, there is the commandant's coxswain, a man named Anderson, who, as Davis relates, had been mate of a whale ship, master of a slaver and had shipped aboard a West Indiaman.

Cuthbertson, against the expert advice of Anderson, attempted to charge headlong into an approaching squall in a boat ironically named the *Bucephalus*—Bucephalus was the name of Alexander the Great's horse. The inevitable happened and Cuthbertson, the would-be all-conquering hero, was bucked into the harbour along with his unfortunate crew. The survivors regrouped around the upturned vessel. Cuthbertson was all for sticking with the wreckage until they were washed ashore. Anderson, however, had had enough. Sticking an oar under his arms he 'whent before the wind and sea' reaching safety. All but one of the surviving members of the boat crew chose to follow Anderson's example. Catter, the convict who chose to remain with Cuthbertson to the last, died with his brave but cruel and stupid commandant.

Ripping stuff, but just in case anybody hasn't got the message, Davis underscores the point with a second story. Following the death of Cuthbertson, the civil officers at the settlement quarrelled over who should take command. Fed up with these petty squabbles, William Douglas, corporal of the 48th, stepped to the fore. He announced that, all other candidates having demonstrated that they were neither 'fit to command a Detachment of Troops' or 'a body of prisoners', he would assume command. According to Davis, Douglas's period in charge was a model of good government: 'there was no murder committed' during his reign 'nor any man took the Bush'.

Contrast this with Surgeon Barnes's report to the Molesworth Committee. According to Barnes, as soon as Douglas assumed command the prisoners attempted a rebellion. The corporal responded by an unwarranted show of force, flogging everyone he suspected of plotting against him. For the record, the reconstituted offence register fails to distinguish anything spectacular about Corporal Douglas's period of office.[25]

The point that Davis makes is that compared to the skills possessed by common soldiers, seafarers and mechanics, the talents of the high and mighty are piffling. But Davis doesn't stop here—one of the impressive things about his memoranda is the range of tricks employed to paint the regime in the worst possible light. Perhaps the most important of these is the way in which he pre-empts middle-class attacks on the morality of the lower order. Davis twists his accusers' spotlight through 180 degrees to expose his would-be critics to the full glare of their own rhetoric. The contrast with published convict narratives is striking. As Ian Duffield has demonstrated, Jack Bushman's *Passages from the Life of a Lifer* contains embedded gender, race and class discourses written into the text by a middle-class editor. The purpose of these passages was to give the text appeal to the readership of the *Moreton Bay Courier*, the paper which serialised Bushman's 'Passages' in the late 1850s. Thus, Bushman's descent into crime is triggered by the death of his first wife—depicted as an angel. He resorts to the alehouse where he meets, and falls in lust with, his second wife. This character conforms to a standard trope within English criminal biography, 'the sexually deviant woman'; pipe in one hand and glass in the other, she lures the 'susceptible' Bushman into a life of crime.[26]

Such 'bad women' were also to be met with at Macquarie Harbour. In the early 1820s a small group of female convicts were transported to Sarah Island. As Commissariat Officer Thomas Lempriere explains: 'The grossest immorality could not fail to reign in a place when there were no means of keeping the sexes apart'. Lempriere singled out one episode to illustrate his point. Four women were sent to assist a male prisoner who was employed at the Heads collecting shells to make lime. Not only was this operation unsupervised, but no attempt was made to provide separate accommodation for the women. Lempriere concludes the passage with a piece of general finger-wagging. 'Numerous were the cases of immorality, but we will pass them over with the silent disgust they merit.'[27]

This same episode is described in Davis's narrative, except here the details are a little different. According to Davis, on New Year's Day 1822 some of the military were seen in company with the female attendant at the hospital. As a punishment Cuthbertson ordered that five women be placed in a whaleboat equipped with some blankets, a pot, a week's rations and an old musket. They were then taken ten miles beyond the Heads and marooned on an ocean beach with instructions to collect shells. This is the cue for Davis to conduct some finger-wagging of his own:

> What would the Good People of England think (they certainly would say that it was false) if they where told an officer in His Majestys service sent 5 women 35 miles from the settlement with no other protection than an old musquet to be used by themselves (and no shelter but the trees and a blanket each) and several tribes of natives known to be within a few miles of them.

And as for sexual contact, Davis relates that the men in the hauling gangs were too weak to even carry the female convicts from the launch to the harbour edge, let alone indulge in any shenanigans.

In his parting shot Davis relates that, rather than the male prisoners, it was Cuthbertson's replacement, Lieutenant Wright, who had trouble keeping his trousers on. This was a man who, according to Davis, possessed all his predecessor's vices but was devoid of his one virtue, bravery. The object of Wright's affection was a soldier's wife of reputed easy virtue. Having set his eye upon gaining the affections of his subordinate's spouse, Wright discovered that he had a rival in the doctor's mate. This was a young man named Elderidge who had arrived free, but had been transported to Macquarie Harbour after being drawn into a cattle-stealing racket. Up early one morning, Wright saw Elderidge heading into the barracks. The Commandant sped after his rival only to run into a seaman from the supply vessel *Waterloo*, the inference being that the married soldiers' quarters had degenerated into a brothel. The sailor was arrested and the search commenced for Elderidge, who was eventually discovered by the Commandant hidden in a large chest in the lady's bedroom. Like all of the convicts mentioned by name in Davis's narrative, George Wray Elderidge can be traced.[28] Elderidge (who was indeed employed as dispenser of medicines, the official title for the doctor's mate) had only one charge entered against his name while at Macquarie Harbour. On April Fool's Day 1824 he was punished for 'Absenting himself from Quarters after hours and being found concealed in a box in one of the soldier's huts'.[29]

According to Davis, an incensed Wright dragged the seaman and Elderidge down to the point to be flogged. This is at odds with the punishment register which records that Elderidge was punished with seven days' solitary confinement on bread and water; a flogging, however, provides Davis with a convenient stage to turn the tables on the Commandant. Arraigned before the assembled gangs, the seaman refused to strip, claiming that he was a free man and that as such Wright had no power over him. The commandant disputed his word and had the clothes torn off him before a message arrived from the supply vessel to confirm the sailor's tale. Davis's narrative finishes with Jack the free seaman throwing his bloody clothes at the feet of Wright before storming off to consult a lawyer in Hobart Town.

In many ways this may seem like a strange point for Davis's story to close. It is certainly unusual compared to the conventional narrative format. There is none of the moralising agenda found at the end of so many supposed convict songs along the lines of 'learn from my story and you will avoid my dreadful fate'.[30] There again, Davis's narrative also departs from the conventional beginning. There is no mention of the crime which brought the author to Australia, let alone the tired old line, 'I was born of poor but honest folk'.

Instead Davis's narrative cracks straight in with a description of Macquarie Harbour, a passage which paints a geographical backdrop against which the author acts out a series of alternate scenes of farce, gore and tyranny.

What we have here is the script for a piece of Norfolk Island storytelling—a set of tales designed to be delivered orally about incarceration and excarceration. These were probably first told by Thomas Brain after he arrived on Norfolk Island in the late 1820s. We can guess that Davis subsequently inherited the mantle of Macquarie Harbour storyteller, since he too had been a prisoner at that notorious hellhole. We should have no illusions about the nature of the 'Davis' narrative. Just like the convict indents employed by the *Convict Workers'* team, this text is the product of power relationships—this is what makes it tick. The written version of the story almost certainly owes its existence to the relatively relaxed regime characteristic of Alexander Maconochie's reign as Norfolk Island Commandant between March 1840 and February 1844.[31] Although Maconochie's regime contrasted with the savage repression of the rule of other Norfolk Island commandants, an open attack on the convict administration could hardly be expected to go unpunished. The long-defunct penal station on Sarah Island was distant enough to act as a cipher. After all, Maconochie himself had attacked the failures of penal administration under the assignment system. For all this, Davis's text is careful to damn the system through allusion rather than outright attack. Yet it should be apparent that the real target of his remarkable Sarah Island tale is all convict administrators.

Can Davis's story be employed to give us a greater understanding of convict experience in the way called for by Evans and Thorpe? The answer to this is no—or at least not if his tale is taken literally. To read this story as evidence of what actually happened at Sarah Island would be to fall into the same trap as that which ensnared the *Convict Workers* team. Davis's tale is not an unproblematic account of life in a colonial penal station (as if such a thing could exist). Instead, it is something much more valuable, a convict representation of the cruelty and stupidity of penal regimes: a counter-vision of immense help in reading the many representations of vicious, lowly, criminal lives authored by commandants, chaplains and other middle-class worthies. The lesson of the Davis narrative is not that such and such happened—but that convicts saw things differently. Without taking that different view on board it is impossible to see the convicts; they remain invisible, disguised by those Dickensian tropes so beloved of the pre-*Convict Workers* histories.[32]

4

Seven tales for a man with seven sides

Hamish Maxwell-Stewart

It was a nightmare voyage. From the start, fierce westerlies bedevilled the passage of the *Sarah*, bound from Portsmouth for Van Diemen's Land. Heavy tumbling waves broke continually over the forecastle, and water poured through the hawser holes whence 'it flowed in torrents over the combings of the hatchways and into the holds'. The prisoners' beds, the ship's hospital, everything in the lower tiers of the vessel was saturated. It was impossible to contemplate opening the portholes, and only briefly between storms could the convicts be released from their foetid quarters and brought on deck for fresh air and exercise. To make matters worse, the prisoners had attempted to mutiny—passing muskets through the deck ventilators to their comrades below. After the suspected ringleaders were secured in irons, the deck ventilators had been ordered shut. Foul, stale air encouraged bacteria to breed, and a virulent streptococcal infection, erysipelas, swept through the vessel. Despite the best efforts of the Surgeon Superintendent, labouring eighteen hours a day, prisoners by the dozen succumbed to the infection with its high fevers and painful raised blotches of red skin on the face and legs. Stoves were lit between decks, and floors constantly swabbed to try and dry the hospital and the prisoners' quarters. The air was regularly fumigated with chloride of lime, and with clouds of acidic steam produced by immersing hot shot into vats of vinegar.[1]

In the stinking gloom, four men whose names did not appear on the *Sarah*'s muster roll were shackled together.[2] When sprung in Valparaiso, Chile, they gave their names as William Jones, James Smith, William Williams and James Connor. No one believed them. They were taken into custody by British naval officers confident they were arresting four of the empire's most wanted escapees, mutineers who in February 1834 had seized the brig *Frederick* at the Macquarie Harbour penal station and sailed her to freedom across the South Pacific.[3] The four pseudonymous villains were sent first to London on the *North Star*, and now amidst the first-time transportees on the *Sarah* were travelling south towards their next round of fate in Van Diemen's Land. When the *Sarah* came up the Derwent and the muster master went on board, he may have taken some dark delight in matching each of the four chained prisoners to a record of physical description in the registers of the convict department. Only ten entries need be consulted, entries for the ten mutineers known to have stolen the *Frederick*. Whatever the four men on the *Sarah* might call themselves, their identification was already fixed:

William Jones—Police Number 280 William Shires per *Maria* (1820);
James Smith—Police Number 299 Charles Lyons per *Asia* (1824);
William Williams—Police Number 819 William Cheshire per *Asia* (1827);
James Connor—Police Number 324 James Porter per *Asia* (1824).[4]

Identity can be more slippery than identification, less set. James Porter was to prove a man of many sides, an elusive figure constantly evading police number 324, even when he was in custody.

Porter entered the records of Van Diemen's Land as an ordinary convict. He had been tried at the Kingston-upon-Thames Assizes, convicted of burglary, and transported for life. When he disembarked at Hobart Town, he told the muster master that his native place was 'Bermondsy' (London), his most recent address was Elephant and Castle, and his father was a weigher at the Custom House. Asked his own trade, Porter replied 'beer machine maker', and if the muster master batted an eye, the clerk at the desk simply wrote down what he was told. Police number 324 was measured at five foot two inches, described as having brown eyes and hair, a dimpled chin, two scars on his forehead, another two on his neck. He was blind in his left eye, and on his left arm he was tattooed with two bare-fist boxers.[5] Like his later companions, William Cheshire and Charles Lyons, he had acquired more tattoos by the time he disembarked from the *Sarah* and was subjected to a second inquisitive muster master. A crucifix embellished his right arm, and on his left the boxers had been joined by a sailor and anchor, symbols perhaps of Christian hope and of Porter's newly professed trade—seaman.[6] The four men chained together during the terrible voyage of the *Sarah* were tried before the Hobart Supreme Court in 1837, found guilty by a military jury (their seizure of the *Frederick* being a case of piracy), and sentenced to die. It sounds a grim tale, and it is, but not in all modes of its telling.

Seven years after the trial, Porter's story was serialised in a Scottish newspaper, the *Fife Herald*, as 'The Convict', the adventures of one James Connor. Told as a romantic saga, it was prefaced with assurances of authenticity (the convict's name went unremarked):

> SIR, – Having become possessed of some MS. notes written by a person named James Connor, a native of Dublin, giving a sketch of his suffer-

ings in New South Wales, and in which there are a few stirring incidents, I have transcribed them. Should you consider the facts worthy of publication, you are welcome to them.

Cupar, 1844 W.[7]

Over the next thirteen editions of the *Fife Herald*, Connor's trials and tribulations unfolded. The narrative's opening pitch was crude but effective: generous dollops of carefully connected sex and 'savages' in the first two episodes. The sex was romanticised and moralised for the readers of 1840s Fife. Titillation depended on imagining a young female body at risk of violation by 'savages' as bloodthirsty and treacherous as any of their competitors in those many nineteenth-century tales set on the frontiers of empire. Connor as convict hero thwarts the wretches, metes out a quick and bloody retribution, and saves the virtue of a beautiful, tender-hearted young lady of sixteen, the daughter of his master. The hero gains her heart, but the convict will never win her hand. There is no future for a convict hero in Van Diemen's Land, and to make matters worse our hero is charged with a burglary that he has not committed and sent to a chain gang. In desperation he escapes, but after an epic chase is apprehended illegally at large and equipped with firearms. To make matters worse he had fired on one of his captors and is put on trial for his life, only to be saved from the gallows by the intercession of his master's daughter. Reprieved, Connor instead found himself 'banished for the natural term of my life to Macquarie Harbour', where once more he resolved to escape.[8]

Once the readers of the *Fife Herald* had finished the serialised version, they were offered a bound, slightly truncated edition.[9] Two years later, another edition appeared in Montreal under the title *Recollections of a Convict and Miscellaneous Pieces by Y-Le.*[10] That might not be surprising, since Canada belonged to the British empire, and there was a considerable Scottish population in Montreal at the time. The genuinely unexpected and puzzling aspect of the Porter narrative is that multiple versions already existed in manuscript well before the *Fife Herald* began printing its serial. The earliest is within the Colonial Secretary's Correspondence for 1837.[11] In 1838 the *Hobart Town Almanack and Van Diemen's Land Annual* published a narrative from Porter. Three years later, on an island hundreds of miles away, yet another handwritten narrative joined the official archive in the penal station on Norfolk Island. Six versions of one convict narrative. Who wrote them, and why? How did the narratives travel such distances in those decidedly pre-internet days? Who read them? Why, at crucial points in the narrative, did the story take markedly different turns?

One story in particular is common to all versions. A group of convicts at the Macquarie Harbour penal station on the west coast of Van Diemen's Land

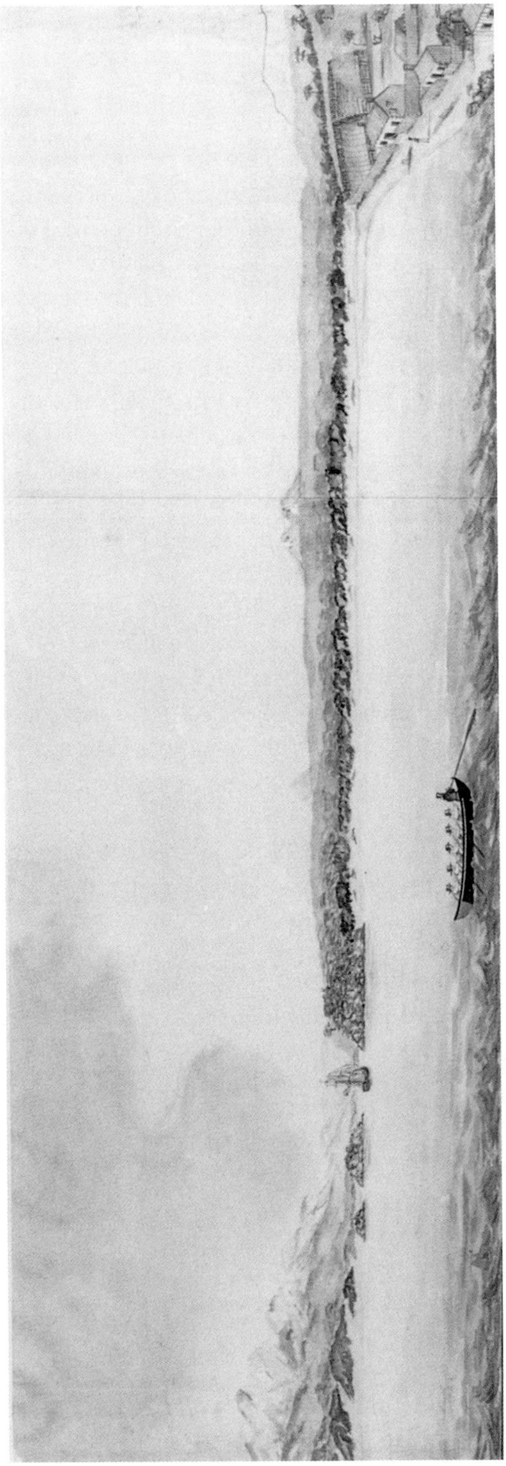

View of the Heads of Macquarie Harbour, with the Pilot's Residence, *artist unknown.*

seize the brig *Frederick* and escape. Macquarie Harbour had been a large establishment with a big boat-building operation, but the authorities in Hobart Town had decided to close it down and relocate everyone to Port Arthur.[12] The *Frederick* was to be the last ship off the slips, and a few convicts remained at the almost deserted station to complete the fittings under the direction of a shipwright, David Hoy. Hoy was accompanied by his servant William Nichols, who stayed to look after his master, and four soldiers from the 63rd Regiment who were detailed to guard the ten convicts charged with completing the fitting out of the brig and with sailing her to Hobart. On her maiden voyage the *Frederick* was to be under the charge of Captain Charles Taw while James Tate, a free sailor, would act as mate.

During the days of relaxed routines and surveillance, the ten convicts—five from the construction crew and five sailors—hatched a plot to seize the vessel. Like so many good plans, theirs was stunningly simple. They knew that once fitted out, the *Frederick* would have to wait at anchor for a favourable tide and wind to carry her over the tricky bar at the harbour's entrance. This would be their window of opportunity.

When the day arrived, everything favoured the mutineers. Two soldiers, Corporal Dearman and Private Henry Gathercole, went off fishing. Captain Taw, Mr Hoy, and his servant William Nichols repaired to the ship's main cabin. The other two soldiers and the mate, James Tate, were on the deck. And then what happened? Versions of the narrative disagree.

In the serial published by the *Fife Herald*, the three free men on the deck were in a companionable mood, and happy to accept an invitation from Connor and the others to join them in the forecastle for a song and a chummy draw on a pipe. Music began when an Englishman with a 'sweet and harmonious' voice sang a sentimental ditty about Connor's native Ireland:

> There is an isle, a bonny isle,
> Starts proudly from the sea;
> And dearer far than all the world
> Is that sweet isle to me . . .

Connor's thoughts turned maudlin: 'Yes, thought I my home is there, all that I ever loved on earth is there; but does not exist—cannot exist for me'. Soldiers and convicts alike were moved by the pathos of the moment. A Scot then sang 'Lochaber no more', the song said to have done 'more to harm some of the Scotch regiments on the continent than the bullets of their enemies'. When this lugubrious rendition had finished, 'each of the company' wore 'a despondent aspect'. The next song, 'Rule Britannia', was the signal for the mutiny. At the line 'Britons never shall be slaves', the convicts arose and overpowered their guards.[13]

A new introduction was added to this stirring tale when the serial was republished in a condensed single-volume version for the readers of Fife. Connor, says the putative transcriber, having escaped to South America, joined the crew of a Yankee ship. In Bombay, he ran into a man he knew. Where have you been? Connor was asked. 'Instead of recounting to his acquaintance the trial he had undergone, he presented him with the notes from which this encounter is taken.' These notes were 'given to the transcriber by a brother of one of the officers of the vessel to which Connor's friend was attached'. The introduction ends: 'an interesting lesson may be derived from this perusal of his history and with this hope it is issued in a revised form'. As usual with published convict narratives, moral tincture made socially transgressive material acceptable to the 'respectable' middle-class who bought books. They could experience the titillation of sex and violence without feeling guilty if the narrative was saturated with moral precepts on its overtly interpretative level.[14] Stories of characters populating the underworld were packaged implicitly as 'lessons' endorsed by Christian teachings, edifying warnings of what happens to those who go astray. The *pleasures* of reading the 'astray' part could be ignored. For the 'lesson' to be effective, it had to be true, had to remind readers that this is indeed the way the world is. The point is made emphatically in the edition published in Montreal. Under the curious nom de plume 'Y-Le', a prefatory note told the audience how to situate their reading:

> The *Recollections of a Convict* must not be looked upon as fiction. The majority of the incidents recorded were experienced in the life of one person. The whole of them were recounted to me by parties conversant with the facts. It has been my endeavour so to arrange them as to form an interesting narrative, in order, if possible, to arrest the attention of young men, and show them the evils and hardships which result from becoming the companions of those who depart from the path of duty and the fear of God.[15]

In the earliest version of the Porter narrative, the preoccupation with learning lessons attaches not to the readers, but to a narrator writing to save his life. While Porter sat in a condemned cell in the Hobart Town gaol, waiting to hear whether the death sentence would see him swing on the gallows tree, he filled his days by composing an account of the mutiny on the *Frederick* and of his subsequent escape. The moment of mutiny begins much as it does in the *Fife Herald*: two of the soldiers had gone fishing; Captain Taw, Mr Hoy and William Nichols were in the cabin; the mate and two soldiers were on deck, and the prisoners were in the forecastle. This time, however, it was Porter who at the request of his fellow convicts started up the music with an unnamed song. After a while one of the soldiers came down to listen.

Distracted by the song he took no notice when James Leslie, William Cheshire, Benjamin Russen, John Fair and John Barker slipped out and climbed up on deck. There they secured the mate and second soldier, and armed themselves. Down in the forecastle a signal was given to Shires who presented his fist to the hapless private. He too was secured with help from Charles Lyons and John Dady. A bemused Porter wandered on deck where he was 'ordered' by John Fair to stand upon the forescuttle hatch. It was from this vantage point that Porter saw Shires make a hasty retreat from the cabin where he had been repelled by Captain Taw and Mr Hoy, who 'defended themselves with astonishing courage'. Despite their best endeavours, Hoy and Taw were beaten back into the cabin by Leslie and Russen. All was silent for a while as both sides took stock of the situation. The deadlock was broken when William Shires ripped the cover off the cabin skylight, and John Barker, John Fair, James Leslie and Benjamin Russen presented their muskets, firing two shots into the cabin below:

> Wm Shires rushed to the Skylight, exclaiming what are you about are you going to commit Murder, they said no—he replied it can be done without he then called to the Captain & Hoy, and asked them if they would deliver themselves up. Mr Hoy replied yes we will if you are not disposed to injure us, Shires replied my life shall be forfeit if we do, we only want our liberty.[16]

Porter has left us an eyewitness account of how the *Frederick* was taken, but is it to be trusted? Consider the circumstances. There sits Porter in his condemned cell thinking about how to avoid the gallows tree. If he could make people see him as misled rather than villainous, sympathy might tilt in his direction. He will tell a story of mutiny in which other men dash about menacingly, while he stands on the forescuttle hatch (in court he claimed he had been forced to join the mutineers).[17] Not my doing, says Porter, I was just in the wrong place at the wrong time. And as to my friend, William Shires, why, if he hadn't spoken out, those brave chaps Taw and Hoy might have been murdered. Barker, Fair, Leslie, Russen, those are the real villains, pity they've never been recaptured.

In November 1837 Porter completed his self-portrait as innocuous bit player caught up in a drama of someone else's devising, and he sent the manuscript to the Colonial Secretary, intent undoubtedly on making a good impression. At some stage, the existence of this convict narrative came to the attention of William Gore Elliston, who had recently acquired the colony's most widely distributed newspaper, the *Hobart Town Courier*.[18] Newspaper proprietor and condemned convict had reason to understand each other very well. Elliston, like Porter, was a self-reinventor who got around. Son of an actor and theatre manager, Elliston went from his studies at Cambridge to manage the reading room in Lymington, then from the spa town to London where he managed the Royal Theatre in Drury Lane, and in 1830 from London to Van Diemen's Land. In the seven years since he arrived, aged little more than thirty, Elliston had opened a store and spirit warehouse in Bagdad, moved the business into Hobart Town, sold it to become an auctioneer, and for four years had run the prestigious Claiborne's Grammar School in the colony's north, renaming it Longford Hall Academy, his eye clearly on what we would call a niche market.

About the time Porter went on trial, Elliston bought the *Courier* for £12 000. That was a lot of money, even with a couple of properties and a nice little money-spinner as government printer thrown in. He had borrowed heavily, and needed to make money. Porter needed a pardon. The colony had been abuzz with stories of the *Frederick*'s mutineers and their remarkable trial. Elliston must have sniffed a potential mass market in this local saga with its ending as yet unknown. As a tale of suspense and escape, Porter's narrative had lurid appeal that later shifted into a register of sex and violence for the readers of Fife. Elliston included Porter's narrative in the *Hobart Town Almanack and Van Diemen's Land Annual*. The marketing pitch to the local readers appears in the title: 'A Narrative of the Sufferings and Adventure of Certain of the Ten Convicts, who Piratically Seized the Brig *Frederick* at Macquarie Harbour, in Van Diemen's Land, as Related by one of the Said Convicts whilst Lying Under Sentence of Death for this Offence at Hobart Town'. Elliston, like his fellow newspaper proprietor in Scotland, needed to tread carefully through dangerous moral terrain. The sensitive area for him was not sex, but the mere publication in a penal colony of a convict narrative. Did Elliston sit drinking porter with Porter in the condemned man's cell, producer and playwright arguing over how exactly their most unorthodox theatrical production should end? Certainly someone added a final paragraph to the script Porter had sent in to the Colonial Secretary. The performance would close on a suitably sombre and submissive note, the convict staying in character as penitent, and on that basis alone permitted to speak, bowing to the authorities as he awaits his fate. At the same time, Elliston had to keep his eye on the business of selling newspapers. If the story wasn't finished, the serial wasn't over, readers would have to buy the *Courier* to experience the pleasure of narrative closure. The interests of convict and newspaper proprietor converge in the condemned man's last words:

> we were placed upon our trial before the Chief Justice of the Colony at Hobart Town, in Van Diemen's Land, and found guilty, and sentenced to be hanged; but which we have every reason to believe will be commuted to transportation for life and our case has gone home for opinion of the English Judges
>
> Gaol Hobart, 1st November, 1837.[19]

Was no one suspicious of a tone so far removed from the clever wordplay of the courtroom where the defendants argued ingeniously against the charge of piracy, claiming that since the *Frederick* had never been registered as a vessel, it should be more properly described as 'a quantity of wood and other materials so fastened as to possess the means of becoming a brig, but possessing no one constituent necessary to justify those materials being then so called'?[20] Another argument ran that piracy by definition occurred on the high seas, whereas the *Frederick* was seized inside the harbour bar. And who was legally in command of the vessel/bundle of wood at the time that she/it was seized? The ship-builder charged only with her construction relinquished his authority when the completed ship set sail on the sea, but against the authority of the ship-builder there could be no 'mutiny'. If the ship had yet to sail, the Captain had yet to take up his command even if it was only of a bundle of wood. If nobody was in command, against whom could one mutiny?[21] The legal pyrotechnics and the doubts surrounding the case were enough to cause Chief Justice Pedder some concern, and the colonial government prevaricated for two years as it wondered what to do. Elliston's publication of Porter's account played an important part in prompting a decision. Not only was it successful in keeping public attention in Van Diemen's Land focused on the case, but a copy was passed to none other than the Secretary of State who wrote to Lieutenant-Governor Franklin to ask what was happening.[22] In May 1839 the condemned men learned that they were to be pardoned on condition of transportation for life. All four were shipped off to Norfolk Island.[23]

Porter's strategy for narrating himself out of the noose had succeeded brilliantly. At this stage, even a man who enjoyed a way with words might have abandoned the *Frederick* and found another subject for his quill. Not Porter. He had a store of jokes waiting to play on those in authority who crossed his path. Clerks and officials were unaccustomed to convicts gifted with black humour, and most of the jokes passed right over their heads. Porter was ready for another go at using language to confuse those who tried to imprison him in text. On Norfolk Island he wrote a narrative about the mutiny on the *Frederick* with himself at its centre as swashbuckling hero.

In this version, the mutiny is again initiated by persuading a soldier to come down into the forecastle to hear Porter sing. This time the song is a salacious-sounding number, 'The Grand Conversation Lies Under the Rose'. Nothing patriotic here, no homesick tears evoked. Porter, unable to concentrate properly on the right words, is prompted by William Shires. The signal to overpower the guards is a simple stamp on the deck (not 'Britons never shall be slaves').[24] At this cue Shires draws a cocked pistol from under the table, holds it to the soldier's head, and together with Porter locks the erstwhile guard below decks, securing the hatch on the forescuttle with a ketch anchor. The mate James Tate and the second soldier have been surprised on deck by Benjamin Russen and James Leslie. Safely secured, they too are conveyed into the makeshift prison. While the mutineers arm themselves with muskets and ball cartridges, they lose the element of surprise when Shires rushes the main cabin where Captain Taw, Mr Hoy, and William Nichols have been drinking rum purloined from the convicts' quota. Shires struggles with the three drunks intent on killing him. The other mutineers rip off the cabin skylight to help their comrade, and under cover he manages to regain the deck without injury. By now the cabin's defenders are armed with muskets and pistols. Seeing that an ugly stand-off has developed, the resourceful and quick-thinking Porter removes the all-important compass to a place of safe-keeping, and the mutineers try to talk the men in the cabin out of their alcohol-fuelled bravado. They refuse to surrender. The mutineers, suspecting that if they rush the cabin guns will go off willy-nilly, try scaring their prisoners into submission. On the command 'fire down upon them', muskets are presented over the skylight combing. One accidentally discharges, the ball knocks the keys to Taw's arms chest clean out of his hands, and the besieged men cry for quarter. Another musket is discharged to attract the attention of the two soldiers off fishing in a whaleboat. When they pull alongside, Porter jumps into the main chains and orders them to make fast.[25] The mutineers are in complete control of the *Frederick* (no suggestion in the Norfolk Island narrative that Porter and his mates went to all this trouble to seize a bundle of wood!).

This figure of derring-do, created ironically under the gaze of a commandant experimenting with convict narrative as convict reform, would captivate audiences on the other side of the world. It is the Nofolk Island narrative that the *Fife Herald* and Montreal editors re-cast for their readers, although it is by no means clear who was responsible for delivering a version of Porter's tale to the office of the *Fife Herald*. As it turns out, however, it was not just to be readers in Scotland and Canada who were to be exposed to Porter's trickery.

When he was landed from the *Asia* in 1824, Porter told the muster master that he was nineteen. If he had still been alive in 1874 he would have been sixty-nine, give or take a year. It is thus just possible that somebody drew his attention to Clarke's description of the seizure of the *Osprey* from Macquarie Harbour in the novel *For the Term of His Natural Life*.[26] What would Porter have done as he realised that whole passages were borrowed from his own account published by Elliston thirty-six years earlier?[27] He may well have smiled, for the net result is a Porter triumph. Clarke portrayed Porter as the least willing of the mutineers. Ordered to stand on the hatchway by Rex, the ringleader, Porter even manages to botch this most marginal of roles, allowing one of the soldiers imprisoned in the forecastle to escape, thus jeopardising the mutiny. As Clarke described it, 'Porter, whose courage was none of the fiercest, and who had been for years given over to that terror of discipline which servitude induces, made but a feeble attempt at resistance'.[28] In the novel, as in the version of his story written in the condemned cell all those years before, Porter is guilty of being little more than a frightened dupe. He is, however, still a frightened dupe who manages to make his escape. Thus it is, that in the pages of the most famous convict novel of them all, James Porter rides again to freedom on the deck of the brig *Osprey* as it is sailed away from the rain-soaked mountains with slopes covered with 'noxious weeds' and the 'foetid exhalations of swamp and fen' which had previously imprisoned him.[29]

The story of the seizure of the *Osprey* is revisited subsequently in the novel. It is 1838 and five years have passed since those dramatic events at Macquarie Harbour. Sitting on 'a rustic seat' at the bottom of her garden Sylvia reads a manuscript 'written in a firm, large hand'. It is headed:

> A NARRATIVE
>
> Of the sufferings and adventures of the ten convicts who seized the brig 'Osprey' at Macquarie Harbour, in Van Diemen's Land, related by one of the said convicts while lying under sentence for this offence in the gaol at Hobart Town.

In the *For the Term of His Natural Life* version, the author of this narrative is the fictional John Rex. Indeed, although 'Shirers', Barker, Cheshire, 'Lesly', Fair, Lyon, Riley and Russen are all named, James Porter is not. Although present in the novel at the point when the *Osprey* was seized, thereafter Porter slips from the page. The other missing mutineer is John Dady who appears to have been scratched from the fictionalised account to make way for Rex. Porter is, however, an absent presence, for the words attributed to Rex are largely lifted from Porter's 1838 account. The effect on Sylvia is dramatic. After reading only a few lines she put the book down and muttered '"Poor fellow" . . . "I think he was not to blame."' She was, wrote Clarke, 'beguiled by Master Rex's specious paragraphs'. When she at last came, 'breathless to the conclusion', she paused to meditate. 'Surely the punishment of "penal servitude" must have been made very terrible', she mused, 'for men to dare such hideous perils to escape from it'.[30] In the guise of John Rex, Porter stands innocent and manly on the shores of Botany Bay.[31] The moment of triumph is brief, however, and it does not take the cynical Maurice Frere long to rumble to Rex's more sinister agenda.

As Clarke wrote in the preface to his novel, 'Some of the events narrated are doubtless tragic and terrible; but I hold it needful to my purpose to record them, for they are events which have actually occurred, and which, if the blunders which produce them be repeated, must infallibly occur again'. He went on to warn that the French penal colony recently established in New

Caledonia 'will, in the natural course of things, repeat in its annals the history of Macquarie Harbour and of Norfolk Island'.[32] Porter of course had direct experience of both these hellholes, and it is thus more than appropriate that his own account of his sufferings should have been used to condemn the two places in which he was incarcerated.

Who was the man who has become known to the world as James Connor and John Rex? We, like the authorities waiting for the *Sarah* in Hobart Town, can identify, under Police Number 324, James Porter per *Asia* (1824). The escape artist too has his history, one secret from all versions of the narrative, but visible once and fleetingly in a hearing before the Hobart Town bench three years after Police Number 324 walked down the gangplank from the *Asia*, and seven years before the mutiny on the *Frederick* created James Connor. The court heard that at 8.30 p.m. on Monday, 23 July 1827, Private Henry Kelly of His Majesty's 40th Regiment was standing sentry by the bonded stores, when two men, clearly drunk, lurched down the wharf. They were convict seamen from the supply brig *Prince Leopold*, who had been upholding the grand old tradition of St Monday (the right to a two-day weekend, Sunday for drinking and Monday to recover). Kelly lowered his musket with bayonet attached, and issued a challenge. Out of the gloom came the reply, 'friend'. When asked what they were about, the two seamen claimed that Captain Welsh said they could stay out until half past eight 'or near nine if they liked'. By this time Kelly had had enough, and ordered the men to stand. They told him to go 'bugger himself'. Beleaguered, the private called out to the watchman while the two sailors continued their abuse. When he threatened them with his bayonet, they retaliated with a promise of '300 [lashes] on his back for breakfast'. The court heard this evidence and sentenced one convict sailor, William Clark, to a flogging of twenty-five lashes. As for the second miscreant, Police Number 324 James Porter was let off with a reprimand: Captain Welsh had given the man gifted with words a 'favourable character' which opened the door for escape.[33]

This is farce, but it is farce with a dangerous agenda and painful consequences. It is a scaled-down version of the mutiny on the *Frederick*, with Porter, as in the main feature, wriggling clear of the worst of the carnage. The hapless Kelly, the symbol of authority, is of course the butt end of the joke. There are other jokes embedded in Porter's story. In his Norfolk Island narrative he describes how, shortly before he was disembarked from the transport *Asia* in 1824, he was told by a Jewish convict not to hail for a sailor. Apparently seamen were in over-supply in Van Diemen's Land and such a confession was likely to result in a billet with a 'dungaree settler'. Here he would have to work from dawn till sunset on 'short commons'. Instead, his Jewish accomplice hoodwinked a blacksmith in Hobart into believing that Porter was a skilled metal worker, thus landing an assignment in town, close to the attractions of the alehouse.[34] This, of course, is one script. A second script is contained in the convict description registers. These reveal that, when disembarked from the *Asia*, Porter (as we have already seen) in fact hailed for a 'beer machine maker'.

There was of course no such occupation. Brewing, though sometimes on a very large scale, was not then mechanised; although the idea of a machine which magically manufactures beer has a certain appeal.[35] Again you can hear convict sniggers and guffaws. Of course what makes the joke complete is the play on his own name, Porter, also the name of a species of dark ale for which London was then famous. He would no doubt have been satisfied to know that the Convict Department never got the joke. When the *Frederick*/bundle of wood sailed off over the horizon, descriptions of the mutineers were drawn up and posted off to London.[36] Armed with this script the Imperial authorities commenced their search for a one-eyed 'beer machine maker': can you hear the roars of laughter? If there is a seventh Porter/Connor narrative it is this joke—another act of deception to place alongside all the other accounts. Such an ending is fitting: seven tales for a man, who in nineteenth-century jargon had seven sides. Being:

A right side,
A left side,
A backside,
A front side,
An inside,
An outside,
And a blind side.[37]

This should be the cue for Porter to wink. But in closing his one good eye he would make himself blind to the dangers of the world, and that is one thing that Porter the trickster is unlikely ever to have done.

Words for the convict women

5

Eliza Churchill tells . . .

Lucy Frost

On 13 April 1840, in the southern port of Plymouth, Eliza Churchill was indicted for stealing 'a cloath cloak and a silk umbrella' belonging to a Dr Moore.[1] She seems to have said nothing in her defence, and as she had pawned the goods, there may have been little to say. The judge before whom Churchill stood was a thoughtful man who preferred sending prisoners to gaol near home (unlike his less feeling colleagues at the Old Bailey), and even consulted with local authorities before sentencing a prisoner he believed 'a mixture of rogue and fool', and hence 'not a proper person to be transported'.[2] His Honour's patience, however, was tried by repeat offenders. These he routinely transported, and because Eliza Churchill, aged nineteen, had already spent six months in gaol for stealing a shawl, she was sentenced on the final day of the Easter Quarter Sessions to fourteen years. Not surprising. What makes her remarkable is that less than two years later, she was walking down the streets of Launceston, Van Diemen's Land, with a conditional pardon in her pocket, and all because she told a story. She bought her freedom with a convict narrative.

As a genre within autobiography, the convict narrative has implicitly been gendered male. In the index to their annotated guide to published Australian autobiographical writing for the period to 1850, Kay Walsh and Joy Hooton list forty-four convict narratives, all with male authors.[3] But some autobiographical narratives of female convict experience do survive, and some like Ariadne's thread lead us into the labyrinthine passages of recoverable story. Incarcerated women can be heard telling their stories from within the circumstances of their incarceration, rather than recounting them when free, as did many of the men whose narratives were published. Among the papers of a committee appointed in 1841 by Sir John Franklin, Lieutenant-Governor of Van Diemen's Land, to inquire into female convict prison discipline are the narratives of five convict women. The committee's final report accompanied by extensive appendices was submitted in 1843 but never published, and today exists as a file of 428 pages held in the Archives Office of Tasmania.[4]

Included in these papers are the autobiographical accounts of four women who on 1 April 1842 received conditional pardons 'for the satisfactory manner in which they gave evidence before a Board for enquiring into Prison Discipline', and of a fifth who on the same grounds was released early from a colonial sentence.[5] Eliza Churchill was one of those who told stories which as testimony were incorporated into the committee's file. She and the other women were constrained in their narratives less by the genre of autobiography than by the technologies of power within a prison system where favours were meted out, as well as punishment. So what did Churchill and the others have to say which was judged 'satisfactory'? And 'satisfactory' to whom? These are the questions I have been pondering.

The narrative: Eliza Churchill's telling

Like most of her shipmates aboard the *Navarino*, Eliza Churchill had been assigned as a servant soon after she disembarked.[6] The idea was that settlers guided female convicts in the ways and rewards of domesticity, and in exchange provided them with food and clothes. That is not the way Churchill tells it:

> I have heard that some of the assigned servants are allowed to do just as they like, they are allowed to be on their own hands [unmonitored] & pay their mistresses for it these instances occur among the petty tradesmen. I have heard of it among gentlemen. Most of the women prefer being assigned in the towns, but some who wish to keep out of mischief prefer being in the country. All the women behave better in the country than in the towns, as they are not so exposed to temptations. Those who are assigned in the country generally stay out of the factory longest. I have been twice punished for being absent without leave. I was assigned in Launceston had I been in the country probably I should not have been absent.[7]

Did Eliza Churchill resent being a servant? On the *Navarino's* description list, she is entered as shoebinder, a skilled occupation.[8] Whether it was the serving she resented, or her master Mr Sprint, or more generally her status as convict, she had been assigned for barely two months when she was officially reprimanded for being absent. Less than a fortnight later she was reported for misconduct, and sentenced to two months' hard labour in the Female House of Correction, known locally as the female factory, or simply 'the factory'. A month after completing that sentence, Churchill absconded from a new master, and was again locked up.[9]

While the two episodes of incarceration gave Churchill something to say in her narrative, they cannot explain why she was chosen to speak, and thus given the chance to trade her way out of the system. Later justifying the unorthodox decision to hear from prisoners themselves, Sir John Franklin would explain that 'several women were selected who had the most experience of [the factory's] interior as well as of the town, and who were promised certain indulgences in consideration of the most faithful and full disclosures'.[10]

Churchill, with her limited experience, relies heavily on what she has heard. To be shut away in the solitary cells on bread and water is 'much disliked'.[11] 'Cutting off their hair' is 'generally disliked'—'I have heard Jane Carr say she would rather take two years in the factory than have her hair cut off & I have heard many others make similar remarks'.[12] Otherwise, says Churchill, life inside the factory is tolerable. Unless dragooned into washing for the Colonial Hospital, there is little work, and even then, 'many prefer being at the wash tub to being in the yards as when washing they get the same ration as the assignable women & do not over work themselves'.[13] For the most part, the convicts simply mill around the yards:

> During the day time the women in the factory amuse themselves the best way they can, dancing & singing etc in fact if it were not for being separated from some friends outside it would be no punishment to be in the factory as the women can get any thing they please if they have money & they generally bring in some concealed where it is almost impossible to find it.[14]

Nothing Churchill says about reactions to punishment or behaviour in the yards could have been very useful to the examining authorities. When it came to trafficking, however, she had information to trade.

Eliza Churchill was in the factory this time not because she had absconded, but because she was ill, and she must have been seriously or infectiously ill to be allowed three weeks in bed. The hospital, on the first floor of the factory where the dormitories were, was the responsibility of the sub-matron, Mrs Littler, assisted by a convict nurse.[15] In the very first sentence of her testimony, Churchill depicts the hospital as the nerve centre of illicit commerce:

> I have seen tobacco constantly brought in and given to the nurse who used to supply the crime class with it. The nurse Mrs Benson gets money from the prisoners and gives it to Mrs Littler the sub-matron who gets tobacco & tea & sugar in the town and gives it to the nurse . . . I have not seen any spirits brought in since I have been this time. They used to be brought in over the wall when I was in before about 10 months ago.[16]

Women who want to write 'get pen & ink from the nurse & paper for which they pay her 6^{d} a sheet & write letters which they send out by women going out. They generally conceal them in their stays'.[17] Mrs Littler runs a thriving black market through the hospital: 'Last Tuesday in particular a pound of tobacco was brought in in the way I have described'.[18] A nice money-spinner to supplement the income of a sub-matron working seven days a week, fifty-two weeks a year, for a measly salary of £20 per annum, with prison accommodation and rations.

At the end of her thousand-word narrative Eliza Churchill, as if determined to make the accusations stick, returns to trafficking:

> I have heard that things are brought to the gate for the women at seven o'clock in the evening when the gatekeeper is at muster, the gate is then opened by his wife. I never knew anything being brought in that way, but I have been told that I might get things in that way. When things are got in they are generally given to some [one] other than the owner to keep, some woman not likely to be suspected.[19]

Eliza Churchill, in telling her story, is trading words for something far more potent than tea or ink. But who exactly is she trading with, and how does the process work?

Trouble among the storytellers

Eliza Churchill, who could not write, spoke her narrative before a man appointed by the Committee of Enquiry into Female Convict Prison Discipline. The committee of four held its meetings in Hobart, the colony's administrative centre. For a month beginning in early December 1841, the gentlemen questioned witnesses who worked in the Female House of Correction on the outskirts of Hobart, or had been there on business, or had employed assigned servants from the 'factory'. They interviewed no female convicts. The women whose accounts were recorded in March 1842 escaped the rigid question-and-answer format of the committee's formal hearings; their stories were taken down as uninterrupted personal narratives. In Launceston, the colony's other principal town and home to its second female factory, three women spoke—Eliza Churchill; Mary Kirk, who had come free to the colony with her grown-up daughters, and was treated more as a member of staff than an inmate when she entered the factory in June 1840 to serve two years for larceny; and Bridget Magahan, who had spent fifteen of her thirty-five years in Van Diemen's Land, and was serving a second seven-years' sentence of transportation for receiving a couple of bottles stolen from the government store.[20]

The narratives of all three women were transcribed by the same hand, presumably that of a convict clerk.

Before the women spoke, the committee's appointee heard from Robert Pearson, superintendent of the Launceston factory. Pearson had not appeared before the committee, and indeed no sense of what was happening in Launceston emerged from the hearings. The Principal Superintendent of Convicts, when asked whether he 'lost sight' of the convict women who were sent up the coast after disembarking in Hobart from the transport ships, replied: 'Yes: I do, except from the Official Reports sent in by the Assistant Superintendent at Launceston'.[21] The same might have been said of the Launceston factory in general. Its superintendent, soldiering on in the north, was desperately short of space and staff.

The building, designed to accommodate eighty to one hundred inmates, had opened in November 1834 with sixty-nine women and eleven children, but when Eliza Churchill testified less than eight years later, it housed 198 women and twenty-nine children (at the Hobart factory that same week there were 447 women and thirteen children).[22] If usage had not modified intention, the Launceston female factory would have been the colony's first venture into the architecture of centralised surveillance, predating Port Arthur's model prison by more than a decade. The original design was for a 'two storey cruciform building set in an octagonal perimeter wall with radial separation walls between the arms'.[23] At the hub were to be four rooms with windows through which guards looked out onto the yards and watched the women. Presumably as a cost-saving measure, no such guards were employed, and the rooms were used instead to house the superintendent and his family, who either lived in rooms with windows closed over, or themselves became the object of easy surveillance by the inmates crowded into the yards on the other side of the Pearsons' quarters. It must have been very stressful for Pearson, his wife the matron, and their several children to live at the hub of a building overcrowded with bored and noisy women. Small wonder that in June 1843, a doctor supporting Pearson's effort to resign on the grounds of his wife's ill-health should attribute her state 'to the constant confinement within the walls of the Building which the nature of her duties rendered it necessary for her to observe'.[24] The matron's confinement was longer and no doubt lonelier than that of most factory inmates.

Besides the Pearsons, the only other non-convict staff were the gatekeeper and sub-matron, Charles and Ann Littler, who lived just inside the building's entrance. Pearson did not trust the Littlers and had already attempted, and failed, to expose their trafficking. In the claustrophobic building where everyone seems to have been spying on everyone else and gossip was life, someone tipped off the Littlers. Immediately they went to Assistant Superintendent Franks and accused Pearson of promising freedom to his assigned servant

Launceston Female Factory

PATERSON c. 1840 STREET

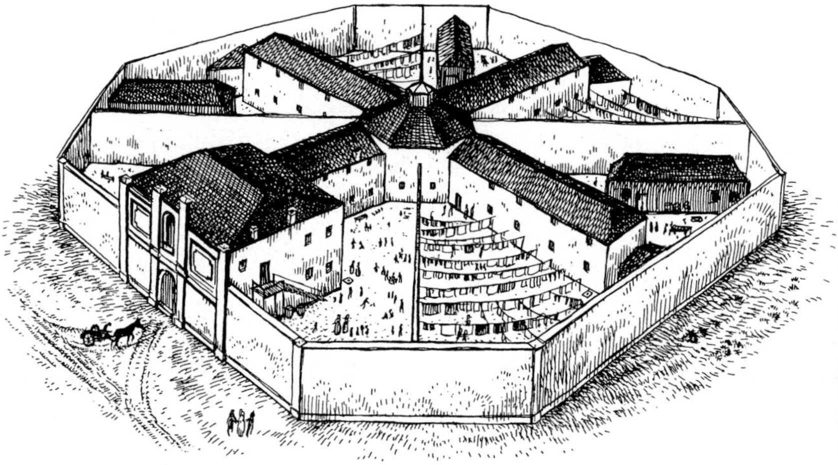

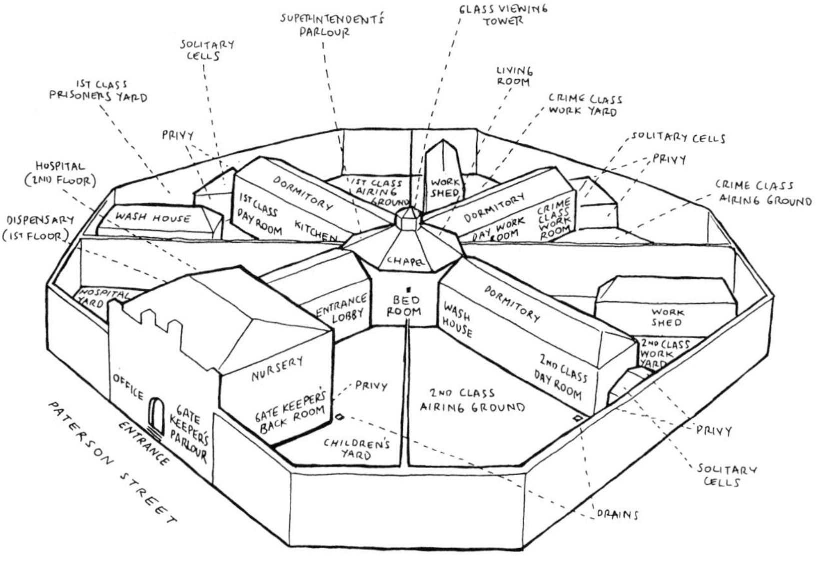

Female Factory, Launceston Gaol Section of Spurling's Panorama, late nineteenth century.

Rebecca Bull if she would help him trap the Littlers. They accused Pearson of going to the house of Bull's husband to involve him as well. Franks admonished the superintendent, and directed him never again to employ Bull in any situation whatsoever. When Franks was replaced by Gardiner, however, Pearson promptly reassigned Rebecca Bull to himself as servant.[25]

Steeped in subterfuge, the superintendent may have received with wry satisfaction the request from Hobart for women who for the promise of 'certain indulgences' would make 'faithful and full disclosures' about daily life in the female factory. Here was a perfect opportunity to stitch up the Littlers if women could be found to finger them: women like Eliza Churchill. Again, Pearson overestimated his own power, and underestimated his foe. Churchill could not have narrated her tale without the Littlers suspecting something. There was a basic matter of bodies in space. Churchill left her bed in the hospital, Ann Littler's domain, to go out. If she testified inside the factory, the gatekeeper must have opened the prison door to the committee's delegate and his clerk, and watched the three convict women go in and out of the superintendent's office, right across the hallway from the Littlers' living quarters. If, as seems more likely, Pearson and the women went into town, Littler must have closed the door after them, and opened it upon their return. Sometime within a fortnight of testifying, Eliza Churchill and Bridget Magahan were recommended for their conditional pardons, and Mary Kirk released from her colonial sentence. Charles Littler, opening the prison gates for these women granted indulgences, must have been livid.

By mid-April 'the Gate Keeper at the Female House of Correction' had prepared his case and lodged a complaint 'against the Sup^{t} of that Establishment'.[26] Littler accused Pearson of reinstating Rebecca Bull against orders, and of persuading Eliza Churchill to charge the gatekeeper (no mention of his wife) 'with supplying the Hospital of the Female H^{o} of Correction with prohibited articles'.[27] The gatekeeper alleged that 'for such Statements . . . this Woman together with two others of the name of Kirk and Monaghan obtained their Liberty'.[28] The assistant superintendent of convicts forwarded the complaint to the principal superintendent in Hobart, who told his subordinate to investigate the matter and report back. On 16 May, Gardiner duly conducted his enquiry, taking testimony from nine witnesses. The allegations involving Rebecca Bull were not difficult to substantiate; most of the time was spent determining whether Eliza Churchill had lied.

Yes, said the convict witness Mary Odeland, Churchill told me she was so unhappy because she'd taken 'a false oath against Mrs Littler as to her selling tea, Sugar, and Tobacco', and she cried and cried and made 'a very great noise she took a penknife and attempted to cut her throat (She cut her throat in three places).'[29] Yes, said the witness Elizabeth Phillips, to me Eliza Churchill confessed that 'Mr Pearson has caused me to false swear myself against Mr and Mrs Littler'. Then she got scared and tried to buy my silence, she 'gave me the Handkerchief and Gold Ring here produced and said "Phillips" don't betray me'.[30] Well, says Elizabeth Studham, painting a brazen hussy instead of a distraught woman riddled with guilt, 'One morning Eliza Churchill and myself went out to draw water "Churchill" called Mrs Littler to the window and asked Mrs Littler if she recollected the Sunday she went out "Churchill" told Mrs Littler that it was all about her that she went out'.[31] And I have a story too, volunteers the freeman Moses Phillips, unexpectedly joining this rather suspect line-up:

> About Three weeks or a Month back I had a Female assigned to me from the Factory at Launceston who asked permission to go and see some women about Mr Pearson & Mr Littler I refused to let her go alone but followed her down the road myself to see that she did not get any Drink from my door she was joined by another Woman of the name of 'Cath Owens' I followed the two to a house where a woman of the name of 'Churchill' lives . . . After a short time all the Women left the house and I followed them close up towards the Tread Mill on the Road I heard 'Churchill' say that she had made a statement and if she altered that statement now she should lose her indulgence
>
> 'Ellen Scott' was the Woman who was assigned to me . . .[32]

The story Phillips tells rings truer than those of the convict women (and what bargains had they struck for their telling?), but he was wrong in imagining that Ellen Scott and Catharine Owens cared tuppence about the vendetta raging between the superintendent and the gatekeeper. The convict women were heavying Eliza Churchill on their own behalf. She had named their names, and somehow they found out. Perhaps the convict clerk recording Churchill's testimony traded information for some other favour in this world of ceaseless illicit transactions.

I suspect that Pearson had made clear to Churchill a second topic to be covered by her narrative once she had exposed the traffickers. The Committee of Enquiry had its own hidden agenda, or at least the Lieutenant-Governor had his. 'Whispers', Sir John Franklin was later to write, had 'reached my ears', and presuming that 'the exterior appearance of things might easily lull the suspicion of so much secret vice', he asked to hear from the incarcerated voices themselves.[33] Eliza Churchill had been most obliging. 'There are many women', she testified,

> who will not stay out of the factory when others with whom they carry on an unnatural connexion are in the building. For instance Sarah Davis and Maria [?Kirby], Catherine Owens & Ellen Scott, Margaret Carr & Rosanne Holcroft, Mary Ann Simpson & Eliza Roberts, Mary Sheriff & Sarah Brown, Ann Collins & Catherine Lowrie. These women are quite

> jealous of each other. The other women are afraid to interfere although they dislike such practices, they are never carried on openly but at night, they are never associated with by the other women, they generally sit together on one side of the yard . . . if any attempt were made to separate the women whose names I have mentioned & others of similar habits a riot would be got up immediately, I heard Ellen Scott say so last night if Catherine Owens were sent to Hobarton.[34]

Catharine Owens and Ellen Scott were formidable characters to take on, even surreptitiously.[35] Owens had been the nineteen-year-old moll for a gang of burglars when she was convicted in 1829 of receiving stolen goods, including silver, after a robbery in Prescot. At their trial she and three men about her age were grassed by a former accomplice. The men were sentenced to death, and Owens to fourteen years' transportation: 'The hardened offender', reported the *Lancaster Gazette*, 'dropped a curtesy, and impudently said, "Thank you, my Lord"'.[36] Three months after Owens curtsied, Ellen Scott appeared at the Old Bailey charged with theft. According to a tailor who claimed to have 'quite lost my property' one night in May, Scott had walked at his side near St Giles Church, teasing him 'to treat her'. Another woman, with whom he had seen Scott whispering, 'made a snatch at my watch, got the chain and seals, and ran away'. When the tailor attempted to follow, Scott 'caught hold of my hand, and struck me several times'. Perhaps because this was not a first offence, the sixteen-year-old was transported for life.[37]

In the twelve years since she arrived in Van Diemen's Land, Scott had developed a reputation for trouble-making, accumulating so many reportable offences that their itemisation filled up the normally allotted space in the convict conduct record book, was almost through a second space in a supplementary volume, and would soon spill over into a third.[38] Most convict women with multiple offences chalked up petty charges like being absent or insolent or drunk or refusing to work, and Ellen Scott had plenty of these, but she had others as well. She had been charged with 'indecent behaviour during the performance of divine service' (doing what, one wonders?), and more spectacularly with 'violently assaulting Mr Hutchinson [Superintendent of the Hobart factory] with intent to kill or do him some bodily harm'.[39] Most recently she had become a public byword for 'the secret vice'. In an editorial of 1840, a scandal-mongering journalist decried in the *Colonial Times* the Hobart factory's 'Flash Mob', who engaged in 'abominable practices', and exerted their influence 'through fear, intimidation, and a kind of masonic and sect influence': 'We will ask Mr Hutchinson—as the Principal Manager of the Factory, to inform us, *privately*, what transpired on the examination of one Ellen Scott, some time since? Was there no evidence of Flash Mob proceedings in this matter?'[40]

In his testimony at Launceston, Pearson as the factory's superintendent admitted his powerlessness against women like Scott:

> at present if anything is wrong it is dangerous to go among the large number in one room. I have [been] set at defiance when I have wanted to take out a woman from the ward & I am obliged to carry pistols, I have had my shirt torn from my back. In almost every case I am obliged to use force to take a woman out as they will seldom come out when called, but call the others to their assistance. Their conduct generally is most depraved & disgusting & their language most obscene, and unnatural intercourse between them is carried on to a great extent . . .[41]

Seven months after this admission of powerlessness, Pearson would find himself confronted by eighty-five inmates of the crime class determined to free Owens from a solitary cell. The police he called 'were beaten off by the women who had armed themselves with the spindle and leg, from the spinning wheels, bricks taken from the floors and walls of the Building, Knives Forks &c and also Quart Bottles in which some of them had received Medicine'.[42] By July the following year, the superintendent in Hobart had become involved, and was trying (unsuccessfully) to find some gaol outside Launceston or Hobart willing to take Ellen Scott, 'ringleader of a desperate set', and 'several of her refractory associates'.[43]

What was Eliza Churchill thinking about when she named Scott and Owens? Had she contemplated the dire consequences if her bid for a conditional pardon should fail, and she remained in the system for the next twelve years of her sentence? Why take such risks? Had she been naïve enough to believe she was protected by confidentiality? Or so desperate that she was prepared to take her chances? Whatever her thinking initially, she must have been beside herself with anxiety on the day Assistant Superintendent Gardiner conducted his investigation. There she stood again as a woman accused. Like the other witnesses, her words on that 17 May 1842 were taken and sworn before the assistant superintendent 'in the presence and hearing of Robert Pearson & Charles Littler'.[44] She stuck to her story, and swore she had spoken 'freely and of my own accord'.[45] Mary Kirk and Bridget Magahan swore the same, all three narrators using a single form of words: 'Mr Pearson never directly or indirectly induced or instigated me to make a statement against Mr and Mrs Littler'.[46] Kirk and Magahan confirmed their evidence with simple Xs, but Eliza Churchill took the time to make her mark meticulously, elaborating it as a distinctive signature, and not just a sign that she could not write. And then she walked out of the unpleasant testing of her truthfulness, and a fortnight later, on 3 June, was married by banns in Launceston's Anglican Church of St John, making her mark on the register to confirm that she was single (though the year before the muster master had recorded her as married) and free (which we know she was not).[47] In exchange for her convict narrative, she had her liberty, and never again was an offence entered on her convict conduct record.

Narrating the lives of convict women

Female convict narratives do exist, if we know where to look, or by chance happen upon them. That no extended autobiographies have come to light, no book- or even pamphlet-length memoirs, undoubtedly reflects the literacy rates of the women, many of whom according to the ships' indents could neither read nor write, or who, during this period when reading and writing were taught as separate skills, could read but not write. And yet literacy alone does not explain the silence. Some women did write letters, and anyone who could write a letter might have written a memoir. The free settler Sarah Davenport pencilled page after page of her 'Sceth of an emegrants Life in austrailia from Leiving England in the year of our Lord 1841'.[48] Of course Davenport could write her struggles into the narrative shape of settler hardship and survival, whereas many of the convict women had stories which were less likely to win approval. Susannah Watson, who had taken with her only one of her five children when she was transported, evoked raw pain when she wrote to a daughter irretrievably left behind: 'It is 48 years, the day after my birthday, since I saw your face'.[49] But many of the convict women became mothers too, starting families who might have cherished their stories of making a life for themselves in a new land. So was the genre of autobiography itself foreign to the convict women, as it was not to the men? Was putting oneself forward as the 'I' of a written story just too radical an act? Did working-class women who enjoyed swapping stories on board ship and in the factories share with middle-class women a reluctance to burst into public disclosure? Or were they resisting the genre itself? Perhaps some day the autobiography of a convict woman will come to light: meanwhile, we look for their words in unexpected places, like the evidence of a committee whose report never went to the printers, and was left to gather dust.

6

A Spanish convict, her clergyman biographer, and the amanuensis of her bastard son

Susan Ballyn and Lucy Frost

It was her courtesy which made him notice her. The bent and toothless old woman who opened the door of the worker's cottage had manners elevated beyond her circumstances, and the clergyman was intrigued. Who was she? How had she learned to sprinkle her elegant speech with quotations from the English poets? Had she been on the stage? To James Cameron she remained a closed book until a sudden and alarming illness frightened her with intimations of mortality, and she spoke more openly than usual to the man who might have been her confessor, if he had been a Catholic priest instead of a Scottish Presbyterian clergyman. Tell me your secrets, the Reverend Cameron coaxed, satisfy my curiosity—and, perhaps he should have added, since I am *not* your confessor and not bound to keep secrets, I will make your telling into my text, I will author you. I will do for you what Richard Cobbold did in 1845 for Margaret Catchpole, buried in that unmarked grave on the edge of town, and buried in the memories of people around here too. Who gave a passing thought to the assigned servant turned shopkeeper until *Margaret Catchpole: History of a Suffolk Girl* created an international bestseller from the story of a woman sentenced to death first for stealing a roan coach gelding, and then for escaping from the Ipswich gaol dressed in the clothes of a man?[1]

During the pastoral visits of days and months and years, the Spanish woman handed over her story to the clergyman. Back at his desk in the elegant house dwarfing the little church at its side (both built by the wealthy landowner whose daughter Cameron had judiciously married), the biographer penned prose that drowned in literary cliché the voice of the woman who spoke. And then, within months of her death, after she lay buried in the same churchyard as Margaret Catchpole, James Cameron put in his bid for fame by publishing *Adelaide de la Thoreza: a Chequered Career*.[2]

The clergyman biographer

The biography is infuriating—the more one looks, the less one sees. No, a biographer is not his subject's ventriloquist, but it would be helpful to know

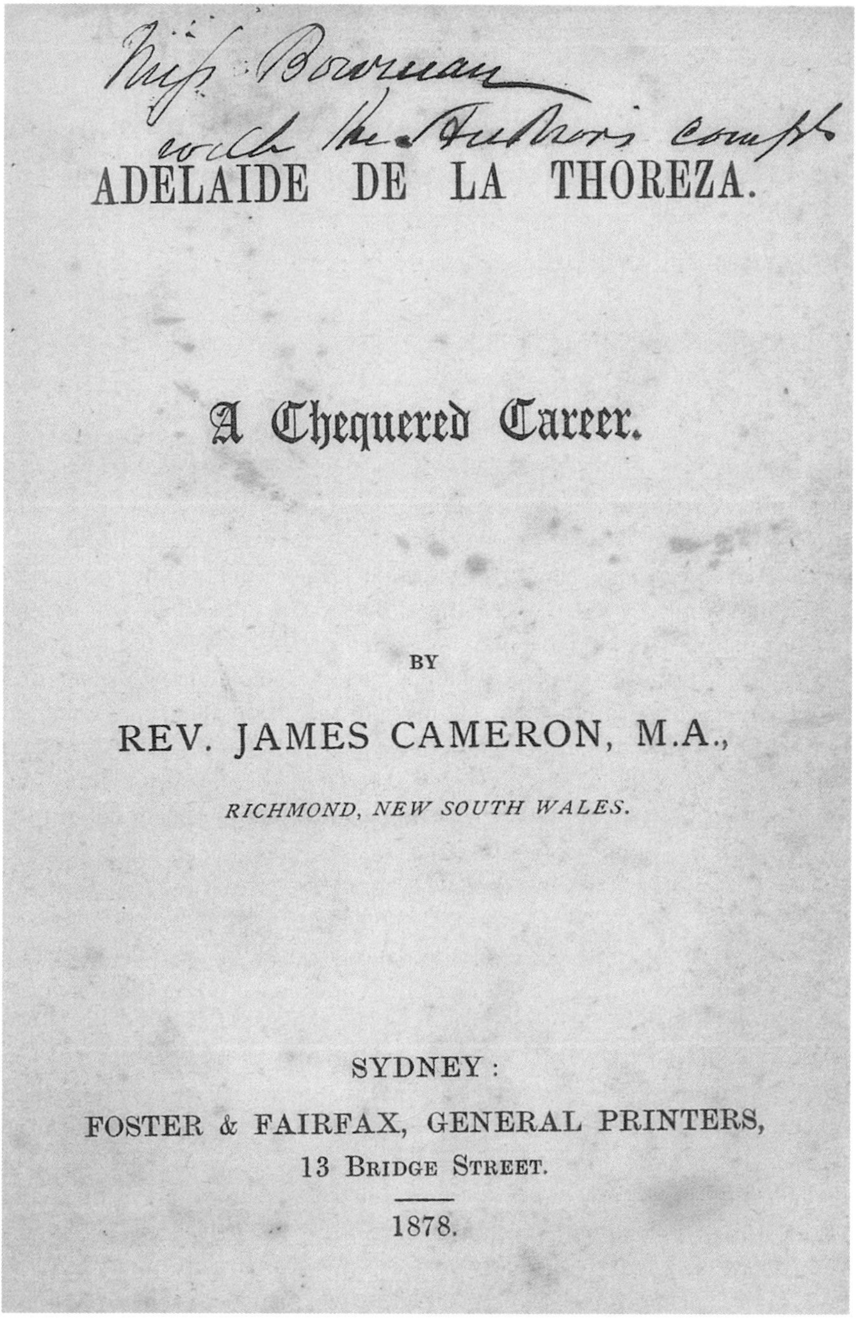

Miss Bowman
with the Author's compts

ADELAIDE DE LA THOREZA.

A Chequered Career.

BY

REV. JAMES CAMERON, M.A.,

RICHMOND, NEW SOUTH WALES.

SYDNEY:

FOSTER & FAIRFAX, GENERAL PRINTERS,

13 BRIDGE STREET.

1878.

Title page from James Cameron's Adelaide de la Thoreza, *Sydney, 1878.*

whether Cameron wrote the story he heard, or used Adelaide's account as the springboard for fiction. If her English was really as eloquent as he claims, why not encourage her to write her own account, offering to edit rather than narrate? Did he wait for the old woman to die because she would deny what only she could verify, the story of her life before she was transported to Botany Bay?

The biographer's version of a childhood in Spain

Adelaide, according to Cameron, was born in Madrid in 1808. Her father, Julian de la Thoreza, was a Spanish nobleman, and his wife was of the 'ancient and honourable house' of de la Vega.[3] Adelaide as their only child enjoyed their 'undivided interest and affection'. One day when she was four, her protective father decided to keep her home from a cousin's birthday party because she had a bad cold:

> The veto thus put on her fondly cherished wish was peculiarly galling to her, and roused into lively exercise the natural heat and vehemence of the Spanish temperament. Her father was busy shaving himself, his foot resting on a stool. Suddenly she sprang on this, snatched the razor from her father's hand, and with it inflicted a wound on her arm, from which the blood spurted over both him and her. 'Will you now let me go?' she exclaimed. Struck with the courageous energy which the deed displayed, her father, instead of chastising her, held her aloft in his arms, and, with a smile of parental satisfaction and pride, exclaimed 'Julian de la Thoreza's own daughter'.[4]

When Adelaide was old enough for school, her fervently patriotic and politically outspoken father sent her to a convent, where during the 'troublous times' he hoped to keep her safe .[5] The abbess doted on Adelaide, the spitting image of the lover for whom the nun so long ago had taken the veil (he had been condemned to death for his politics, and 'with a barbarity worthy of such a country, his affianced bride was compelled to be present at the execution').[6] Only eleven young ladies boarded at the convent, an elite set whose liberal education was carefully nurtured. Here Adelaide learned English, giving 'long recitations from our standard authors in prose and poetry'.[7] She escaped such disasters as befell the beautiful schoolmate cousin who collapsed and died at the convent door, just as the carriage arrived to bear her off to be married (she died from an orange pip around which a ball had grown in her stomach).

When Julian de la Thoreza was eventually forced into exile, Adelaide left the convent to flee with her parents first to France, and then Italy. Because her father—the son, grandson, and great-grandson of ministers of state—

supported the liberal cause, his life was in danger from the royalists after Ferdinand VII was restored to the throne in 1814. During her exile, Adelaide fell in love with 'a young Italian gentleman' of engaging manners and good family.[8] He proposed, her parents said yes, and the lovers impatiently waited out the two months until Adelaide would turn fourteen, and they could be married. On the moonlit night before their wedding day, they strolled in the town's public gardens. As they imagined the ceremony to come, the eager bridegroom pulled from his pocket the wedding ring

> to place it by anticipation on the finger of his betrothed. But lo! when in the act of putting it on, a gleam as of lightning dazzled her sight. It was the gleam of glittering steel, and that steel was being plunged by a vengeful hand into her lover's bosom.[9]

A hot-headed Spanish rival, to whom 'according to a vile custom of the country' Adelaide was betrothed as a child, had followed her to Italy, and killed off the love of her life. 'Her own hand had been wounded by the weapon in its passage. The ring even had been severed, and the mark of the wound received on that memorable night, she bore about with her through life, and carried to her grave.'[10]

A year later, on her fifteenth birthday, Adelaide was back in Madrid. Political allegiances had shifted, and Julian de la Thoreza was a public man once more. On her birthday morning, he 'presented his daughter with a beautiful book' and 'a crown of flowers, which he placed on her head, and called her "Queen Adelaide"'. But he seemed troubled. 'Three times he returned to kiss his wife, ere taking his departure to the Senate House.' All day in the Cortes and on the streets of Madrid there was political turmoil, but within their home, Adelaide and her mother were busily preparing a gala celebration.

> The evening came; the guests had assembled; the music had begun; and Adelaide was waiting for her father's arrival, to open the ball. Of a sudden, a confused noise was heard in the great square. Her mother rushed to the window to ascertain the cause. A sorrowful sight burst upon her view. A bleeding corpse was being borne toward her house. It was her beloved husband, struck down by the hand of an assassin.[11]

Adelaide's mother fainted, lapsed into unconsciousness, and died, recovering only briefly 'to give some directions as to the future custody of her orphan child'. Beside the deathbed stood 'an Indian lady of rank, and of English extraction. She was the widow of a military officer who had been killed in the Peninsular war.' To this childless aristocrat, the Countess Coutts Trotter, Adelaide was bequeathed. She came penniless, 'for all the family property was confiscated, and she was cast a forlorn orphan on the care of others'.[12] She had no Spanish family to turn to:

> Her uncle Adolphus, like her father, had been basely assassinated. Her uncle Alonso had been immured in a dungeon, and on one occasion when he wanted water to quench his thirst, blood was brought to him instead, while the skull of his murdered brother was made to serve the purpose of a drinking cup. It was time to leave a land where political rancour was making blood to flow like water.[13]

The evidence

Not a shred of evidence supports the story Cameron tells about Adelaide's childhood. No record of birth fits his account of an aristocratic lineage (signalled by 'de la') on both sides of her family. 'Thoreza' is not a Spanish surname: 'th' itself is unusual in Spanish, although it might be a corruption of a name beginning with 'z' and thus *pronounced* 'th'. Adelaide's birth is recorded neither under 'Thoreza', nor under any surname beginning with 'z'. Cameron gives no first name for Adelaide's mother, but there is no record anyway of a 'de la Vega' marrying a 'de la Thoreza' (or variant thereof), or giving birth in the Madrid parish to an Adelaide. To complicate matters further, our search must remain inconclusive because the records are incomplete. Adelaide was supposedly born, and her parents married, before Spain had a centralised system for registering births, deaths, and marriages. Few parish records for Madrid survived the Napoleonic wars, Carlist wars, and the Spanish Civil War.

There are state records, however, and if the family of Julian de la Thoreza had indeed included three generations of ministers of state, they would have been appointed by the Crown, and their names printed in the *Gaceta Oficial* in Madrid. No such appointment appears under any version of 'de la Thoreza'. Neither is the assassination of Adelaide's father or her Uncle Adolphus reported. No edict exists authorising the confiscation of property of Julian de la Thoreza. And if Adelaide had borne on her hand the scar from the weapon which killed her Italian lover, the mark useful for identification would have been written into her convict record. It was not.

From orphaned aristocrat to convict woman

In London, says her biographer, Adelaide lived with the Countess Coutts Trotter on Grosvenor Square. The Countess, a Protestant, attended to 'the proprieties of religion', but was very much 'a woman of the world, haughty, imperious and specially desirous of cutting a respectable figure in fashionable society'.[14] Dutiful Adelaide, though with little heart for such frivolity, went off to 'balls, parties, the opera, the theatre'. After two and a half years, the match-making Countess introduced her ward to an Indian nabob described by the press as having wealth 'so vast that he could pay off the National Debt'.[15] Though admittedly twenty or so years older than Adelaide, he was 'still in his prime . . . tall and handsome, and as attractive as we can imagine an Indian to be'. Adelaide declined his offer of marriage. The Countess was furious with the ingrate: 'seek for yourself another home'.[16]

Adelaide found refuge with Lady Kirkwall, who was 'not merely intellectual and accomplished, but also pious'. All went well until summer, when Adelaide 'for various reasons' preferred remaining in town, while Lady Kirkwall went to Scotland, leaving a cousin to stay with her new ward.[17] Adelaide came down with typhus, and almost died. While she was recovering from one sort of fever, the lower orders in the household (butler, housekeeper, and upper housemaid) contracted another: they were stricken with lottery-madness and bought £100 worth of tickets by pawning the Kirkwall silver. They won nothing, as the cousin quickly discovered, seeing in their crime the perfect opportunity to remove a 'hated rival' because, yes, the cousin was in love with Lady Kirkwall's brother, Major de Blatchford, and the Major was in love with Adelaide.[18] The cousin 'laid information against Adelaide, affirming that she had overheard her conversing with the servants about the pawning of the goods'. Adelaide was arrested, and as she left for gaol, 'the cousin, with a fiendish grin of triumph, whispered in her ear the caustic words "What will Major de Blatchford think of you now?"' The trial excited much interest. The Major was there, and Lady Kirkwall, and when Adelaide was convicted along with the servants, 'such a shock did this give to Lady Kirkwall, that she fainted, and shortly thereafter expired'. The judge said he was sorry to sentence to Botany Bay 'one so young, so engaging, and moving in such a circle as Adelaide did'.[19]

The evidence

Nothing supports Cameron's version of Adelaide as the orphaned aristocrat betrayed. Still, there are traces in the biography of actual people. Though the Coutts Trotters do exist and in the 1820s owned a house on Grosvenor Square, nowhere is Adelaide mentioned in their extensive household papers, even as servant.[20] Neither the family nor Debretts, which guards the Coutts Trotter genealogy for *Burke's Peerage*, countenance the suggestion of an Anglo-Indian countess.[21] There was a Lady Kirkwall, and although she did not die until 1831 when Adelaide was two years into her sentence, her maiden name of 'de

Blaquiere' is close to Cameron's 'de Blatchford'. There is nothing in the London newspapers about a fabulously wealthy Indian nabob, or an alluring lottery (though public lotteries at this time were illegal). There is, however, the printed record of a trial held at the Old Bailey on the sixth day of the fifth session, beginning Thursday 11 June 1829, and transcribed in shorthand as case 1286 in which 'Adelaide De Thoraza was indicted for stealing, on the 28th of April, 6 sheets, value 15s., the goods of Martha Davis'.[22]

Davis spoke first:

> I live at No. 15, Finsbury-street, Finsbury-square. I am single, and am a dress-maker—the prisoner was a servant at my house for fifteen months and a fortnight; she was there I believe at the time the sheets were stolen—she was the only female servant in the house; it was her business to mind the bedding and the bed-room; a butcher came to me to ask for a sum of money which I did not owe—I then went and searched the prisoner's box; I found a sheet and a night-gown belonging to me—I knew the sheet was mine, it had been worn a little, but was not dirty—it was a sheet from her own bed, but it was mine; I examined her bed soon after, and both the sheets were gone—this was on the 28th of April; I never saw the corresponding sheet; the officer produced some duplicates, by which we found six sheets; I knew them to be mine, as I had assisted to spin them, and made them up myself.[23]

Susannah Perry then told the court that one evening some months earlier Adelaide appeared with 'a pair of sheets and a bolster in her apron', saying that the bailiffs had been to her mistress's house, and Adelaide had already pawned a bed for her. Now she was tired, so would Susannah please pawn the sheets on her mistress's behalf? Yes, she would, and she did, and gave eight shillings to Adelaide. The pawnbroker's assistant said that Susannah had been in the shop, and he thought she had pawned the sheets—her name and address were on the ticket later claimed by Martha Davis.

Davis was recalled: 'These are my sheets, they are marked with my name; the prisoner had no authority to pawn them—I never authorised her to pawn a bed; I had an excellent character with her.'[24]

A pawnbroker took the stand, saying he had 'four sheets pawned at two different times', not in the name of Susannah Perry but Eliza Wilson: 'I do not know who pawned them'.[25] He thought that because they were not marked, Davis had not sworn they were her property, but as the policeman John Bee would tell the court, the tickets for those sheets were found on Adelaide when she was taken up and searched. Again, Martha Davis was recalled:

> COURT *to* MARTHA DAVIS. *Q*. Look at these four sheets, and tell me what reason you have to claim them as yours? *A*. I made up part of them—

> some of them were kept in a cupboard and some in a box, they are both kept locked; I never sent the prisoner to take the sheets out; I always do that myself.
>
> GUILTY. Aged 23.
>
> Transported for Seven Years.[26]

Adelaide might have spoken during her trial, said something about her circumstances, entered a defence. We might at least have heard her voice through the clerk's shorthand. Her silence deepens our uncertainty.

Is it relevant that Finsbury Square, where Martha Davis lost her sheets, is no more than a ten-minute walk from the Finsbury Barracks, and 'dressmaker' was often a euphemism for prostitute?

From convict woman to pioneer mother

Aboard the *Lucy Davidson* bound for Botany Bay, James Cameron's Adelaide is still treated as special. 'Every consideration' was shown her during the voyage, and she carried letters of introduction to men of influence, including the Governor:

> This secured for her as much regard for her comfort as was compatible with the position she occupied. She was assigned to an old Spanish gentleman, Arietta by name, who lived at the Cow-pastures. It was thought that this would be a congenial home for her; but in her countryman's household she did not, by any means, find things wholly to her mind. Her next place was in the family of Commissary Birch.[27]

This was much better. Here she cared for a little girl who decades later would remember distinctly 'an assigned servant that we called *Theresa* . . . I was very fond of her and often wished to see her again'.[28]

Unfortunately, mingling with the lower orders as 'a servant among servants' did Adelaide's morals no good. She became pregnant to a fellow servant, George Smith, who 'afterwards drowned'. Though he offered to marry Adelaide, 'her feelings recoiled', and she 'declined'. Alfred Smith was born, the 'energetic and trustworthy' drover 'still sojourning among us'. Adelaide went next to an estate on the edge of a village, Richmond, where the Cox family lived like English gentry. They treated the cultivated Adelaide as 'companion' rather than convict servant, and attempted to dissuade her from 'stooping' to marry their butler John Masters.[29] A few months after 'companion' and butler were free, and before they married on 8 September 1836, Masters (formerly apprenticed to a solicitor and tempted 'in an evil hour' to forgery) wrote his bride-to-be a touching letter. Enclosing the first money earned 'since I have been in bondage', he was in a mood for promises: 'Your own dear child was first to call me father; in me he shall find a father; in me you shall find a kind and loving partner'.[30]

To John and Adelaide Masters two children were born, Adelaide and Thomas. The ex-convict parents 'set up a small shop in Richmond, in which confectionery and other wares were sold'. They prospered and moved nearby to the larger town of Windsor, where John Masters 'followed the trade of a painter'. And drank. And grew unpredictable and violent. And was sent away by his wife, desperate for 'some measure of peace and comfort'.[31] From the distance of Maitland, Masters wrote his 'wounded feelings' into poetry:

> Yes, thou didst wrong me, A. . ., I fondly thought
> In thee I'd find the love, my heart had sought . . .[32]

And in response from Richmond, where Adelaide lived with their unmarried son Tom, and kept herself by washing for the Hawkesbury Benevolent Asylum, came 'verses, believed to be her composition', verses in which 'she bewailed her estrangement from him in whose affection she had hoped to find a solace amid the trials of life'.[33] Years later, an old man 'bowed down with infirmities and sorrows' returned to Richmond to talk with his wife once more, and die. The Adelaide who was by this time confiding in James Cameron lived out the rest of her days in gloom, quoting often the words she wished engraved upon her tombstone:

> I've lived to prove
> There's darkness in the brightest dream,
> And sorrow in the deepest joy.[34]

On 26 December 1877, in the year before her seventieth birthday, Adelaide Masters née de la Thoreza was 'united to Christ'.[35]

Amanuensis to the bastard son

Some thirty years later, on 13 November 1909, the *Windsor and Richmond Gazette* began a series which would run for a year under the title, 'Some Ups and Downs of an Old Richmondite, Mr Alfred Smith'.[36] The reminiscences were introduced by Robert Farlow, who had for some time thought 'the experiences of my esteemed old friend, Mr Alfred Smith, of Richmond, ought to be worth chronicling and should make interesting reading'. Smith might be in 'his seventy eighth year', but his 'memory is very good and clear and carries him back to his early boyhood days'. In this project, says Farlow, 'I shall place myself in the background as much as possible throughout and allow Mr Smith to tell his own tale'.[37] With the exception of one brief comment, the amanuensis calls no further attention to himself until the story's end, and what he then says rings true: 'Throughout I have left the narrator as original as possible, and I think the reader who knows the narrator has often fancied they have been chatting with the old man.'[38] Rather different from James Cameron's designs on Adelaide.

Alf Smith begins at the beginning:

> I was born at Hobartville on July the 13th 1831 . . . I have heard them say father at one time kept an hotel near Bungarrabee, on the Western road, and was found drowned near Liverpool by one of the late Mr Lowes. Old George James having only one child, a daughter . . . adopted me as his own child. They were kind to me, and I never forgot their kindness, and always tried to do as much as I could to repay them, as long as they lived.[39]

Only once does Smith mention his mother. He has been describing the cottages along Bosworth Street (did Farlow walk with him along these village streets, inviting the old man to recollect the vanished?):

> Mrs Masters, my mother, stands first in my mind. I was taken down to see her one day, and told she was my mother, but I couldn't make out how it was possible to have two mothers. I had always known Mrs James as mother, and I was too young to know anything about being adopted at the age of fifteen months.[40]

For whatever reason, Alf Smith never called John Masters 'father' as Cameron's account seemed to anticipate, but he weaves his mother's husband into memories of the small community where they all lived:

> Going down March street . . . there was a skillion standing just past the corner. The front portion has been put on since I first knew it. The first person I have any recollections of living there was John Masters, father of Tom Masters in Windsor. He was a painter and decorator by trade, and a splendid tradesman. He was an artist also, and could paint animals or any other pictures. Weller, I think, who was a publican of Windsor in the early days, had a sign done by him. It represented a blackfellow and a large lump of gold in his hand.[41]

John Masters, father of Tom. Tom Masters, mate of Alf Smith. Thomas Mathew Masters, born in Richmond on 23 May 1843, must have been no more than twelve when he started working for Alf, who was twice that age.[42] 'Tom was well liked all along the road. Civil, obliging, and a real good fellow was Tom.' Again and again as Alf recounts his stories of those days 'when droving was droving', Tom is mentioned, the lad whose erratic father had by this time been banished to Maitland. The fatherless half-brothers fend for themselves, and look after each other as they travel the vast distances from the other side of Bourke down into Ned Kelly country, even 'entertaining bushrangers unawares'.[43] And Alf weaves Adelaide's daughter into the story too, Adelaide Eliza Masters, born in Richmond on 8 January 1838.[44] Outside Richmond, a clergyman kept a boarding school, where 'Mrs Etherdon, of Marrickville, a sister of Tom Masters, was a pupil'—while her brothers were on the road, young Adelaide was at school.[45]

Alf Smith's recall of detail is phenomenal: in his mind's eye the Richmond where his mother lived for forty years after she was free is rebuilt, and reinhabited. But nothing is said of the convict factor (and Alf's adoptive father had been a convict too), and with names like 'Smith' and 'Masters' the Spanish element seems to vanish as well. Except for one evocative detail. Alf remembers a six-roomed house on Lennox Street, 'old weatherboard, and "brick nogged" inside', run as a pub by a man named Menease, who hailed from Spain, and was my godfather'.[46] A Spanish godfather . . . Adelaide's gift to her bastard son?

Secrets and cover-ups, or, what to make of this story . . .

Quite a beginning for a child born in the Parramatta Female Factory—an exotic Spanish godfather growing vines on the river terraces outside Richmond, and a completely untraceable father named 'John Smith'.[47] Or was the almost comically determined Englishness a cover-up for the actual father, recently married and socially pretentious? A father who flourished his signature as 'John, Baptist, Lehimas, De Arrieta' or sometimes with dramatic brevity as just the aristocratic-sounding 'De Arrieta'.[48]

Arrieta had heard about 'a spanish woman' aboard the *Lucy Davidson* from Sydney's harbour master, who 'promised to endeavour to get her assigned to me'.[49] Perhaps a Spanish-speaker would not tax the vocabulary of a man of whom a bored houseguest had unkindly said, 'De Arrietta's whole range of the English Language did not include above Fifty Words!'[50] Arrieta had been in New South Wales since 1821, and was the recipient of a 2000-acre grant of prime land adjoining the Macarthur property at Camden Park. Why was he so well treated?[51] Among his contemporaries, Arrieta's call on the public purse was explained by saying that he was a spy during the Peninsular War, or a prisoner of war, or a witness during the trial of Queen Caroline, or, more plausibly, that he was attached to the Commissariat and acted as a contact between the Army and the local contractors, but he had lost money through speculation, and was therefore pressing his British contacts to help him start again in the colony.[52] Arrieta was in his mid-fifties when 23-year-old Adelaide joined his household, and the nineteen-year-old he had married the previous year in what looks like a shotgun wedding was already the mother of a baby girl.[53] Remembering the household, a neighbour would later recall

> an excitable man, Senor D'Arrietta [with] a gay, charming, but equally excitable wife . . . on one occasion, as he sat brooding after a quarrel, she smashed a prize pumpkin over his head. If D'Arrietta was excitable, he was also practical.
>
> 'Dios!' he cried. 'What I do now for the pumpkin seed?'[54]

Adelaide's volatile young mistress was English, and it was not for her that Arrieta requested 'the spanish woman'.

Convicts assigned to Arrieta had in the past been reported for absconding and barnburning, and in at least one case, a complaint had been lodged against the master as sexual predator.[55] Three years before Adelaide's arrival, a convict husband petitioned the Colonial Secretary, saying that 'in consequence of some private motives Mr. D'Arietta took advantage of Petitioner in order to separate him from his wife'.[56] Adelaide may have been another victim of Arrieta's 'private motives'. Certainly she was pregnant within ten months of being assigned to his property 'at the Cow-pastures', as Cameron put it, although Arrieta's name, 'Morton Park', sounds more elegant (he was probably evoking the name of the well-connected British Member of Parliament, Morton Pitt, who wrote letters of introduction for 'a good friend of mine, a Spaniard, but who has long resided in England at different times').[57] One visitor, having described his host as 'a happy, good-humoured, hospitable Spanish gentleman', conjures up a paranoid intruder into the landscape, who 'has, by way of protection from burglars and bush-rangers, drawn a regular chain of videttes around [the homestead] in the shape of fierce growling devils of dogs, pegged down to the ground at such exact mathematical distances, that two can just meet to lick each other's faces, and pinch a mouthful out of any intruder's hip'.[58] The peculiar personality behind this arrangement of dogs, uncannily like that of the beasts chained across Eagle Hawk Neck to stop convicts escaping from Port Arthur, emerges from the letter from an acquaintance of the Peninsular War years to his wife. After forty-seven days at Morton Park (he counted them), the guest wrote that Arrieta's 'interminable list of mortifications which his embarrassments subject him to—has encreased the irritability of a temper originally warm and hasty till it is become a disease, and the gay warm, easy open hearted man of thirty is become at forty eight envious, suspicious, gloomy and irritable'.[59] And no doubt overbearing when it came to making demands upon a young Spanish woman, who found herself assigned to work inside the circle of dogs on a property sufficiently far from any town for a social life beyond the homestead to seem unlikely.

Whoever was the father of Adelaide's child, and it could have been another servant at Morton Park, it was the master who by returning the pregnant convict woman to the Female Factory at Parramatta extended her bondage from two years to almost seven (Adelaide served all but three months of her seven-year sentence, whereas John Masters received his ticket-of-leave before he had served half his fourteen years).[60] The pressures on Adelaide must have been intense, and if she was not the victim of dastardly aristocrats, as Cameron would have it, she undoubtedly felt the crushing power of forces beyond her control. We know that she gave birth to Alfred Smith in prison, and relinquished him when weaned to George and Ann James. If she had kept her baby longer, she would have risked his being sent to the Orphan School, as usually happened with the children of convict mothers.[61] Even when she was free, she did not reclaim Alf, or establish regular contact with him. But whether she tried, we do not know, and after all, when Alf went to the Jameses in 1832, Adelaide managed to get herself assigned to William Cox at Hobartville, on the edge of Richmond where the Jameses lived.[62] She and John Masters could easily have moved after their marriage to start a family in some place where people did not know about Alf, or about their convict past, and yet they made their home in Richmond. When Masters turned out to be a disastrous husband and father, Adelaide made him leave the area so that she could stay. We know, too, that before Adelaide relinquished Alf, she generated an official document implying legitimate origins when she had him baptised at St John's Church of England, Parramatta, as the son of Adelaide De Theorisa and John Smith.[63] By espousing 'Smith', that blandest of English names, Adelaide told the person registering the baptism what she wanted him to know.

And when did Adelaide begin to realise that power often resides not in the 'facts', but in the way a story is told? Did she as a child in Spain hear details from her life reshaped into stories a mother or father told to make things happen in the way they wished, or at least to try to make them happen? Was she, like her first child, the bastard offspring of a man who used her mother and then pushed her aside, perhaps a British soldier fighting with the Spanish to free the Iberian Peninsula from Napoleonic invaders? Did Adelaide's mother make her way to London in search of the child's father, and then die or abandon her daughter to fend for herself as prostitute or servant? If the past were marked by an English father's betrayal, would that explain her clinging to a Spanish surname, and to Spanishness itself as a source of identity? Or was she after all the victim of some complicated set of circumstances, reconfigured by Cameron in his fantasy of gothic Spain and the romantic aristocratic child?

We have fossicked in the archives of Australia, Spain, and the United Kingdom, pondered all sorts of possibilities, argued between ourselves and with others, and now we are left with a female convict narrative which remains at crucial points as murky as ever. At its end, however, there is closure. We can see Adelaide clearly at her moment of death, the matriarch whose three children all live within easy walking distance in Richmond, and who have each named a daughter Adelaide in honour of their mother: the daughter of Alfred Smith was born in 1860; of Adelaide (Masters) Etherdon in 1866; and of Tom Masters in 1871.[64] But 'Adelaide' was after all the name of an English queen, a name which need not sound 'foreign' to British ears, so was our convict woman even Spanish? Cameron says so, of course, but who are we to trust Cameron? Just as we are about to collapse into the despair of researchers who have found much, only to know nothing, we suddenly notice details on the certificate of death. Tom, the son with whom for decades Adelaide had lived, tells for the authorities the story he knows: his mother was born in Spain, the daughter of 'Julian Delatheresa, a Spaniard, rank not known'.[65] Whatever may or may not be true about Adelaide's origins, we are satisfied now that this convict woman who became an Australian pioneer mother and grandmother began her improbable journey in Spain.

7

'your unfortunate and undutiful wife'

Eleanor Conlin Casella, Ellen Cornwall and Lucy Frost

Convict narratives are often heard through a process of serendipity. This is a story of a solitary female voice, discovered accidentally and recovered through the combined fortunes of archival detective work and simple luck. Within the social sciences, researchers use the term 'triangulation' to describe the interweaving and juxtaposition of historical details into a patterned narrative chorus of verified facts.[1] This mystery unfolds by triangulating voices from the past to discover and recover the story of Ellen Cornwall.

From Launceston (Cornwall) to Launceston (Tasmania)

Eleanor Conlin Casella

It was a photocopied letter—two pages of neat handwriting hung in a frame on the bottom floor of the Lawrence House Museum of Launceston, Cornwall. I was in the area to participate in an archaeological dig on a Bronze Age settlement in Bodmin Moor. One of the project directors had suggested I visit the museum; she remembered an Australian convict letter on display, and knew I was 'into that sort of thing'. The letter had been sent from Van Diemen's Land. Missing its signature page, the photocopied narrative communicated a solitary voice of regret and redemption from its anonymous convict author.

Who wrote this letter? Could the woman's identity be retraced? Museum staff did not know how the mysterious photocopy had come to the Lawrence House collections. Nor were they sure of the location of the original letter. Perhaps she had been transported to Launceston, Tasmania, their sister town within the infamous penal colony? Certain details of the lonely narrative hinted at possible triangulations. Could she be found through her specific date of arrival in Hobart? Or through the tragic description of her young son's death in the convict nursery? Or through her description of a leg injury and resulting accommodation in the 'Government Hospital'? I promised to share any new voices recovered by my colleagues in Australia.

But first, the voice we were trying to hear.

ELLEN CORNWALL'S LETTER

Van Diemans Land
February 25th 1848

My Dear Husband
This comes from your unfortunate and undutiful wife hoping it will be received with as much affection as it is sent. you will say how can I expect it. but I know that you would at any time be glad to hear of me being leading a different life to what I led from the time I became your wife till such time as it pleased the Lord to stop my wild career and I hope and trust it may be for the salvation of my soul as it the most Important of all things that I neglected I hope the lord has given me a sight of my Wickedness and folly and gives me grace to lead a new life seek his will as he has said that he that cometh to me I will in no wise cast out you have said my Dear Fred^{k} that you would pray for me I hope your prayer will be answered I hope you still do the same not forget me for I need it.

I am happy to inform you that I am with a kind religous Family who wishes me and all in there House to lead a good life and from whom I receive every Instruction necessary to show me the rule of life I ought to go by, I attend the Church of England service and I bigen to like it very much I also read the Protestant Bible you know I was very ignorant of the Lord I feel that [illegible] The only way that I can find out what I am and what I would come to if I do not seek eternal life and now my Dear Husband though I am not worthy to call you by that name you that has so many times forgiven me and taken me back when I broke my false promises of amendment O could I but redeem the times gone by I would try to make amends to you for the many Troubles I brought on you but to give you an account of my life since I left England and the end of our dear child whom I was not worthy of the lord taken him from me

I ought to have told you before that we landed in Van Diemans Land on the 4th of January 1847 and all the Females that had no Incumbrance were taken on board of a lage Hulk that lies in the bay for the purpose of receiving Every Female convict that comes into the Colony and they obliged to serve six months on it and then they are sent out to service and receive wages to turn to their own use but I was let go with my child to a Nursery with my child tho he was twelve months older than the children are when the are taken away from their Mother but our Superintendant obtained permission for me to go with him but the Country did not agree with my dear boy the hot winds in the months Jan^{ry} and Feb^{ry} was too much for his delicate constitution although he had Medical attendance and everything was done that could be done but it pleased the lord on the 7th of March to take him to his Heavenly

The eyes and figure of a female convict assigned as servant (G. T. W. B. Boyes' Sketchbook, 1825).

abode out of this vain & wicked world but my Dear Fred[k] I shall pass over this scene of sorrow

I only add that it was the greatest trial I ever had I followed his remains and saw him laid in the Churchyard in the Town and on the 17th of the same month I was sent to the Hulk above named to serve my Probation the situation is not disagreeable there as you may suppose as Everything is found for there use there is about 500 women always on board and I was at Needlework all my time there on the 22nd of Sept[r] I was hired off the ship as needlewoman you know that is the only thing I was capable of doing I had not been long in my situation when I had the misfortune to scald my leg very bad and I was sent to the General Hospital where I remained for two months and then was taken back to my place again I staid as long as my service was required and on the 28th of Dec[r] I was recommend to the Family that I am now living with as Needle women and receive twelve pounds a year I have been here nor two month and I can assure you that I feel quite at home I hope the lord will give me grace to fulfil my duty in whatever station of life it shall please god to place me in you know my dear Fred[k] that I am a poor creature now without a protector. I often think of your words but I know by experience . . .[2]

In search of shards

Lucy Frost

I have never seen Ellen's letter, and yet I can imagine it vividly from what I've been told, its thin blue pages so well worn along the folds that the paper has split and rendered a few of the words illegible. This is a letter which has been read and reread over the years, speaking its intimacy to a man who was loved. Now, hanging on the wall of a museum, its personal voice has entered cultural memory.

Ellen obviously had not written to her husband since she left England, so how did Frederick react to this letter of contrition from a wayward wife? Did he blanch from the opening pages as histrionic breast-beating? If anger were all he felt, he could have torn the insolence into pieces, or watched as good riddance was burnt in the fire. But he kept the letter. Perhaps he never replied, and I know that he and Ellen were never reunited as husband and wife, and yet I have come to believe that something about her undoubtedly touched him. He let her go, and kept her words.

If Frederick did not discard Ellen's impassioned plea as mere cliche from an incarcerated woman who always turned to him when she got herself into trouble, perhaps I too should give her the benefit of the doubt. And yet the real issue seems less a matter of believing or not believing the letter's literal truthfulness, and more one of trying to understand the emotionally charged narrative it calls into play by evoking for readers down the years the voice of a convict woman speaking intimately to her husband of broken promises and a dead child. From textual fragments scattered over time and space, it becomes possible to piece together a story which gives shape to a marriage. Within the Archives Office of Tasmania, I have dug for personal detail in records created to serve institutional ends. Returning to my home at Lower Snug with photocopies and notes, I would start up my computer, and find email messages sent by Eleanor Casella from Berkeley and later from Manchester, messages which transmit electronically the English shards unearthed by Carol Richardson-Bunbury from The Friends of Lawrence House Museum, Launceston, Cornwall, who had marshalled relatives and friends. Gradually the letter's meanings have grown sharper, until I now think I understand something of what Ellen was saying to Frederick.

In hindsight and from the outside, the Cornwalls seem an ill-matched couple. The husband was a local man, Birmingham born and bred, the wife a grey-eyed lass from County Mayo. All I know of Frederick's family is that his father Daniel was a plasterer, a worker with specialised skills in the building trade. It was within the families of such men as Daniel Cornwall that an elite was formed within the working class, an elite for whom independence and domestic respectability were central values. Frederick, as a bricklayer, had followed in his father's footsteps. Ellen's family was different. Her father, Anthony Rowland, was an Irish labourer with ten children whose names Ellen recited as she stood on the deck of the convict transport: three brothers, Thomas, James, Martin; six sisters, Bridget, Catherine, Sarah, Ann, Margaret, Mary. Ellen's horizons, however, were broader than her family circumstances, and although we know nothing in detail about her childhood, we do know that, quite remarkably, Ellen had learned to read, and to write confidently. This is surprising: initially I assumed that the letter had been written for, and not by, Ellen. The attention to particular dates seemed, however, a mark of a literate woman rather than one formed within an oral sense of life's telling. The style fits what I've learned of Ellen, too, and the second part of the letter in particular is devoid of stock phrases and the linguistic flourishes of a paid letter-writer. When Carol Richardson-Bunbury received a copy of the Cornwalls' marriage certificate and compared Ellen's signature with the script of the letter, she became convinced that the hand was the same—and the other people she consulted agreed. Ellen may have come from one of Ireland's most impoverished rural areas, but she was literate.

Literacy seemed to go with leaving, or at least one can say that it was the literate and skilled who were more likely to leave Ireland than those who stayed behind.[3] The letter itself calls attention to her accomplishment. Carol Richardson-Bunbury tells me that Ellen writes with confidence and fluency—only once throughout the letter is a word crossed out, and only once are words (those which are now illegible) added in the margin. The letter is the meticulous production of someone proud of her literacy—a practised hand. But how did she practise? Paper and ink were by no means readily available to a convict. Had she written regularly to all those brothers and sisters when she first left home for a new life in England?

Ellen was part of the vast flow of young men and women who crossed the Irish Sea in search of better prospects in industrialising Britain. Indeed, for many in Ireland it seemed as though the lifeblood of the nation flowed out of Cork harbour.[4] How old Ellen was when she left home we do not know, or where she first went. We do know that when she married Frederick they were both living in Handsworth, a village on Birmingham's northwest where the Black Country began.[5] Thousands of unskilled workers had been pouring into the Black Country, a leading producer of iron and coal and a centre of iron manufactures; and among them the Irish, both women and men, had a reputation for drinking and brawling.[6] If Ellen ran true to national type, and there is evidence to suggest that she did, a respectable bricklayer would have been taking considerable risk in marrying her.

Maybe Ellen offered comfort to a lonely man. Although Frederick was only in his mid-twenties, he was already a widower when he married nineteen-year-old Ellen on 26 November 1843. The service was performed after banns at the Handsworth Parish Church, according to the rites and ceremonies of the Church of England, Frederick's church. Later Ellen, who told the prison authorities she was a Catholic, would try to persuade Frederick that she was genuinely drawn to a religion which in the past separated them. 'I attend the Church of England service and I begin to like it very much', wrote the supplicant wife. I really have changed, she seems to be pleading, I am like you now, not rebellious and different, I am ready to be your wife.

As she had not been when they married. 'I left my Husband two years', Ellen told the muster master as she prepared to disembark from the convict ship, 'he paid me 5/ a week'.[7] The Cornwalls had been married a mere two years and three months before Ellen was sentenced to ten years' transportation.

> *My Dear Husband though I am not worthy to call you by that name you that has so many times forgiven me and taken me back*

During their brief and intermittent marriage, Ellen twice gave birth. The Cornwalls had moved in from Handsworth to central Birmingham when Ann was born little more than four months after their marriage. Did Ellen use her pregnancy to pressure the widowed bricklayer, who had married his first wife after she became pregnant as well? On 1 April 1844 Ellen gave birth to a daughter at home, 42 Warf Street. On 5 May at the local parish church of Saint Thomas, the baby was christened Ann, and on 11 May Ellen registered the birth. And then what? After six months' of marriage, did Ellen decide that domestic respectability didn't suit her wild Irish ways, and take off with the baby? That could explain why Frederick paid her five shillings a week. But if Ellen had a tiny baby with her, and no family around to spell the mother while she went to the pub, work must have been hard to find, and daily life a battle. And what became of little Ann? She simply disappears from the records, and Ellen never mentions her when she tells her story to the muster master, or when she writes to Frederick. Did something happen of which the mother was ashamed? Was it after the baby's (unregistered) death that Ellen left the home she and Frederick had made together? Or did Ellen take Ann with her and get a job for herself while she gave Frederick's weekly payments to one of the notorious baby farmers who would not have registered a child's death?

Whether or not Ann's story was a mother's shame, there is no evidence that Ellen neglected her second child. But there is also no evidence that Frederick ever supported the child registered by his mother as Henry Edward Cornwall, or even recognised the baby as his son. Henry was born on 5 May 1845, just thirteen months after his sister. Although it must have been during this period that Frederick had so often forgiven his wife and taken her back, she does call herself 'undutiful', and her 'wild career' may have been sexual as well as criminal. If the Cornwalls had been living together, as they were when their daughter was born, Ellen might have avoided the Birmingham Lying-in Hospital, where the city's poorest and most desperate women '(although they seldom knew it) were exposing themselves to a risk of dying that was many times higher than if they had stayed at home in the worst of slums and been attended in their birth by no one except family and an untrained midwife'.[8] Ellen was lucky to escape puerperal fever. Since she left the hospital for a tenement address she gave as No 2 in House 4 on Brass House Passage, when she registered Henry's birth on 3 June 1845, Henry was fortunate to survive his first weeks of life. But how could a mother with a child to whose welfare the putative father was not contributing find the money even to pay for a bed in a tenement? Was it Ellen's determination to keep Henry, as she had not kept Ann, which led her to steal?

On 17 October 1845, before the Birmingham Court of Quarter Sessions, Ellen Cornwall was charged with stealing wearing apparel at Aston, near Birmingham, convicted, and sentenced to gaol for three months.[9] Henry, who less than a year later would sail with his mother for Van Diemen's Land, was probably with her from the time she entered prison to await trial. In mid-January 1846 Ellen would have been due for release. A month later she was arrested and charged with the theft of 'one sheet 2/- 1 blanket 2/- 1 Tablecloth 2/- 1 pr Boots 2/-', the goods of Thomas Wallis, her master.[10] Ellen, most likely with baby in arms, travelled to Warwick where her case was held on 31 March 1846. In the Grand Jury Room, a judge on the Midland Circuit presided over some two dozen trials. Ellen's offence was nothing special, and the local newspaper simply recorded charge, conviction, sentence.[11] All charges against her were dropped, except those of stealing the blanket and sheet. For this theft she was sentenced to ten years' transportation beyond the seas.[12]

In the record of sentence which accompanied Ellen when she and Henry were transferred to the Millbank prison in London, Ellen's trade is recorded as 'milliner and dressmaker'.[13] Had she been working for little more than a room in her master's house where she looked after her baby and plied her needle? Was it as a live-in worker that she stripped linen from her bed and pawned or sold it to buy something for Henry—food, clothes, medicine? Or was she trapped in outwork, living with her baby in yet another tenement room, where she made the hats for which Wallis paid a pittance? Did she arrive one day to find him absent, leave her hats and take the bedding which at least might keep her warm?[14] Was the theft an impulsive gesture of defiance against a master who would have no trouble identifying the culprit? Retaliation for a dispute over money promised and unpaid? So many questions, so few answers.

We are on firmer ground when it comes to Henry's first birthday. He spent it in Millbank prison, where Ellen had been on the register since 28 April.[15] Poor Henry, such a short life, and almost all of it spent incarcerated. How strong was he? I would like to imagine a rambunctious toddler of fourteen months, who had inherited his mother's spirited ways and learned to walk so confidently at Millbank that he was ready to try out his balancing skills on the deck of the *Elizabeth and Henry* when it sailed on 17 September 1846, bound for Van Diemen's Land. Though an active toddler would have been a handful for his mother, a winsome little boy would have attracted attention from other women who would have shared Ellen's watchfulness. Among the 169 convicts on board, some would have missed dreadfully the children left behind with husbands, family, and friends. Others on a voyage of 109 days might have found the child an amusing diversion, and gladly helped Ellen look after him.[16]

Not surprisingly, however, the child of prison cells was far from robust, and it was Dr Harvey Morris, the ship's surgeon, to whom Ellen turned for help. On 22 October, five weeks into the voyage, Henry was admitted to the hospital, where he remained until 4 January 1847 when the *Elizabeth and Henry* docked at Hobart Town. Children did not fare well on this voyage. The two who were born aboard ship both died, as did Isabella Bush, aged six months. 'I did not doubt the child's Illness was caused by want of maternal love and tenderness', wrote the censorious surgeon in his report.[17] Ellen Cornwall, in contrast, he praised for being 'as intensely affectionate towards her offspring as [Isabella's mother] was culpably regardless of the same'.[18] Poor Henry was in a distressing state. 'A severe attack of Diarrhoea reduced this child in a short space to the greatest possible state of Debility consistent with life', and yet 'he eventually recovered under the palliative plan of treatment by which I mean combating symptoms as they presented themselves'.[19] Surely the surgeon had an eye on the superior who would read his report rather than on the child when he entered 'cured' beside Henry's name in the register.[20] As we know from Ellen's letter, the little boy now twenty months old was far from 'cured'. The surgeon's smugly moralistic equations of bad mother/dead child, good mother/cured child collapse into a pattern of dead children subjected to highly dubious medical care. Two months to the day after Henry was discharged, he was dead. This was 'the greatest trial I ever had', wrote Ellen to Frederick, and there is no reason to disbelieve her.

About the rest of that year we know from Ellen's letter. She was sent after Henry's death to serve her six months' probation on the *Anson*, a hulk anchored off Hobart. As she sat day after day at her needlework, the sheer sameness and predicability of the routine may have soothed her nerves. The situation was not, she told Frederick, disagreeable. In a changed regime during this final decade of transportation to Van Diemen's Land, convicts were now hired out to settlers instead of being assigned and unpaid. Needlewomen were much in demand, and Ellen was hired immediately, only to have her life seared once more by pain, this time the physical agony of a leg so badly burned that for weeks she was in the stinking and overcrowded General Hospital, where disease was spread as often as cured. Once more, Ellen survived institutionalised medical care, and picked up her needle. 'You know that is the only thing I was capable of doing', she reminded Frederick, and capable she proved herself. The account she gives is of a reliable worker, integrated into respectable domesticity, and earning the yearly wage which implies long-term employment. Here, too, she tries to persuade Frederick that she has become like him, has espoused his values. In the letter's final missing page, did Ellen plead for reconciliation? The whole purpose of the letter seems to move in that direction. Why else write now, rather than earlier?

And did Frederick reply? Perhaps he wrote saying stay away for good this time, perhaps he had paid her the 5/ a week to leave him alone before, and had always been seduced by her physical presence, drawn by sexual desire. Our marriage is never going to work, he may have written, better for us both if you remain where you are. Whether Frederick actually rejected his wife's appeal, or simply failed to respond, Ellen's determination to keep to the straight and narrow seems to have weakened. On 9 January 1849, almost a year after she wrote to Frederick, Ellen blotted her convict conduct record for the first time. Charged with 'Neglect of duty mismanagement of work and absent without leave', she was sentenced to three months' hard labour in the Female Factory. On 28 August that same year, she was charged with absconding.[21]

Perhaps around this time the rejected wife met Henry Macarthy, an Irishman from County Cork, but a Protestant like Frederick and a skilled tradesman too, a cabinet maker. Like Ellen, Macarthy had left his home country to work in England, where he was convicted. Both had been sentenced to ten years, though Henry's offence, as he stated to the muster master, was 'manslaughter in Bristol I was attacked by 3 men and I struck one of them with a pen knife of which wound he died after 2 days'.[22] Sometime around February 1850, two years after she wrote to Frederick, Ellen became pregnant with Henry Macarthy's child, a daughter to whom she gave birth on 18 November and named for herself. A fortnight later the parents were married at Holy Trinity in Hobart Town, according to the Rites and Ceremonies of the United Church of England and Ireland.[23] Henry, who had described himself as married when he disembarked from *The Duchess of Northumberland* in 1843, claimed to be a widower, and Ellen to be the widow she was not.[24] Henry, who already had a ticket-of-leave, received his certificate of freedom in 1852; Ellen got her ticket-of-leave in 1851, and her conditional pardon in 1853.[25] The Macarthys disappear then from the records, and may have left the colony. As for Frederick Cornwall, he surfaces in the Birmingham census for 1851, a

Toeing the official line?

Some hope! Though transported for seven years in 1833, he was continuously a prisoner till 1844. Within that period, he accumulated seventeen recorded additional punishments, including repeated additional terms of up to two years in road parties and chain gangs and one flogging of twenty-five lashes. His related offences included drunkenness; absence without leave; theft from his master; fraudulently attempting to obtain money, and public begging. On top came the additional twelve months' hard labour in 1847–8. His only indulgence was bestowed on 7 September 1847, when his employment at Hobart gaol as cook (one of his pre-transportation skills) was approved.[21] Further, in a perverse turn revealing that the colonial eye saw what it chose and 'authenticated' what it saw, his birthplace was consistently misrecorded as Sierra Leone.[22] That implicitly and conveniently discounted his claim to humane sympathy.

'Me want free too—Ah pity!!' Alexander Simpson's story

Prisoner number 1664 Simpson, Alexander, appeared before Hobart's Muster Master aboard the *Jupiter* in May 1833.[23] He was an unusual prisoner, convicted by Portland General Court Martial, Jamaica, 20 January 1832, of 'Seditious Language, Conspiracy & Rebellion' and sentenced to be 'hung by the neck . . . in the Market place', although this was later commuted to life transportation.[24] These facts are important. They identify Simpson as involved in a huge if brief slave uprising—Jamaica's 'Baptist War' of December 1831 to January 1832.

Simpson's recorded statement of offence was: 'Mutiny & exciting the Slaves to Rebellion. I was a slave myself'.[25] These twelve words—note the crucial 'I'—discharge an intense 'in your face, white boy!' effect, through their defiant confidence of being splendidly in the right before captors who shame themselves. In 1833, the year of Westminster's Emancipation Act, he may well have felt that he had neither suffered, nor many comrades died, in vain. Unlike Brown's micro-narrative, there is no implicit supplication: Simpson was already inwardly free when shaming the Muster Master. The contrast forces recognition of strong variables anchored in specific experiences among formerly enslaved convicts' senses of self. Brown had lacked opportunity to confront his enslavement under arms. Simpson had urged freedom must be seized, not passively awaited, in a context where Jamaica's plantocrats were out of step with increasingly pro-abolitionist metropolitan Britain. Given the anti-planter tide in Britain by December 1831, of which Jamaican slaves were well aware,[26] Simpson's political analysis was shrewd in one sense, mistaken in another, for slave mass self-liberation was desired neither by Abolitionists

Convict gang at rest, showing a black prisoner with his back against a tree (Tasmanie/Groupe de Convicts dans un defrichement, *by Victor-Marie-Felix Danvin*).

nor Parliament. *They* envisaged emancipation as an 'indulgence' from above, under terms decided entirely at that elevated level.

The Baptist War intensely embarrassed Westminster, because it occasioned a 'white terror' in which hundreds of slaves were executed and others severely flogged. These punishments were rubber stamped by settler-militia courts martial. Subsequently, the Colonial Office made a lengthy compilation of all the court martial records—virtually an official enquiry.[27] This source reveals Simpson underwent not one, but two courts martial. While their transcripts are in obvious respects records of a determination to terrify, degrade and in the case of his second trial, eliminate, they perforce expose the slaves' liberational 'hidden transcripts' too.[28]

Simpson's first trial was at Port Antonio, 6 January 1832. Major Cozens presided over twelve other officers of the Portland Regiment of Foot Militia,[29] which had been active in combating the insurgents. Cozens was the former overseer of Fairfield estate, located in the eye of the recent storm and close to Fairy Hill estate, where Simpson belonged.[30] This settler lynch party in uniform tried Simpson for 'attempting to rescue a Prisoner from a Party of Maroons on the morning of Sunday the first of January instant—in breach of the Rules and Articles of War'. The Maroons—a semi-autonomous community of free descendants of runaway slaves, feared for their irregular warfare skills—were auxiliaries of the whites in this conflict. A Maroon band had captured Simpson's sister (among others) at Fairy Hill's slave provision grounds.[31] Even in the context of post-rebellion mopping-up operations, this was brutally arbitrary. Jamaican slaves had long enjoyed customary rights to till their provision grounds on Sundays. Indeed, Alexander Ogilvy, Fairy Hill's overseer, volunteered that, 'the Negroes had come in and were ordered to go to their grounds'. Simpson was incensed to see his weeping sister dragged along by the Maroons. Thwarted by their weapons from rescuing her, despite a gathering crowd of angry slaves carrying stones, he bandied words with her scornful captors. The Maroons jeered: 'Buckra [white master] plant Cane and who were to work them if the Negroes got free?' Simpson riposted:

> dont you free[?]
> me want free too—Ah pity!!

And stamped his foot. All this was recklessly courageous in the circumstances, although 'the Overseer came out and told the Maroons that the Prisoner and his Sister were not runaways'.[32] Nevertheless, a detachment of the 77th Regiment stationed at Fairy Hill was summoned. On arrival their commander, Captain Buchan, said he would have had Simpson shot instantly, had he behaved similarly to *his* troops.[33] The first court martial found Simpson guilty and sentenced him 'to be led to the Gallows with a rope around his neck—

there receive one hundred lashes over his Shoulders, be confined twelve months in the Work-House and receive fifty lashes on coming out at the expiration of that term':[34] by the standards of these tribunals, a 'light' sentence.

Settler 'justice' was not yet finished with Simpson. A fortnight (and 100 lashes) later, on 20 January 1832, Simpson now faced capital charges, including 'Seditious language, Joining and engaging in conspiracy, Traitorous, Rebellious or Hostile Acts'.[35] Even a white official later aptly minuted, 'was it not hard to try him again?'[36]

The first witness was African-born John Taylor, head driver (field-gang overseer) at Fairy Hill. Taylor had already received fifty lashes for 'Being aware of a conspiracy and not revealing it'.[37] Although he was a key prosecution witness, he nevertheless provides striking evidence of slave experiences and feelings. Simpson, said Taylor, was 'a very good negro in the field, one Morning deponent flogged Prisoner and some others for turning out late'. Even *good* field hands felt the lash on Jamaican plantations. A slave woman, Taylor reported, then spoke up defiantly:

> every place for get free
> no more Fairy Hill.

Simpson capped this with:

> if we no eye no strong[,]
> we wont get free.

The sense in standard English is, 'if we don't look sharp, we won't obtain freedom' but the original has greater pith and power.

The next witness, Fairy Hill's second slave driver, George Pussier, claimed Simpson had said 'they would carry the women to the wood make hut and come down and fight Buckra. When they see fire from Look Out[,] Boston and Fairfield would join at the Mango Tree[.] Sion Hill were to be at the Goat Pen.' It is extraordinary how, in slave speech, the names of slave-owning plantations became appropriated as the names of freedom-minded slave communities. The world constructed by slave owners was being turned upside down through this potent liberational discourse and the actions it nurtured.

Another Fairy Hill slave, Nicholas Simpson (later hanged), Pussier said, was to fire the cane. Then Alexander Simpson 'was to lead the others to break Busha's [the master's] house take the Guns and the provisions for the women in the woods and then all the men and women were to come down to fight'.[38] Edward Francis, a Fairfield slave, reported speaking with Simpson in the master's kitchen at Fairfield at Christmas 1831 just before the uprising:

> Allick said after Christmas if any one Negro go to work or put themselves with white people he would take his cutlass and chop off their head[,] that he would set fire to the cane piece at Fairy Hill and when the white people run out he would go in Busha's house & take the Guns.[39]

In the intimidating circumstances of this trial, slave witnesses were certainly under pressure to deliver evidence to hang Simpson. His one recorded brush with authority in Van Diemen's Land, however, circumstantially supports the gist of their evidence, since his tongue remained subversively persuasive there. On 18 September 1834, he was convicted of having aroused 'general disatisf$^{\underline{n}}$ among his fellow servants' in his master's absence and was returned to the government gang at Green Ponds for reassignment.[40] That released him from serving his previous master, which was probably his objective. Also, he manipulated the system of allocating convict labour. As seen, he had been a very good plantation field hand, which required skill, stamina and a strong physique. At five foot nine inches, Simpson was taller than most transported convict men.[41] Prospectively, he was fodder for grindingly hard public-works labour. However, his indent entry, based on his own pre-disembarkation statements, solely listed his trade as 'house servant'.[42] It is possible that Simpson had worked inside Fairy Hill's 'big house'. Slaves too young for field labour often waited attendance in the 'big house'. Plantation slaves, like transported convicts, were also subject to occupational promotions and demotions, in similar 'carrot and stick' management systems. Nevertheless, Simpson successfully laundered his Van Diemen's Land record of any mention of canefield work. The motive was to avoid, if possible, ultra-exacting toil. After 1834, he never again irritated the official eye. Under those circumstances, the colonial state showered this embarrassing reminder of the injustices of slavery with major indulgences. He received a ticket-of-leave on 14 November 1838, the same year so-called apprenticeship to his former owner in Jamaica would have ended, had he not been transported. On 31 October 1840 he received a conditional pardon, upgraded to a free pardon on 21 January 1841.[43]

Simpson was the only 'Baptist War' slave rebel transported to Van Diemen's Land, but several were sent to New South Wales. All have long been concealed in a profound historical silence.[44] Even by George Rudé's narrow criteria concerning 'protest and resistance' convicts, these men surely qualify. Bamboozled perhaps by then existing Australian historiography's exclusive recognition of white 'protest and resistance', Rudé reproduced the exclusion of Jamaica's transported freedom fighters in his book *Protest and Punishment*. It is high time for Simpson and his transported comrades to receive honoured remembrance.

A slave woman's honour: Maria's story

Maria, too, was a Caribbean slave,[45] from Britain's settlements (now called Belize) on the Bay of Honduras, where George Arthur had once been Superintendent and Commandant. She can be numbered amongst the many Caribbean slave women, long neglected by historians, who resisted oppression fiercely and valiantly.[46] The Muster Master already knew, when commanding Maria's statement, that her offence was murder and her death sentence had been commuted to transportation for life, though not that Robert Peel (later Prime Minister) helped secure the commutation.[47] Her answer to the Muster Master was highly mitigating and totally unapologetic:

> Murder [—]
> William Mair, a builder.
> I was beat by him and he got a knife.
> We scuffled together and in the scuffle the knife entered his body and killed him.[48]

Maria was eighteen and four feet eleven inches tall when she reached Hobart in 1828; probably smaller at her conviction in September 1825.[49] Unfortunately, no full record of her trial was sent to London. Thus details about Mair's assault, or his status, are lacking.[50] Was Maria resisting rape? This is distinctly possible for notoriously, even very young female slaves were sexually abused by white males. Mair, however, was not Maria's master. Before conviction, she had last lived with her mistress, Mary White, as a skilled servant of all work, who could wash, iron, and do needlework.[51]

Maria's other responses to the Muster Master's questions are equally informative. She named her father as Bryan Middleton, mahogany cutter (archetypal slave employment in Belize) and mentioned a mother, brother and sisters. She had a family, although the official record stripped its name away. In her indent record, her name is merely given as 'Maria (a slave)'. Middleton, the name under which Tardif's compendium of women convicts' records catalogues her, was not at first her officially validated name in Van Diemen's Land.[52] Her familial anchoring, nevertheless, perhaps influenced her actions. With established family and kinship, slaves gathered a strong sense of belonging, a treasure to conserve and defend. Such a grounded slave would, arguably, feel the more empowered to resist Mair's assault.

There is further evidence that family mattered to Maria. On 26 October 1830, she successfully applied for permission to marry John Murray, a free man. Approval received, the couple married at Hobart on 22 November 1830.[53] Even to officialdom, she now gained a surname, signifying her marital status. Thereafter but one blot to her conduct was recorded. At Hobart Town Quarter

Sessions on 13 July 1832 she was tried for stealing goods belonging to Peter Rush. Her trial record, however, also allows glimpses of her marital household circumstances in several important respects.[54] The trial briefly punctuated an upturn in the affairs of Maria and John Murray. Six months previously they and their assigned convict servant, Ann Davis, had ceased lodging with Rush at the former 'Hope and Anchor' inn, moving to another residence, where the Murrays set up as lodging-house keepers. While this was not a high-status enterprise, it provided some hope of basic material security.

Ann Davis stated that even before the move, she 'used to cook and do everything for the Murrays'.[55] Thus by early 1832, through her own assignment to her free husband, the former domestic slave had become the mistress of a white convict maid of all work, such as humbler households employed. This diametrically reversed Maria's former enslaved bondage to Mary White. Now, self-respect required decisive authority over her convict servant. Ann Davis was perhaps reluctant to submit to a fellow assigned convict, who was her mistress only through marriage. If Maria supposed this new status was secure, she was soon disabused.

At Maria's trial, Ann Davis admitted (probably under questioning): 'My disagreement with the Prisoner went on from the first week of my service, and "niggling, niggling" every day'. As 'there were Four or Five Lodgers in the house', heavy domestic chores were probably a major site of conflict with her mistress; good business for the Murrays was bad news for Ann Davis.[56] Did she resent serving a black former slave? Nothing of that was indicated at the trial. The common opinion is that convict women assigned as domestics were isolated defenceless creatures, at the mercy of the caprices and worse of their employers. Kirsty Reid has effectively shown otherwise for Van Diemen's Land in the 1820s and 1830s. She reveals instead that convict-women domestics often had agendas of expectations and what they thought intolerable; and would escalate conflict with obdurate employers. Especially resented were hectoring employers who attempted to impose minute surveillance and regulation of their workplace activities. Employers who persisted could expect payback, often starting with lip.[57]

In the Murray household, escalating conflict of this sort led to what Reid reveals as many assigned women's trump card; walking off the job to complain to authority. Unlike convict men, convict women were not flogged after 1817, even if judged guilty of making false accusations against employers. At worst they faced a spell in the female factory, a space the women themselves often largely controlled, followed (with luck) by reassignment to a more pliable employer.[58] Ann Davis was perfectly happy to recall her walk-out in open court: 'I told her I would not bide with her, and went and gave myself up to Mr Spode [Superintendent of Convicts] as the Prisoner used me very ill, and struck me several times'.

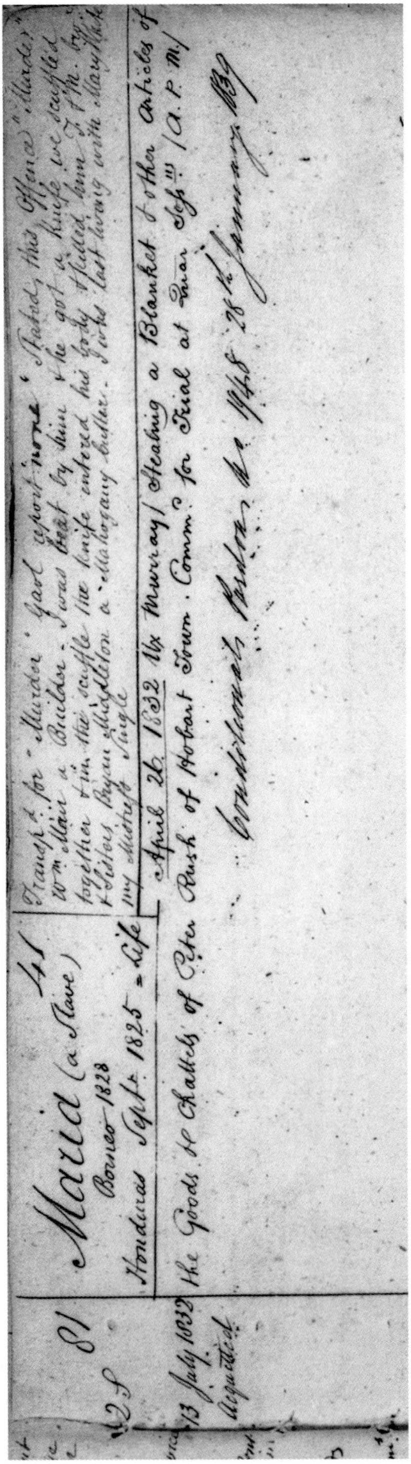

81 Maria (a Slave) 41
Borneo 1828
Honduras Sept. 1825 = Life

Transp.d for Murder. Gaol report none. Stated this Offence "Murder"

13 July 1832 April 26 1832 w/ Murray / Stealing a Blanket & other articles of the Goods & Chattels of Peter Rush of Hobart Town. Comm.d for Trial at ... Sess.ns / A.P.M. /

Acquitted.

Conditional Pardon No 1448 28th January 1839

Maria's Convict Conduct Record.

This last accusation was serious enough. Employers were forbidden to strike their assigned convicts. It could not be proved, however: Davis had no witnesses. She had, however, far more serious accusations to place before Spode, then the Police Office and finally the Quarter Sessions. She raked up altercations between Mrs Rush and the Murrays (carefully exonerating her master), about property of the former allegedly taken by Maria when moving from the Rushes' place. The items mentioned were bolsters, pillows, blankets and a tin dish. Davis also alleged that on Maria's orders, she reluctantly put the blankets on the lodgers' beds, 'As my mistress said, if the Constables come to search the house—they would think the Lodgers had stolen them'. Davis asserted that on Maria's orders, she had reluctantly torn up the pillows and stuffed their feathers into Maria's marital bed.[59]

On 6 July 1832, Constable William Peel, armed with a search warrant and accompanied by Mrs Rush, searched the Murrays' premises. Three blankets and the tin dish were claimed by Mrs Rush as her property. In court the Constable was only able to swear, 'I know one of these blankets by a small hole burned in it'.[60] It is certainly rum that Mrs Rush failed to involve the police six months back, when the thefts allegedly occurred. Recalled to the witness box, Ann Davis, while insistent about the tin dish, admitted she too could not 'swear to the blankets' produced in court.[61] Beyond these uncertainties, other evidence unravelled the prosecution case and secured a not guilty verdict. Thomas Johnson, the Hobart Town District Constable who a few days after Peel searched the Murrays' bedroom in the presence of the couple and Ann Davis, found 'nothing that I could take away', although observing the mattress seemed to have been sewn up twice.[62] John Bodny, a Hobart dealer, swore he once sold two blankets to John Murray similar to those produced in court. Walter John Skey, a tinman, swore he had sold the Murrays 'two or three pounds worth of Tinware and I think there was a dish among them . . . the Dish produced is one of my Patterns . . . I do not know Rush or his wife'.[63] These two witnesses certainly put the tin hat on the prosecution. Consequently, the honours were roughly even. Ann Davis had the satisfaction of dragging her former mistress through criminal proceedings and escaping a disagreeable assignment; Maria Murray had the satisfaction of the verdict.

Like many other convicts, Maria had lost a far-away family. Given all family meant to slaves, one can imagine her yearning, in Van Diemen's Land, to create another, and with it, respected belonging. By 1832 her marriage provided the additional attractions of being mistress of a convict domestic, in a materially viable autonomous household; an honourable feather bed for Maria to repose in. Further, a husband able to expend two or three pounds—then a significant sum—on tinware to equip their lodging house, seems a good provider as then ordinarily understood. Her marriage, like many other convict and free plebeian marriages of the period, was probably pragmatic; which does not exclude room for mutual affection. The union was evidently workable, for her 1832 trial did not shake it apart, though it may have damped her ardour for scolding, perhaps even slapping, assigned servant women. At the 1835 Muster, Maria was still assigned to her husband, and on 18 November 1837, after seven years of marriage, she gave birth to a daughter, her only child. Baptised at St David's Parish Church, Hobart, by Rev William Bedford, on 28 August 1838, the little girl received names no child had ever before been recorded as receiving in the colony: Fedicia Exine.[64] The conclusion must be that these names were meaningful to Maria herself and that she, not her husband, chose them, for they were certainly not from the common stock of British and Irish female names then in use. Her husband's surname suggests a Scotsman or an Irishman. Perhaps these enigmatically poetic names preserved the cherished memory of Maria's mother, some other close kinswomen or a loved and respected woman elder in her former slave community. There is no Tasmanian record of Fedicia Exine eventually marrying or even of her death. Perhaps she left the colony for mainland Australia. It remains open, therefore, as to whether Maria has Australian descendants today but we can hope so, as they have a foremother they can in many (if not quite all) ways be proud of.

By 1838, the material underpinning of the Murrays' marriage had changed. At the time of his daughter's baptism, John Murray was a whaler. By 1838, bay whaling in the Derwent Estuary was residual, so he would certainly have been absent for long periods at sea. Probably, for her part, Maria continued to take in lodgers, though if so, on too modest a scale to be listed in contemporary Hobart directories. A conditional pardon, recommended 28 January 1839 and approved 20 November 1840, suggests her marriage was still functioning, as that indulgence necessitated a recommendation from Maria's assigned master, her husband.[65] This, and her almost blemish-free colonial conduct record, suggests that Maria, wife of John Murray, became maritally respectable and respected if in a humble station in life. Reasonably tranquil marriage would certainly have eased her path to an early conditional pardon, signifying that the official eye now regarded her as socially anchored in the 'proper' order of things. Maria, on the other hand, probably understood her marriage as a self-achieved life with honour.

Sometimes exertions were needed to defend her achieved honour. Having heard her character publicly besmirched by Ann Davis, she counter-attacked by cross-questioning her accuser about previous drunkenness and her actions between stalking out and informing to Spode. We do not have Maria's questions but they are indicated by Ann Davis's answers.[66] Anyone in court would have taken the hint that Davis really quit the Murrays' house for an improper, perhaps sexually immoral purpose and then, to escape the consequences, sought out

Spode and laid false accusations. Hobart's many sly-grog shops attracted convicts of both sexes, seeking leisure while at large without permission and against regulations. Sly-grog shops also commonly doubled as disorderly houses where sexual services were vended and clandestine liaisons facilitated.[67]

Maria appears never to have completed her transition towards freedom from a lifetime of bondage as first slave, then transported convict. A Hobart woman called Maria Murray died of consumption 17 months before the recommended conditional pardon was approved.[68] That no further mention of our Maria occurs in the colonial records suggests that, just as she had been born into servitude, her release was perhaps through natural causes, not official indulgence. This putative death is unmentioned in her conduct record—a possible aberration in standard recording practices concerning convicts still under sentence, which queries the records' absolute reliability.

Speculation in depleted social capital: George Barrow's story

Prisoner number 1153 Barrow, George, was never a slave. Born in Demerara (now in Guyana), his description was recorded in Van Diemen's Land as: 'complexion, dark brown'; 'hair, jet black curly'; 'eyes, black'; 'nose, medium long flat at point'; 'lips, thick'. To clarify, the clerk added 'man of color, Mulatto'.[69] Barrow was a lawyer. Transported lawyers were often fraudsters. His seven-year sentence was for fraud against Anstey & Nettleton of George Street, Hanover Square, London.[70] Barrow's profession, like his offence, was then accessible to a free, educated, 'man of color' from Britain's sugar colonies, where such people formed an uneasy stratum between the white plantocrats and the mass of slaves. A 'mulatto' lawyer might be the acknowledged, or anyway supported, son of a white planter by a 'favoured' slave woman. Barrow also crossed a European cultural divide *via* the Dutch law of Demerara's former rulers. Did he ever *practise* law anywhere? In London, his social status, 'mulatto' gentleman, was implicitly limbic; his alien professional status, explicitly so. Aged thirty-four on arrival at Hobart aboard the *Georgiana*, 13 April 1829,[71] he was of the first generation of Demerarans under British rule.

When confronted by the Muster Master, George Barrow delivered a radically different micro-narrative to those preceding:

> I am an Advocate admitted to the Courts of Holland and Demerara. I was educated at Westminster School, neither F[ather] nor M[other] alive my Sister is married to the American [*sic*; probably British] Consul at New York—I know Mr Montagu well who is here—lived in his Father's House [for some] months.[72]

This narrative is easily decoded. Barrow was puffing his accumulated social capital, to appear as no common felon but a professional gentleman educated at a swanky London school, whose sister's husband was Consul in an important foreign city. Bidding for treatment as 'a cut above', he flourished, in the manner of *free* gentlemen immigrants, [73] connections with a gentleman already established there.

Captain John Montagu was the son of Barrow's probable former patron, Lieutenant-Colonel Edward Montagu of the East India Company's Army of Bengal. In an age when those things counted, acutely so in Van Diemen's Land, these Montagus were kinsmen of a great aristocrat, the Duke of Manchester. Captain Montagu had accompanied his friend and uncle by marriage, George Arthur, to Hobart when Arthur was appointed Lieutenant-Governor. He remained Arthur's friend and protégé[74] and would have become his uncle's official right hand as his Colonial Secretary, had Secretary of State Lord Bathurst in London not vetoed the appointment. Further, Montagu was outside the colony from 1828 to 1831.[75]

One can admire Barrow's *chutzpah* in seeking, *via* the web of patronage and connection, to lift himself above the common herd of transported felons. His accumulated social capital, however, had been hopelessly depleted by the taint of felony, rendering this speculation futile in Arthur's Hobart. Formerly, a transported lawyer in Australia might engage lucratively in legal practice. The colonial career of the Irish lawyer and fraudster, Edward Eagar, measures this change. Transported to New South Wales in 1811, after a conditional pardon from Governor Macquarie he practised law in Sydney from 1813 to 1815. This promising career terminated abruptly in 1815, when J. H. Bent, Judge of the new Supreme Court, ruled him ineligible to practise law because tainted by conviction.[76] Even then, Eagar found other career outlets, becoming a paladin of the colony's emancipists in their conflicts with the exclusivist 'came-free' gentry.[77] No convicted lawyer, of whatever colour, arriving in Van Diemen's Land under Arthur's governorship had such opportunities. Barrow died in the Colonial Hospital on 17 July 1833, the sole trace of his post-disembarkation existence in his conduct register record.[78] His story might as well have been spoken to a brick wall. Symbolically, his early death while still under sentence figures his collapsed sense of self in Van Diemen's Land, where he was in every sense socially *dis*placed and perhaps unable to find any alternative social space he could bear to inhabit.

Conclusion

This study may stand accused of offering four sandwiches whose skimpy convict-narrative filling is enclosed in stodgy doorstops of official-record

Billy Blue, the Old Commodore, *by Charles Rodius.*

bread. The defence against such a charge hinges on James C. Scott's point that the 'official transcript' of colonial (or any other) power relations mostly silences the 'hidden transcript' of what subordinated elements think and covertly express. However, Scott's 'hidden transcript' has a latent capacity to surface and challenge existing power relations. These four micro-narratives, as powerfully dramatic 'action narratives', attempted just that and the more strikingly because within a site explicitly designed to *secure* existing power relations. Thus, the meaning of the official record becomes subverted from that intended. Indeed, the very zeal to compel humiliating confessions backfired. These statements' first-person focus on selfhood's understanding of its crucial life experiences wrenched the colonial eye's optical apparatus off its chosen focus. All—even Barrow trying to grease his way into the status of privileged gentleman-convict—managed to evade being inventorised solely as specimens of the 'criminal classes' transported.

The varying outcomes for this study's four convicts—whether early pardon, long subjection to the Government Stroke or early death—indicate how different convicts' penal experiences could be. While not fully sharing Alan Atkinson's belief that there was never a 'convict system' in Australia's penal colonies, I regard the official 'colonial eye' as, though possessed of real power, not omniscient and so not omnipotent. I also share Atkinson's belief that individual convict lives are enormously fruitful to study.[79] Such studies can dissolve the illusion that the convicts' managers were totally effective and restore the convicts to us as historical actors. For an incorrigible historian of the African Diaspora, it was irresistible to select four African-Diaspora convicts' micro-narratives for this study. The Atlantic African Diaspora was more connected to early colonial Australia than most Australian or British readers might suppose.[80] Linebaugh and Rediker's recent brilliant study[81] places Diaspora Africans within the subversive 'motley crew' of the international dispossessed (including prisoners transported to or within the Americas), whom they place at the heart of Atlantic history from the early 1600s to the early 1800s. They never, however, connect this vast coerced movement of peoples with Australia's convict settlers, who were more multinational and multiethnic than is usually thought and included about 800 Africans[82] originating from both sides of the North Atlantic plus the Cape Colony, St Helena and Mauritius. This study proclaims that connection.

Its *method*, however, is not only applicable to African and African-Diaspora transported convicts and could assist studies of other Van Diemen's Land convicts who inserted 'I' narratives into their statements of offence. There are plenty more where these four come from. Of course, all the problematics of convict narratives apply. These micro-narratives challenge conventional *genre* typologies too. In three of the four stories scrutinised here, two conventionally separated autobiographical *genres*, slave and convict narratives, collapse into each other. Further, in these brief, supercharged tales, the convicts' agendas are not effectively hijacked by the agendas of Convict Department record-keeping: the convict voices are vividly if briefly audible. Exciting prospects now open for extensive unpackaging of similar 'I' for an 'Eye' micro-narratives, thus enriching our understanding of the relationship of convict narrative to convict lived experience. Marx, in an ironic parody of 'legitimate' capitalism, asserted that 'criminals' produce crime and, by extension, many ensuing esteemed productions, including literature.[83] In this light, convict micro-narratives may also query crime's fundamental social location.

9

'These are but items in the sad ledger of despair'

Tina Picton Phillipps

Our cast is small, at least in respect of the estimated total of 160 000 individuals transported to the Australian penal colonies. None of the three main actors, Richard Bankin, John Sanderson and Thomas Francis, would merit more than walk-on parts within the convict drama which unfolded between 1788 and 1868. Not surprisingly, when the panorama of colonial history marched across early volumes of the *Australian Dictionary of Biography*, Bankin, Sanderson and Francis were not included, and they had been far too insignificant before they left home to be named in Britain's *Dictionary of National Biography*. None of the three mattered much either to the clerks in England who methodically compiled ledgers for the Home Office, or for those employed by the colonial administrators of New South Wales.[1] In the brutal impersonality of formal record-keeping, the lives of our players shrank to information required for institutional purposes.

Records of people are not people but merely marks on pages. But even within the neatly ruled lines of ledgers where bodies were transformed into script, there remain traces of domestic life-scripts in which men who were reduced by the process of convict record-keeping break out of the unindividuated pack, and push their way towards centre stage. Through their approaches to the state we can track the scripts of their interrupted lives. The stories which emerge are different from the record compiled by the state, so different that a collapsing of their lives into the generalised category 'convict' seems a cruel distortion of their own varied experiences.

The rural labourer

Our first protagonist, Richard Bankin, was transported in 1814 under a fourteen-year sentence. The *Marquis of Wellington*'s indent does not disclose his crime. At the time of Richard's conviction the Napoleonic wars had had a severe effect on the economic security of farm labouring families. Military conscription had given rise to wage increases but these were offset by a sharp increase in food prices. The decline in woollen spinning during the same period had drastically affected the financial contribution wives and daughters had made to the household economy. Petty thefts of basic foods resulted in harsh sentences; theft of a fowl or a bushel of wheat could result in a transportation sentence of seven years or more.[2] More drastic indications of rural poverty during this period were demonstrated with the East Anglian riots of 1816, occurring after Richard's embarkation. We can be fairly certain that he had not committed any act of an incendiary nature.[3] Until 1837, those found guilty of arson, or 'firing', received capital sentences; few, if any, of these sentences were commuted to transportation. He had been tried at the Essex Assizes on 7 March and sailed on the *Marquis of Wellington*, which arrived at Port Jackson in January 1815.[4]

Richard's voyage to New South Wales was not a solitary undertaking. The prison ship *Marquis of Wellington* contained another 119 outcasts.[5] Parliamentary debates reveal that individual male convicts were given less space than that recorded for slave ships. Six convicts were often crammed into a crib measuring 'six feet and a half broad by five feet and a half long'; three or four cribs—upwards of twenty-four men—were squeezed into a cabin twelve foot square.[6] Richard would have recognised some of the faces in the crush. Amongst the transportees there were eight who had been tried on the same day as Richard at the Essex Assizes, others would have been familiar from the hulk. At fifty-five, Richard was one of the oldest convicts on board. Most of his fellow passengers were under the age of thirty and 13 per cent were younger than twenty. There were even two ten-year-olds. This variation in age was mirrored in the geographic spread of 'native places'. This spread surely gave rise to some problems in communication. There were the regional dialects of Scotland with convicts from Glasgow, Edinburgh, Jedburgh and Forfar. Those from England came from the rural areas of the south and west (and Richard of course from East Anglia), or from London and the urban centres of the Midlands as well. In addition there were others who, although tried in England, were born in Ireland. Others came from continental Europe, including France, Spain, Sicily, Germany, Prussia and Poland. Some of these may have served in the Peninsular Campaign, perhaps in the ranks of the King's German Legion or as an alternative to incarceration as a prisoner of war.[7] A veritable hull of Babel! So many vowel differences, elisions, verbal stresses and accents all contained under the sails of the *Marquis of Wellington*. So utterly unlike Richard Bankin's home.

We move from these claustrophobic quarters to a rural backwater of Essex, where parish divisions were marked by the medieval term of hundreds.[8] Scrutiny of the seventeenth-century reprint, *Theatre of the Empire of Great Britaine*, reveals the tiny hamlet of Little Warley.[9] In 1811 the population of

Little Warley, lying in the Chafford hundred, amounted to some 177 souls.[10] To compare the population of Richard's 'native place' with the numbers of those on board the *Marquis of Wellington* gives some indication of the shock of confinement for those from similarly small rural areas. Amongst those counted souls in Little Warley were most certainly Richard's wife Prudence, and his elder daughter Mary. Prudence and Richard Bankin had married in 1806 and Mary had been born the following year. Their youngest surviving daughter Sarah had been born in July 1814, just two months before Richard embarked on the *Marquis of Wellington*. [11]

Richard's first communication to his family 'gave great satisfaction to all your relations and friends'.[12] Although the original letter is now lost, the reply sent by John Bankin, Richard's nephew, survives as an attachment to Richard's application to the colonial authorities for his wife and children to be sent out. John's letter reveals that Richard had written to his family on 14 March 1824—exactly ten years and one week after the day he had been sentenced to transportation. Is there a symbolic significance in the attempt to renew contact with his family? That he had marked the ten-year anniversary of his court appearance with his communication? Is it untenable to suggest that there had been a personal pledge, a pledge made and a pledge kept? Romantic? Yes, indeed; but human beings are complex in their personal vows and silences. From John's letter we can only guess at the contents of Richard's first communication to his friends and relatives. He had obviously written of his progress in New South Wales. John comments with pleasure that 'you have been favoured by the bountiful protection of providence'.[13] Richard's industry had indeed brought material advantages. On his indent entry, Richard's occupation was noted as 'labourer'. By 1822 he had gained his ticket-of-leave and was described as a 'Landholder' in Richmond.[14] His efforts in his new environment were well regarded by two local landowners who were also well-known justices, William Cox and Archibald Bell. Cox described Bankin as a 'very sober and remarkably industrious man' who has managed to 'lay by a portion of Money'.[15] Perhaps it was this material advancement prompted his first letter back to Little Warley. And it is through the reply sent by his nephew that we gain insight into a close-knit family circle.

In his role as amanuensis for the wider kin group, John frugally wrote out the messages from Prudence and Sarah, one of Richard's sisters. These, along with his own letter, covered two sheets of paper. The document itself has been torn in places but enough remains to put together some of the pieces of a jig-saw of a family tree. Richard Bankin was one of a family of five. His two brothers were named John (senior) and James and his sisters were Sarah (who had married a Mr Bennet) and one unnamed woman who sent 'good wishes' through his nephew John (junior). There is an irony which may not have been lost on Richard, when he read that his brother James and his wife

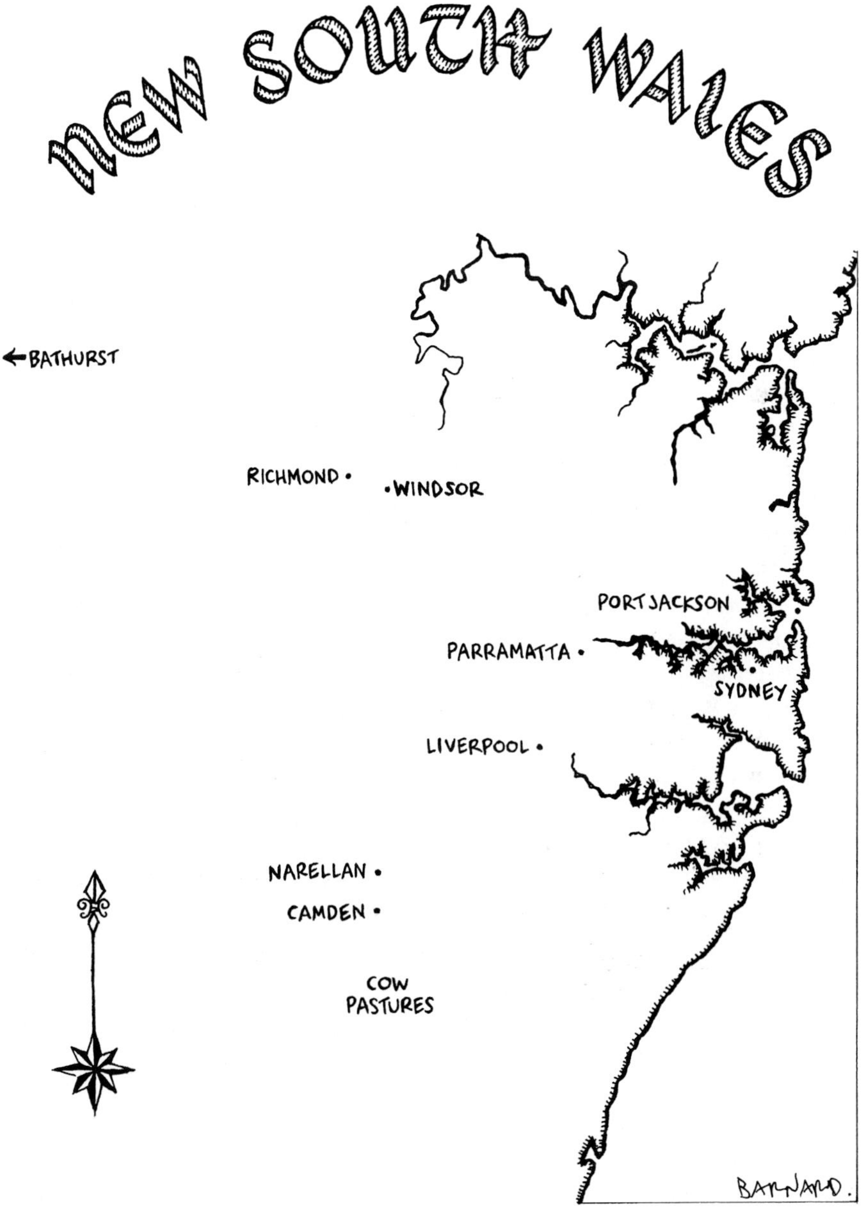
NEW SOUTH WALES
←BATHURST
RICHMOND
WINDSOR
PORT JACKSON
PARRAMATTA
SYDNEY
LIVERPOOL
NARELLAN
CAMDEN
COW PASTURES
BARNARD.

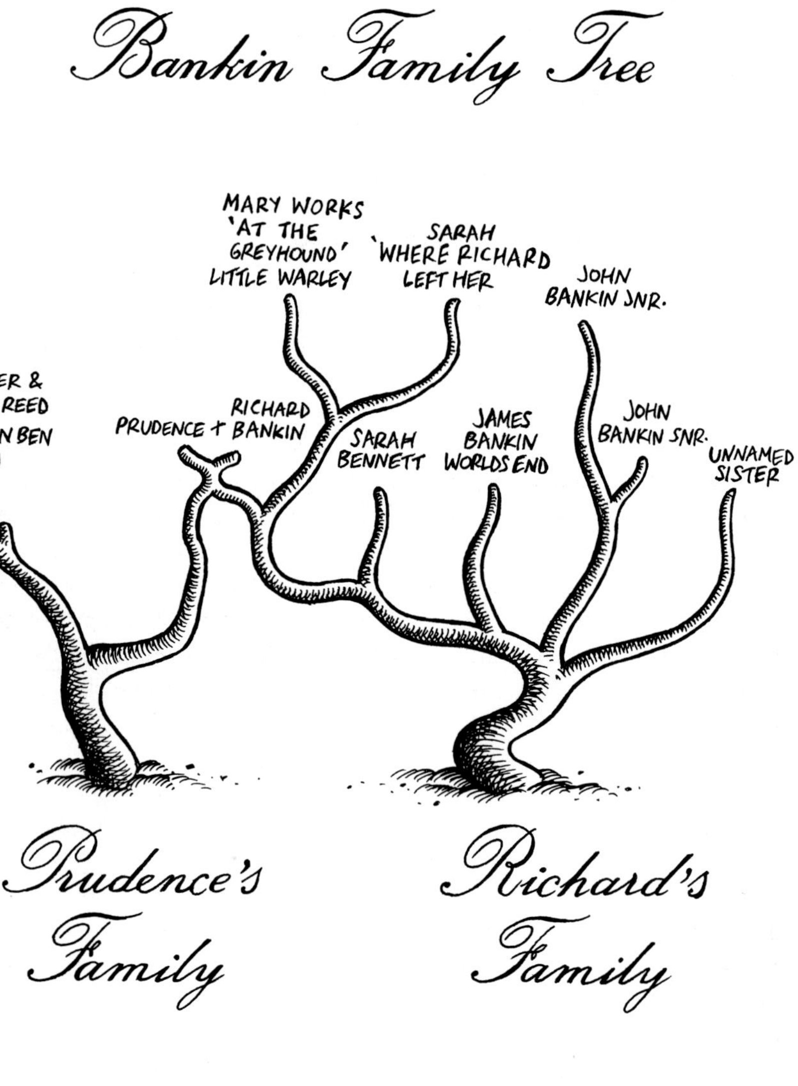
Bankin Family Tree
MARY WORKS 'AT THE GREYHOUND' LITTLE WARLEY
SARAH 'WHERE RICHARD LEFT HER
JOHN BANKIN SNR.
BROTHER & SISTER REED BULPHAN BEN
RICHARD PRUDENCE + BANKIN
SARAH BENNETT
JAMES BANKIN WORLDS END
JOHN BANKIN SNR.
UNNAMED SISTER
Prudence's Family
Richard's Family

'are living near Worlds End . . .'.[16] If any of the Bankin family were near World's End, surely it was Richard.

John sent a verbal message from Richard's elder daughter Mary, and anticipated seeing the younger daughter Sarah. From John's letter we learn that Mary was working 'at the Greyhound' in Little Warley, close enough for her cousin John to have spoken to her. John also had contact with Richard's wife Prudence. She was living with her brother and sister Reed at Bulphan Fen (a slightly larger hamlet, close to Little Warley, with a population of 206 in 1811).[17] These three hamlets were located close to each other; a distance of no more than seven miles (as the crow flies) between Bulphan Fen and the Warleys, Great and Little. The distance between Little Warley and Chelmsford (where Richard was tried) is about fifteen miles.[18] In the letter Prudence dictated to John she informed Richard that 'Sarah is where you left her'. Though Sarah was just two months old when Richard was transported, the letter is strangely silent about the circumstances that could have separated a baby from her mother. There is a puzzle here as to the young Sarah's whereabouts. Had Prudence been unable to support her younger daughter and, through Richard's exile, been forced to leave her in the care of the parish? Why did a member of the extended family not take her in? This silence is all the more curious since, as the letters make clear, despite the domestic upheavals which had separated Richard's family there is no suggestion of a rupture in their social relations. Indeed, the extended kin group seem to have been in regular contact and there appears to be no ill-will towards Richard. Even Prudence's siblings, referred to only as 'Brother and Sister Reed', sent him their 'love'. John's letter makes it clear that he would be seeing his young cousin Sarah for he assured his uncle that he would ascertain from her whether or not she would be willing to make the voyage to the colony.

Prudence's response to Richard's request initially appears cautious: 'I and your children will be very happy to see you, if you can convey us into your country'. Such caution is hardly surprising when one considers that Richard and Prudence had been separated for ten years of their eighteen-year marriage. Was it youth, or John's gloss on Mary's reaction to her father's suggestion? On Mary's behalf John declared she would 'venture life and all that is dear to her to be again under the protection of her Father'. Richard's family understood that his future lay in New South Wales. John refers to 'your settlement'; Prudence says 'your country'; Sarah Bennet regrets her brother's distance from 'your native country' but assures him that even there, he will be 'under the protection of the same good and gracious God'.[19]

Richard, like others in the archive where his application lies, sought to reconstitute his family unit in New South Wales. His application to this end was received by the Colonial Secretary on 25 May 1825. The annotation to the printed application form states, 'In list sent home Informed 23 March 1827'.

Richard then had a further wait, along with the other husbands and fathers who had sent in similar applications. Richard's entry in the *Census* of 1828 suggests a downturn in his fortunes. He had left Richmond and was then working as a labourer, at Lower Portland Head for Mr Andrew Doyle.[20] The later 1820s were not so good for the smallholder in New South Wales.[21] However, in 1828 the *Borneo*, a female convict ship, sailed from Britain for Hobart with seventy female convicts on board. [22] The additional human cargo included Richard Bankin's female relatives, his wife Prudence and his two daughters, Mary and Sarah, who travelled 12 000 miles for their reunion. Prudence, according to the Surgeon's Report dated 19 August 1828, had experienced ill-health on the voyage. She was described as being 'an old and infirm woman'.[23] When the *Borneo* arrived at Hobart on 8 October she was taken to the local hospital where she died on 24 October aged forty-five.[24] The *Borneo* left Hobart in December 1828 with Mary and Sarah on board, continuing their passage to Sydney. Each woman applied for permission to marry in New South Wales: Mary in 1829 and Sarah in 1831. In each case the governor's consent was given for the Banns to be called; Mary married Thomas Williams at Richmond and Sarah married John Adams at Narellen. Richard, having lived to be eighty-eight and dying in 1845 at the Benevolent Asylum in Windsor, may have seen his daughters married and his grandchildren born.[25]

The military deserter

John Sanderson is the most anonymous of the three players. He is remembered here through the few words he left in his petition requesting not to be transported. A private in the 2nd Battalion of the Grenadier Guards, Sanderson was charged with desertion, found guilty, and sentenced to fourteen years.[26] Desertion created a perennial problem for an army in which most ordinary soldiers enlisted for a term of twenty-one years.[27] In the two years 1819 and 1820, years of high unemployment in Britain, more than 1500 soldiers deserted.[28] Those deserters who were caught and court-martialled sometimes petitioned the administrative centre of the army (known as Horse Guards) for favours or clemency. Invariably they recorded their military careers, but about his John Sanderson said nothing.[29]

Courts martial were part of the formal process of dealing with military, as against civil, offences. A soldier found guilty of the military offence of desertion by a court martial had that military offence officially transformed into the civil crime of 'felony'.[30] A contemporary critic of military discipline and courts martial referred to their arbitrary nature and application.[31] In the

1820s the threat and application of flogging as a disciplinary measure was an issue of public concern.[32] Courts martial maintained the sanctioning power of life and death over individual soldiers in times of war. In times of peace corporal punishment was a more frequent means of maintaining control.[33] It was not unknown for soldiers to die under these circumstances. In 1825 a man received 1200 strokes of his 1900-stroke sentence. This sentence was despite the 1807 General Order that 'the maximum number of lashes to be awarded was 1000'.[34] The issue of corporal punishment was of course strongly related to the civilian movement away from 'punishing the body' to 'punishing the mind'.[35]

Sanderson's mind was obviously distressed when he composed his anguished appeal. It was sent from the Portman Square barracks, before he was moved to a civil prison. Like many other petitioners, he begged recognition of his responsibilities as a family man as grounds for asking not to be transported. 'The motive which actuates . . . this request' is concern for what would happen to his family.[36] Social control in the army extended at that time to the private soldier's domestic arrangements. Marriage was viewed as a disadvantage for those amongst the ranks, and men wishing to marry were expected to apply for permission to their commanding officers, who should 'discountenance marriage among their men'.[37] In part this was related to the rates of pay, which were deemed insufficient for the support of dependants. The soldier's daily rate of pay was 1/1d, a measly sum reduced even further by deductions made at source. According to Spiers, 'few soldiers depended entirely on their regimental pay'.[38]

Despite the official dictum of 'discountenance', the men quite clearly did marry. The Adjutant-General, H. Taylor, in his General Order of 1829, referred to a previous General Order of 1824. These two Orders related to 'the number of women and children with the several regiments in Great Britain'. The Adjutant-General drew attention to the disparity between the number accommodated in regimental barracks and the number 'allowed by His Majesty'.[39] Several commanding officers differed from the official opinion discouraging marriage, and described married soldiers as steadier, more likely to save, and less likely to desert.[40] Married men and their families shared barrack accommodation with the single soldiers. Privacy was a blanket as a makeshift wall. Such accommodation was regarded as an indulgence, and the soldier who married without his commanding officer's approval could be made to live in barracks, with his wife compelled to live elsewhere.[41] Benefits for 'living in barracks' included fuel and candle allowances as well as 'barrack bedding'. As late as 1837 accommodation for the ordinary soldier in the barracks was deemed to be on a par with 'Asylums for the insane or some of the new poor houses'.[42] Even so, the numbers of soldiers quartered in barracks throughout the French wars increased dramatically from 20 487 in 1792 to 97 269 in

Prisoner in cell of military prison, Anglesea Barracks, Hobart, *artist unknown. These sketches of military prisoners reading and writing were found behind the skirting boards in the cell block.*

1816.[43] And if a soldier's wife was with him in the barracks, she could wash for the Regiment, earning as much as four or five shillings a week.[44]

But what would happen if the soldier was transported, and his family thrown onto their own resources? Where would they go? Who would look after their needs? Sanderson's impassioned plea not to be transported resonates with his anxiety about his role as husband and father. Adopting prophetic mode, he wrote darkly of his wife's future as 'an helpless, young and now unprotected female with two small children'. Without his presence as the head of his small family, they would be 'desolate and friendless'. How could he fulfil the promises he made in his marriage vows? How could he live? Transportation would remove him from the 'Society of a beloved faithful wife and family'. If, on the other hand, he served his sentence in England, he could promise reform, because being with his family would 'materially assist him in pursuing that line of conduct'.[45] Wives, after all, were noted for their check on husbandly excess. And imagine what would happen to his wife, left 'to the mercy of the wide unpitying World', a young woman in a military town. Army barracks were not popular. Barracks were said to drive down adjacent property prices, and attract prostitutes.[46] Would that 'wide unpitying

World' make of her a prostitute too? Would she become the prey of his erstwhile companions, who would be only too well aware of his absence? Remember that public shame and disgrace within a regiment formed part of the military *esprit de corps*. Those who were found guilty of the offence of desertion were publicly 'sent off' the parade ground in front of their fellow soldiers.[47]

For how many did Sanderson speak? How many married transportees experienced a similar anguish? How many of those male transportees accepted that their role and function as husbands and fathers included protection and guardianship? Such questions cannot be answered, but surely Sanderson was not unusual in his worries and fears of what his transportation sentence foreboded for his wife's future. Perhaps the Horse Guards heard Sanderson's plea, and pronounced a reprieve. Certainly he appears neither on the New South Wales 1828 *Census*, nor in the index of convicts landed in Van Diemen's Land.

The urban labourer

Our third protagonist, Thomas Francis, was convicted in August 1817 at Monmouth Assizes; he arrived at Port Jackson in September 1818 on board the *Isabella*.[48] He too can be numbered amongst the statistics collected by the state: the total number of those transported from Wales to the Australian penal colonies between 1788 and 1860 was 2200.[49] Although convicted in the industrial port of Newport, Thomas Francis was a labourer from Somerset.[50] He may have moved, like so many other nineteenth-century migrants, in search of work. Industrial development had begun in Newport with the exploitation of the inland coal deposits and the completion of an associated transport network. To this end, a canal connecting the mining operations with the port was begun in 1792 and completed in 1798. Before the mid-nineteenth-century railways, a complex system of three canals remained the main communication network.[51] The promotion and initiative behind these and other industrial developments in the area were reflected in the subscriptions to the local joint stock company authorised by an act of parliament.[52] The local magnate, Sir Charles Morgan, benefited from the tolls he was able to charge as a result of the bisection of his estate, Tredegar Park. As one of the subscribers to the joint stock company, he also profited from the communications between the mining works and the port itself. The resultant heavy industrial development altered the landscape. Mr Donovan, a contemporary traveller, remarked with regret that the beauty of the area had been sacrificed. It was not, however, only the countryside which had been transformed. Employment opportunities had attracted labour to the area, requiring accommodation in Newport itself. The change to the town provoked Mr Donovan to state, 'Most of the houses are very mean, the streets ill-paved and, what is worse, remarkably dirty'.[53]

Five years after Thomas had been transported, Susannah Francis posted a letter in Newport, Monmouthshire, which resonated with the pleasure of a woman who had at long last received news of the man she loved: 'I had almost gave up that I should ever hear from you more, and that you had forgotten me and your Children, or that you were number'd with the Dead . . .'.[54]

Susannah Francis was Thomas's wife and the mother of his four children—Elizabeth (born 1807), John (born 1809), James (born 1813) and Jane (born 1816). She had written to her husband in response to the first letter that she had received from him since his embarkation for New South Wales. Her response to his statement that he had 'written several Letters to me' was 'I never received them'.[55]

The archive in which Susannah's letter is now lodged contains petitions from prisoners in New South Wales requesting passages for their families to join them. Her reply to Thomas lies forgotten in the same series of documents as Richard Bankin's application for Prudence, Mary and Sarah. All but one of the applications in this series has the formal minute appended 'In list sent home. Informed March 1827'. The exception to this bureaucratic formality is the document sent by Susannah to her husband Thomas. On it, in the scratchy writing of a clerk, appears the following statement, 'A memorial was written for this man for his Wife and Family a long time since; but he never put it in'.[56] Did Thomas ever receive that precious letter from his wife? It was addressed to 'Mr Thomas Francis at Wm. Redfern's Esq., Port Jackson, New South Wales'. This presumably was the address Thomas had given his wife. Indeed, Susannah expressed an identical ignorance to Prudence Bankin, 'I should have written before this but was at a loss to know how and where to direct'.[57] Yet, by 1822, when Susannah wrote her reply, Thomas Francis had moved on and was working for Mr Thomas Wells in Liverpool.[58] By the time of the 1828 *Census* he had moved on again, this time to Bathurst.[59] Other than the minute on Susannah's letter there is no other information held in the archive. If the letter from Susannah had not been collected by Thomas it would have been returned to the General Post Office in Sydney. Occasional notices in the *Sydney Gazette* announced that unclaimed correspondence was available for inspection but, unlike in the sister colony of Van Diemen's Land, the paper did not publish the names of the intended recipients. The itinerant Thomas may well have been unaware that a precious reply from his wife was waiting for him in Sydney.[60]

Consider, just consider, the situation. A man writes several letters to his wife; he asks if she is willing to join him so that he may regain his position as a husband and a father; and he waits . . . and he waits . . . and he writes again; and again; and he never receives an answer. He does not know that there is a letter declaring that his 'Children are well thank God and in transports [of delight] with the thoughts of our once more meeting together and of seeing their Father'. He has no idea that his wife has written that 'if I could but obtain leave or find the Means I would not loose one moment and be the bearer of this myself'.[61] He does not know that she was 'doing every thing in my power to obtain a passage to live and die with you'.[62] At what point does a person stop hoping for a favourable response?[63]

Nine years later Thomas Francis, now holding a ticket of leave, applied for permission to call the banns in the parish of Narellen, New South Wales.[64] His intended wife was Anne Little, who was free by servitude. Anne had arrived in the colony in the same year as Thomas Francis—1818. The governor's consent was given. If Thomas knew of the existence of the letter from his wife, then this was an act of bigamy. If not, he might have reasonably assumed that, having no word in the years since he was sentenced beyond the seas and over the seas, it was likely she was now 'number'd with the dead'.

We do not know whether or not Thomas Francis committed bigamy. His 'story' is incomplete. We make no predictions for the future of our protagonists or make statements about their outcome. What these three stories disclose instead is a revision of the personal qualities our three convicts held. Each member of our small cast was a husband and a father; each in his own way attempted to regain his position in his household; each recognised his duties and his responsibilities to the members of his household. In 1831 the Superintendent of Convicts, John Henry Capper, drew attention to one group of prisoners for whom transportation was an appalling threat. That group was identified as 'a married man with a wife and family [who] would rather stay here, enduring all the fatigues and dread of punishment, that he may have his wife and family near him, and with the hope of returning to them hereafter'.[65]

This is not a story of a farm labourer who was aged fifty-five, with grey hair and grey eyes who stood five feet four inches tall;[66] nor of a soldier who was one of the 1539 rank and file who deserted in the year 1819–20; nor even of a migrant worker who can be numbered amongst the casualties of industrialisation. Of these three men it could be said 'these are but items in the sad ledger of despair'.[67] Our farm labourer strove to make a materially secure future for his wife and family; our soldier feared for his wife's future if he were transported; and our industrial labourer may never have learnt of his wife's steady devotion. In none of these three stories did the crime which had caused the disruption of family life count for so much as a jot on the abacus of affection.

10

Raising Lazurus

Tamsin O'Connor

It rained the day John Hawes and Stephen Smith were hanged, so perhaps the spectators were grateful that Smith kept silent and Hawes kept it quick. According to Edward Hall's radical *Monitor*, 'He addressed the spectators in *nearly* the following words':

> Take warning by my fate, But I would sooner be hanged here this morning than return to Moreton Bay. Starvation and ill usage there have brought me to this untimely end. It is not my natural disposition to commit an inhuman act. *I forgive all my oppressors*. [my emphasis][1]

The wet weather notwithstanding, there was discomfort enough attached to the elegant brevity of Hawes's (or perhaps Hall's) words. For despite the customary warning to the wicked and the language of piety, he had introduced a discordant note to the careful orchestration of his execution. The scaffold was, after all, a place from which to beg, not bestow, forgiveness.

For the first and only time in their short lives Stephen Smith and John Hawes were important men: 'the chains they wore, even the rope itself signified their special status both as the wretched subjects of legal retribution and as the hopeful participants in their own redemption'.[2] Not even a Sydney shower could deter the eager mob from gathering on the rocks behind the gaol yard. Here they watched and waited, 'amusing themselves with . . . the unmeaning nothings of ordinary gossip, full in view of two fellow-beings for whom, in ten minutes, time would have passed away'.[3] The clean institutional lines of a pattern-book prison and the sharp natural edges of an exotic rock face had collided to create a new colonial landscape and a new penal theatre. The audience came to see the faces of the condemned, to hear their prayers, to smell their fear and for a few thrilling moments to share that most liminal of spaces—the space between life and death. And on this day they came to see John Hawes and Stephen Smith hang for the brutal murder of a fellow prisoner at Moreton Bay.

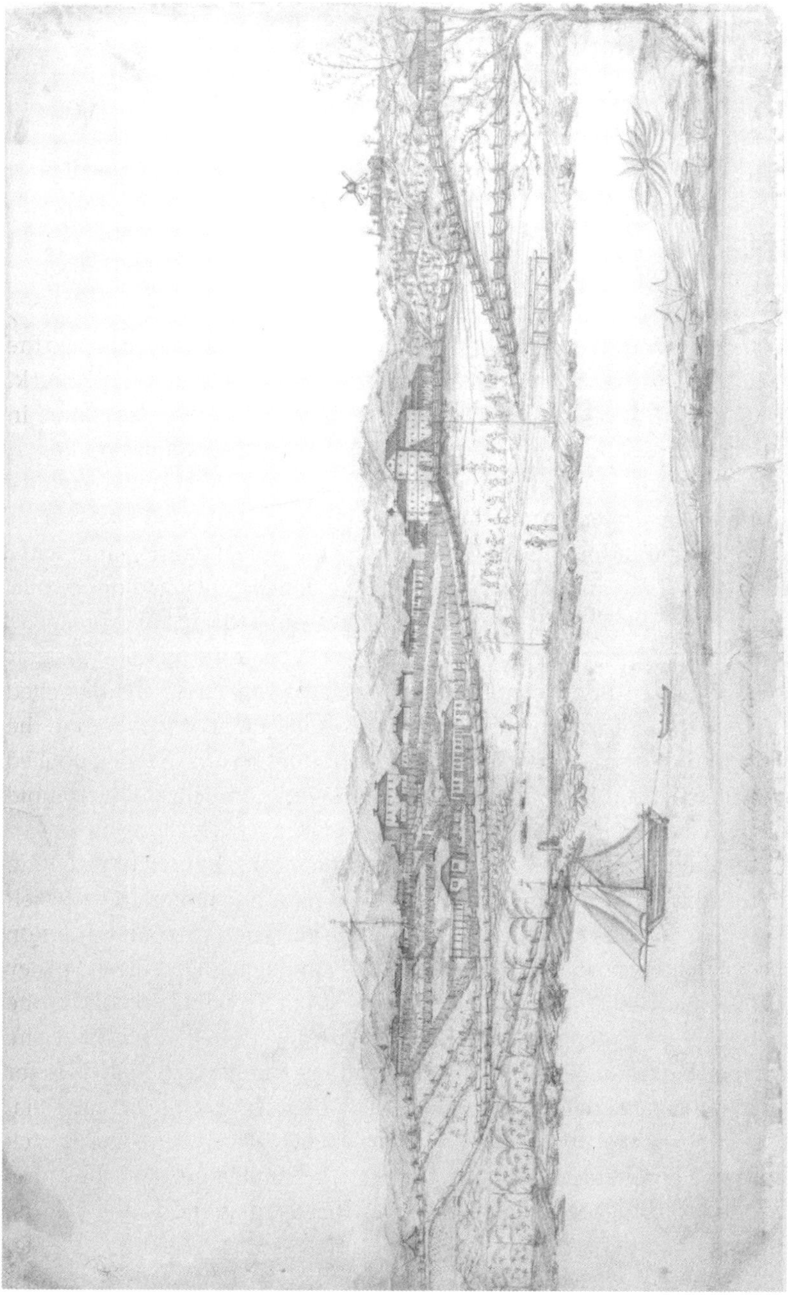

Moreton Bay *[penal station]*, New South Wales, *by Henry Boucher Bowerman, c. 1835.*

In the rhetoric of the day murder was 'the foulest crime which can be committed by man' against nature as well as against God, and society demanded full reparation with unconditional repentance.[4] For their part Hawes and Smith had to do a great deal more than die. Public executions were one of 'the most important colonial contact points between the elite and the non-elite, between ministers and magistrates on one side and "the mob" on the other'.[5] The condemned were not only required to demonstrate the fatal effects of a sinful disobedience, they were also expected to mediate a range of sacred and secular messages—articulated or merely implied—for the mass consumption of a hungry mob. In return they would be blessed with the physical comfort of a tight rope and a long drop and the spiritual comfort of God's grace. Moreover, Williams suggests that the dignity of a ritualised public death could confer the sense of public worth that had been so forcibly denied in life. Equally, though paradoxically, a measure of self-abasement could establish a degree of self-esteem.[6] But so too could a measure of defiance.

Smith died suitably penitent for nameless sins—perhaps too weary now to continue proclaiming his innocence of this one. It was Hawes who gave the drama of their death its narrative force and its dangerous edge.[7] As Lincoln Faller explains, murder 'opened fissures in the social fabric, and when murderers died silent and unresponsive . . . the damage they had done could never quite be undone. Their confessions, however—redacted and broadcast by the popular press—could allow those fissures to be (quite literally) papered over'.[8] Hawes had certainly confessed, but he had also accused and there was more than a hint of self-justification in his subsequent forgiveness. The *Monitor*, at pains to paper over some of those fissures (while opening others), reminded its readers that for all his suffering, Hawes's crime was nevertheless 'matchless in infamy'.[9] Still, it could not quite erase the disturbing impression that Smith and Hawes could be what Daniel Cohen calls 'injured innocents'.[10]

With his last words Hawes demonstrated his refusal to permit the exploitation of his death or the effacement of his life. His brief narrative gave a context to his crime, engendered a distrust of authority and demanded the sympathy of the mob. He would die penitent to please God but he would not take on the role of the desperate, depraved convict to please government. The elite could engineer the execution, establish its conventions and enforce its rituals but they could not control the way tales were told or the way people listened. The crowd was ever ready to support a bad man who died well, especially one who left a good tale bravely told. In this way the condemned and the crowd would collude in the subtle subversion of official ritual and in the creative formation of unauthorised sub-texts.

Those who did not participate in the damp drama of this particular death could relive it in the days and weeks to come as Sydney gossip and the *Sydney Gazette* made their respective rounds. Eventually both would make their way to the distant penal station of Moreton Bay, and here, the men who knew how the story had begun would finally learn how it ended. They could choose the official textual truth of the government *Gazette*, or, if they were lucky, the radical challenge of the forbidden *Monitor* or the more elusive, evolutionary truths of convict gossip. These conflicting narratives converged and collided in the curious isolation of the penal station world, where they formed new shapes, acquired new meanings and inspired fresh new plots with fresh new blood.

For while Hawes's and Smith's crime seems remarkable only for the banality of its violence, the 'spectators also understood [Hawes] to signify, that being a long sentenced man he wished to make sure of death by committing murder'.[11] In violent deed and valiant (last) word his tale of crime and punishment echoes that of men like John Gough, Thomas Matthews, Thomas Allen, Patrick Sullivan and Henry Muggleton, who all, in their different ways, transformed the fatal drop of death into a grand gesture of deliverance by declaring that 'life was of no use to them at a penal station'.[12]

Faller argues that 'in the mythic interpretation of familiar murder . . . there is no clear suggestion of any ambivalence about the worth of that society . . . or the legitimacy of its authority . . . the murderer raised troublesome questions . . . but he never threatened, as the highwayman [and bushrangers] often did, to become a social critique'.[13] However, as the last words of the Moreton Bay men reveal, the boundaries between murder and social criticism had become dangerously indistinct. Moreover, it escaped no one's notice that these murders were identified as a species of suicide—a cunning convict adaptation that carried all the advantages of death, but none of the dangers of eternal damnation.[14] Neither the motives nor the measure of guilt attached to each man can ever be truly known. But this matters less than the myth itself, so quickly spread by the convicts and so eagerly manipulated by the *Monitor*. This was not the world of lawyerly facts, this was David Malouf's 'different history' in the making, 'a myth history', an alternative convict 'history of experience in the imagination' and imagination in the experience.[15]

The Moreton Bay murders have slipped from memory and the meanings attached to these familial convict killings have been safely contained within the folklore of penal station life—adrift, distant and reassuringly aberrant. Yet the final act of these penal station tragedies was almost always played out in a crowded Sydney court and on the sturdy scaffold at the Sydney gaol, where, it will be remembered, Stephen Smith did not address the assembled spectators at his execution. But he did have something to say. The day he died he wrote this short note to a friend in prison:

> I now write my final words to you . . . and I for ever bless you for your kindness, and now hope that my blessed lord and Saviour will be my

> friend in heaven. I hope you will not forget to send my letter, as I wish my friends to know that I have departed this life. My time is short, I cannot write any more.[16]

It is poignant, but it is also private and hints at the enormity of Smith's sense of separation and loss. We shall never know what was contained in that letter home or how his friends and family reacted on reading the last dying words of a man who had been so long in exile and, by then, so long dead. First oceans and then eternity kept Smith from his home and family and it is no wonder that the fear of exile and isolation were recurring themes in convict life and convict tales. When Robert Taylor contemplated his 'doleful sentence' of fourteen years' hard labour in chains, it was the prospect of a life 'deprived of any society, or friend, to whom I may tell out my sorrows' that he seemed to dread most.[17] Stephen Smith did have a friend, but his last days were haunted by the fear that his distant family would know nothing of his fate and this anxiety—that life could pass into death in one hemisphere unknown and *unfelt* in the other—echoed in the words of those who the convicts left behind.

In 1827 when Agnes McMillan put scratchy pen to flimsy paper in a small village near Stanraer in Scotland, her thoughts were divided between the family she was struggling to support, 'the house rent very dear' and the husband she had not seen for seven years.[18] 'I wish to know if he is in life', she asked the Colonial Secretary, and this simple little phrase recurs as an emotional refrain throughout a letter loaded with loss and a cautious hope: 'If your Exelence can find him out thanks be to god for it . . . if may husband wishes me to go I will be very desierous to go I add no more at present . . . PS plas send me an anseur as soon as this coms to hand.'[19]

But it would take well over a year before her letter came to hand. By then her husband had slipped out of government sight and disappeared into the relative anonymity of his free life. Agnes and William were divided by the length of his seven-year sentence and by a lived experience that was, and remains, so very difficult to convey. And of course, for Agnes, perched as she was on the edge of the Irish Sea, they were separated by a distance so vast and a geography so diverse as to be almost unimaginable.

Sophia Frayer knew something of distance and diversity, for she had made the long journey to New South Wales as a convict, but there was always more to learn about exile. In May 1825 she married James Henshaw shortly before he was transported to Port Macquarie, promising to join him as soon as permission was granted. But, with sudden cold feet at the prospect of a penal station before her, Sophia left town. She was found at her husband's behest, and then placed in the Parramatta female factory at the Colonial Secretary's, an outcome that was as painful as it was predictable. There she waited uncertain, uninformed and unfree. By September 1826 her impatience and anxiety had become tinged with insecurity and anger:

> My Dear Husband
> With A sorrowful heart I once more write to you in hopes that these few lines will find you in good health as it fine me at present. I have wrote in litters to you and can get no Answers . . . witch leves with a sorrowful and broken heart . . . if please god you do get this safe pray for god sake write me a few lines to lett me know how you are sittuated and pray lett me know what the cause of you treating me in such a manner as you well know I am not deserving it from you. my long confinement in this misserably place ought I think Move you to pity and compassion to write to me . . . I wood never have Married you if I had not a sencere regard for you, but I am sorry to say that my marriage at present is very fatal to me. I have continually in my mind being married Alas . . . I have never had the comforts nor consolation of a husband nor even the happiness of a few lines to know if he is or dead or A Live . . . judge what my unhappy thoughts must be. It is the last time I shall ever trouble you with writing any more if I due not hear from you I shall endeavour to go out to a place of service as I am thank god quite capable of earning my hone livehood . . . your unhappy wife . . . sophia henshaw.[20]

Sophia was more forthright than Agnes—more certain of her ground, more confident of her ability and more resentful of her lot—but these two letters, written a world apart, share the same sense of a barely articulated betrayal and the same palpable fear of irretrievable separation and loss. Moreover, Agnes's letter reminds us that the relationship between the paradise of home and the hell of penal Australia was already ambiguous. After all, she was destitute in Scotland and was now 'very desirous' to leave, while her husband was free in New South Wales and may well have been desirous to stay. Sophia's letter tacitly demonstrates the cost of this ambiguity. A new paradise needed a new hell and there was always further to fall—to Newcastle; to Port Macquarie; to Moreton Bay and finally to Norfolk Island.

These centres of ever-increasing pain and ever-decreasing hope were truly intended to measure a Miltonic scale of exile and disgrace, where the fallen convict was 'As far remov'd from God and light of Heav'n / As from the centre thrice to th' utmost Pole'.[21] George Molyson captures this sense of metaphorical and physical distance in his disjointed despair: 'I am this day warned for my destination, I believe for Port Macquarie—very badly prepared—my concern lies at a great distance and bad roads—by water a great part. I am ordered I must obey—I am willing to meet my fait whatever happens.'[22]

As a veteran of the Second Fleet, long since 'comfortably settled in life'. George Molyson had been confident of his character and secure in his well-earned freedom. That is until 1822, when he was sentenced to fourteen years' heavy labour for harbouring bushrangers on his lonely Hawkesbury farm.[23] For an old man, even an old sailor, who had twice crossed the oceans to Australia, first as a convict and later as a settler, the journey to a new place of exile at Port Macquarie was truly daunting. 'I am doomed', he wrote. Indeed the long double vowels of his doom are echoed again and again when he writes 'where I am to goo', 'where I will doo', 'seventeen days agoo'. Here the poignancy is heightened as oral and literary cultures collide to reveal the *sound* of an exile's lament. George Molyson's uneven, ill-formed script barely disguises the panic in his plaintive wail. His awkward spelling and syntax may reveal a limited education but they also capture the sound and structure of his own Edinburgh accent. The sheer effort of written articulation is evident in every word. This is the convict voice and it is brave and true and almost unbearably sad. For George Molyson would never return to his fine Hawkesbury farm with its forty hogs and fifty fruitful acres.[24]

Sophia and James Henshaw felt acutely the tyranny of this distance. As James explained, 'with the greatest deference', to the then Colonial Secretary, Thomas Goulburn, 'our separation if possible is more painful than the heavy sentence I now lie under'.[25] But while Sophia fretted in Parramatta, James did his best to bring her to him. 'I have frequently addressed his Excellency upon the subject', he told Commandant Innes, 'but being at the sugar plantation I am fearful that those with whom I had entrusted the delivery of my petitions have failed'. The following month Sophia and James Henshaw received identical letters of official 'non compliance'.[26] It appears, though no-one told her, that Sophia's forthright character was deemed undeserving of such 'kind indulgence' from his Excellency the Governor.

Margaret Connor would become all too familiar with these short notes of refusal and she would also learn that in New South Wales freedom—like Paradise or a convict's character—was easier to lose than regain. She had come to the colony a free woman with her husband David Connor, a private in the 57th Regiment of Foot. She had spent nineteen years following the drum and was every inch the regimental wife and mother. Then, in 1829, Margaret was sentenced to fourteen years transportation to Moreton Bay for the possession of stolen property. Nothing, not even the protestations of her friends in the 57th could save her from the Governor's determined assault on female receivers.[27]

However, like Robert Young, James Henshaw and George Molyson, she had one last theoretical glimmer of hope—'the Humble Petition'. These documents of dutiful deference and occasional mercy 'occupied the centre ground of a judicial system whose very basis was the discretionary application or mitigation of penal pain'.[28] They are paper proof both of the symbolic power attached to the Royal Prerogative of mercy and of the bureaucratic control necessary to apply symbolic power.

This process, that began in the gaols and hulks of the British Isles with the composition of plaintive pleas to the King or Home Secretary—some adorned with the mixed blessings of judges and nobles—was imperfectly reflected through the colonial looking-glass. Thus, endless appeals, sometimes to magistrates and masters, but more often to the colonial secretary or the governor, were composed in the Sydney gaol, on the *Phoenix* hulk and at the penal stations themselves as the process of punishment moved inexorably on from its metropolitan centre to the farthest frontier. Each petition begged the bestowal of gracious pardons, merciful mitigation, or kind indulgences of every description in exchange for the exaltations and gratitude of the humble petitioner. Elizabeth Davidson, a native-born woman from Windsor, summoned a special flair and fluency when she petitioned the governor and promised to teach 'her babes to lisp their prayers to the throne of heaven for its choicest blessings to pour upon [him]' if only he would grant her permission to join her husband at Moreton Bay.[29] This was not the mawkish language of melodrama but a searing *cri de coeur* from a woman who loved her husband and feared for her children. Similar petitions, stamped with their own version of this familiar pattern of pain, plea, and promise, were sent on behalf of Margaret Connor. This one was sent by Margaret herself from the Sydney gaol on 19 November 1829. It is a typical example of the stream of petitions that poured from the gaol following every session of the criminal court and preceding every new draft of penal station prisoners.

> To His Excellency Lieutenant General Ralph Darling, Captain General, Governor and Commander in Chief, in and over the Territory of NSW and its Dependencies etc—etc—etc.
>
> The Humble Petition of Margaret Connor, Most respectfully shewth
>
> That Your Excellency's Petitioner was convicted at the Supreme Court of Criminal Jurisdiction on the 19th September last, for having stolen property in her possession, and sentenced to fourteen years transportation. —
>
> That Petitioner came free to this colony with her husband (Private David Connor of the 57th Regiment) by whom she has four children (Now living) the eldest of whom is serving as Drummer in the same corps with his father —
>
> That Petitioner most humbly represents that from the period of her intermarriage to her present unforseen misfortune, her character has not been impeached by any act of impropriety whatsoever and Petitioners

> fatality was occasioned more by ignorance than by any motive of fraud—
>
> That Petitioner most humbly implores Your Excellency's humane and Kind consideration and gracious design to commute your humble Petitioner's sentence of Transportation and for such benevolent act of Your Excellency's kindness, Petitioner as in duty bound will ever pray.
>
> Margaret Connor
>
> That Petitioner begs leave most respectfully to request reference be made to the character which she held for many years in the 57th, which no doubt will exactly accord with what she herein represents.[30]

It is brief, but the clerk's exquisite copperplate hand and his ability to compress a life into a series of well-turned—and well-tried—phrases would have cost the Connors dear. The drawing-up of professional petitions was a lucrative sideline for the convict clerks of the colony. Victor Gattrel, the historian of Home Office petitions, suggests that these formal appeals for mercy take us away from the public domain of the court and the scaffold and closer to the private 'attitudes and feelings of those convicted and doomed to face death or distant exile'.[31] They take us into an unknown archival world, a storehouse of stories from which 'people could draw, if they wished a scolding, a sermon, a moral lesson or a literary tale'.[32] In theme and form the petition echoes closely the narrative structure and moral style of the scaffold speech. It too captures a life in connection with a death—in this instance the slow social death of the penal station. It too features the self-defence of a hapless 'hero', the narrative craft of persuasion and the literary conventions of familiar ritual. Yet for all their compelling detail, the stories of the humble petition almost never crossed into the published world of broadside and ballad. Natalie Zemon Davies offers a persuasive explanation: 'pamphlet writers wanted something clear cut with exemplary punishment and the privileged last words of the condemned. A grateful supplicant and a [theoretically] merciful king were not persuasive enough as a finish.'[33]

The power of a persuasive finish also eluded Margaret Connor as she struggled to explain her life and excuse her crime. If her attitudes and feelings seem a little deadened by the formulaic structure of her first appeal, and if her voice seems a little smothered by linguistic devices, it is not entirely surprising. The petition may not have been in the public domain, but it was a public document. There was a style book to follow, conventions to heed and advice to be solicited before most convicts dared invest their hopes and meagre means in the written word—particularly one like Margaret who was so new to the narrative rituals of sin and supplication.

For all that, Margaret and her nameless clerical collaborator tell us much about her family and her sense of self as an integral part of regimental life.

Later petitions would tell of her husband's agony as he and their sons were posted to Madras, leaving their young daughters alone in the orphanage at Sydney; of her prosecutor's belief that justice had been more than satisfied, and of Margaret's increasing despair as her life ebbed away at Moreton Bay. But each plea for a pardon, or mere mitigation, told another terse tale of refusal in the scribbled minutes of successive governors—'Cannot be allowed', 'Cannot be Complied with', 'No answer'. One can only imagine the sense of elation, even disbelief, and perhaps fear (after all her husband and sons were long gone and her daughters were almost grown), when, in 1836, Governor Bourke finally relented and restored Margaret to life with one word—'allowed'.[34]

James Davidson longed to be allowed to see his wife Elizabeth and his four young children. His heartfelt plea for deliverance from the physical and psychological ordeal of Moreton Bay is expressed with all the anguish of a man mourning his own social death.

> I *Entreat* you and *Implore* you sir for the sake of my unfortunate wife deprived of a husband for the *sake* of four *innocent* children deprived of their father that you will have the benevolent humanity to use your interest with His Excellency . . . to allow me to remove from Moreton Bay . . . Situated as I am sir *I have no hope*—deprived of even the *slightest* indulgence without the *common* necessaries of life—deprived in my affliction of my wife and dearest babes . . . Indeed sir my pen is at a loss to express . . . my forlorn situation surrounded as I am by affliction and the worst of ills—my pen sir is inadequate to describe the mental agony of my heart . . .[35]

However, this appeal was destined for the desk of Governor Ralph Darling and there would be no hope of resurrection nor any hope of reunion with his 'dearest babes'.

Myriad expressions of deferential hope punctuated the narrative of every petition. Thus, Denis McHugh 'hop[ed] that the Governor [would] be graciously pleased to grant the indulgence [he] begged'; Edward Downland 'hop[ed] his Execellency [would] pardon the liberty' he took 'by writing these few lines'; George Molyson promised to 'bear the yeok of fourteen years heavey . . . in hopes that [his] honour [would] grant [his] earnest request'; Neil Smith simply waited in 'humble hope'; and William Cooley hoped that the Colonial Secretary would continue 'the full enjoyment of health and happiness'. However, such generous good wishes were doubtless conditional upon the success of his petition.[36]

Indeed, the cringing and needful tones of dutiful deference were sometimes hard to sustain in the face of an indifferent silence. When James Holland became disenchanted with the quality of the Governor's mercy he began to cut the cloth of his deference accordingly. After a cursory show of formulaic humility he issued this unwise rebuke: 'I hope his Excellency will consider [my liberty] due me again. I have repeatedly passed in petitions and forms according to the regulations but to no effect . . . [I] wondered why I am objected to after being so long in the colony.'[37] He would wait and wonder for some time yet.

From the lonely shores of the continent's far north John Francis and Henry Taylor made this staggering request:

> Hon'd Sir, As we are prisoners for life we hope you will grant us the indulgence of sending us two women as we are very bad off for the want of them as there is not one woman among us to do any kind of work for us and we shall marry them if your honour thinks fit.[38]

Perhaps this extraordinary little petition was prompted by the boredom of Melville Island and the bravado of men with nothing to lose. However, Gatrell reminds us that there can be no categorical readings, and this may also have been a sincere appeal from simple men who naively believed they had something to gain.[39] Yet regardless of their mood or motive Francis and Taylor clearly felt they had rights to demand that the Governor was obliged to meet and thus with deliberate insolence or misguided ignorance, they reduced the Governor's pomp to convict's pimp: a sharp lesson for the powerful with a short petition from the powerless.

In contrast Warren Kerr was a little too well-practised in the art of the humble petition. For almost twenty years he would besiege Government House with his relentless appeals and his irrepressible hopes. Here, to misquote Montaigne, *le Plaidoyer et histoire*—the plea is history and the history is pure picaresque.[40] For with every humble request Kerr chronicles his astonishing life as a soldier and his tragi-comic misadventures as convict. Over time his tones of reflexive self-abasement and rhetorical self-justification grow ever more confiding and ever more familiar, edging dangerously close to contempt:

> praying your excellency will pardon my entrusion, I am subject to many of the frailties of human nature, it is the nature of man to err. I am not without my faults and he that is without Sir, let him first cast a stone . . . I had the misfortune to fall in my life time but . . . I steal not, I offend not, I kill not and bare not false witness nor do I drink to excess, I love god above all things and if I do not love my neighbour as much as I ought to I pray god to cause me so to do . . . I have been separated from [my] companion and my children five years and upwards. *God had enemy's on earth, kings and governors have theirs and why me exempt* ... my families distress is hid from the wourld, and [they] has

> borne their affliction with Christian fortitude, not sounding the Trumpet of their distress to the Editor of a radical Newspaper, but has from time to time submitted their case to your Excellency . . . had the hungry cries of my children . . . ascended to your Excellency's ear your Excellencey would have said long ere this time suffer little children to come unto me . . . I am an aged man serving on the first expedition to Egypt . . . I received several wounds one on the head that I suffer much from . . .[41]

Kerr's homely Christian values would do him no good, nor would his veiled criticism of the *Monitor*. His war record and his war wound had long since lost their currency, and old age and exile were too commonplace for compassion. Kerr would receive no answer, but he would receive yet another black mark against his already 'incorrigible' character.[42] For the convict had presumed to range himself with God, governors and kings, and for this violation of the humble petition—the ever so flattering self-portrait of the ruling elite—he would not be forgiven.[43]

No doubt dashed hopes provoked violent curses, but they could also inspire astonishing appeals. Warren Kerr had articulated this persistent belief in the transformational power of the humble petition when he told Governor Brisbane that 'all our hopes depend on your Honours' Humanity'.[44] Some of course had more hope than others and those serving life sentences at a penal station had almost none. An American prisoner in a modern penitentiary captures the lifers' sense of social death with an awful eloquence, 'Oh I'm dead—they just ain't thrown the dirt on yet'.[45] Over a century earlier and a continent away a group of Port Macquarie lifers composed an elegant petition that was both a meditation on hope and a manifesto for justice:

> The prisoner who is so deprived of hope views the world with indifference; he beholds everything with apathy,—and cares little for being virtuous, who think he has no motive to make him so. Reformation upon a principle of honour, of philosophy or even of real religion will never actuate the exile while 'hope's deferred' and that primary stimulus to personal exertion, the certainty of reward, is withheld.[46]

In exquisite language they (or rather their delegated scribe/s) manage to convey the impression of an unambiguous, if strategic, deference for authority while delivering an unmistakable, if careful, censure of its agents. We learn that they had been sentenced to a penal station by an over-zealous magistracy for breaking the convict regulations, for offending their masters and above all for life—'a conviction distressing and despondent'. These men were well acquainted with the law—with the detail of its letter and with the inequity of its spirit. And their measured tones of reasonable restraint suggest that they were equally well acquainted with the capricious vanity of those who flexed and stretched the sinews of colonial law. For all that they could only pray that the Governor would 'give ear to statements that are founded upon the truths of a sorrowful and melancholy experience'.[47] The dutiful deference of this petition cannot disguise the conflict between a determined belief in success and a dismal expectation of failure. In fact the letter of a new law and the Attorney-General's determination to apply it in the face of an obdurate magistracy would eventually bring reprieve—though not immediately and not for everyone. For while the due process of law was so quick to incarcerate, it was slow and suspicious when called upon to 'ex-carcerate'.

The humble petition is unique among plebeian texts, for it is both a counterpoint to and a component of the 'official transcript' and its 'panoptic quasi-scientific viewpoint'.[48] It is a cultural collaboration of sorts, but the historian of French letters of remission overstates her case when she insists, 'We have not here an impermeable "official culture" imposing its criteria on "popular culture" but cultural exchange, conducted under the King's rules'.[49] The official culture of convict society never offered an *equal* exchange and it must have looked impermeable enough to Sophia Henshaw, Margaret Connor, James Davidson and George Molyson.

Nevertheless, scattered through the endless bundles of Colonial Office correspondence these letters of appeal are among the most evocative textual fragments of colonial life. They are, to steal a phrase from Natalie Zemon Davies, 'one of the best sources of relatively uninterrupted narrative from the lips of the lower orders . . .'.[50] A phantasmagoric array of characters has been bundled, boxed and buried, not under the 'centuries' ingrained dust and grime' of Gatrell's 'archival soil', but under a century's deep dismissive disbelief.[51] We must raid these cardboard graves and raise their paper dead, for they tell of men and women; of innocence and guilt; of bushrangers and bush constables; of native lads and lasses; of torture and terror; of reward and remission. They are written with the legal fluency of the unnamed lifer or with the unlettered genius of a born storyteller like Warren Kerr or with the sad, awkward anguish of the semi-literate George Molyson. Some are scratched on flimsy scraps of paper, while others are scrolled on the finest parchment. They almost always conjure dreams of liberty and sometimes dreams of creation. They are the work of soldiers with battle stories and battle scars and of dissolute young merchants led astray. They share the fears of informers and the skills of artisans. There are brickmakers, blacksmiths, caulkers and carpenters. Most have accents heavy with the dialects of England and the Gaelic of Ireland, Wales and Scotland. And deep in this colonial archive paper fragments echo the murmuring voices of Europeans, Americans, Mauritians, Africans and West Indians telling their rich tales—some in a foreign language—all to a foreign power.

To be sure, these peculiar convict narratives are often constrained by the conventional syntax and vocabulary of deference and humility. Equally, they are often carefully shaped and moulded to achieve the most flattering likeness of a life. Yet all these features are less problematic and more interesting than many would suppose. For, whatever the limitations set by form and tradition, and by means and materials, the petition offered the convicts a rare opportunity not only to tell but also to *record* their version of their life. This was especially meaningful in a society devoted to the judgemental documentation of their every move. Each convict plea had to offset the prejudicial knowledge encapsulated in the damning brevity of the indents, in the sceptical scrawl of the superintendents' police histories and in the commandants' terse assessment of a convict's 'character'.

Men like Michael Duggan were no longer identified by their sentence or by their ship but by a new colonial acquisition—their character—and Duggan's was deemed 'desperate'. His tale of mutiny and escape and of punishment and pain was tersely told in the neat columns of a punishment book and with a visceral force in the deep scar tissue of his back. His police record encapsulated his past at one penal station and would ensure a bleak future at the next.[52] To steal a telling phrase from Alan Atkinson, this was a world where 'print in black and white had its reverberations in flesh and blood'.[53] And on occasion it was also a world where flesh and blood had its reverberations in black and white. Lewis Lazurus had a police record long in the damning detail of recalcitrance and resistance that so limited convict hopes of resurrection. It stretched from Newcastle to Port Macquarie and onward to Moreton Bay. He refused, he robbed and he ran and his lingering social death must have seemed interminable. That is, until the day he gently carried home the battered corpse of his murdered master—the infamous Patrick Logan. In time the Commandant's violent death and the convict's solemn duty would bring news of reward, release and resurrection. It is ironic that the 'Fell Tyrant's' last act at Moreton Bay was raising the convict Lazurus.[54]

Penal station stories converge on these liminal spaces between life and death, between exile and execution. To misquote Seamus Heaney we must 'take our squat pens and dig', gently sifting and searching the rich soil of these unmarked paper graves. Only then can we fulfill long-dead dreams of resurrection. Only then can we raise Lazurus and all the rest. They are our ghosts and 'sometimes they glitter'. They are our stories and 'sometimes they shine'.[55]

‘When this you see’

11

'Wherever I go I whill right to you'

Bruce Hindmarsh

Richard Taylor received a sentence of ten years transportation for receiving stolen goods at Pontefract Assizes on 6 April 1840.[1] Five days later he wrote from the confines of York Castle gaol to his father, George Taylor, in Burnley telling him of his sentence.[2] In July of the same year Simon Brown, Richard's half-brother, was sentenced to ten years transportation at the Quarter Sessions at Preston for burglary.[3] The *Preston Chronicle* noted that 'the Calendar was rather heavy, there being about one hundred prisoners for trial', reflecting the depression of the local textile industries.[4] Simon was indicted with two brothers, Abraham and William Rodgers, for 'burglariously entering the house of Mr. Joseph Pomfret of Blackburn', and therein stealing clothing, including a waistcoat, coat and hat, on 4 May. Simon and William pleaded guilty, but Abraham continued to protest his innocence.

Dr Brown presented the prosecution. He stated that on the day following the theft the three men had attempted to pledge the stolen items. A witness swore that Abraham had been with Simon and William in the pawnbroker's. Abraham's fate appeared uncertain. T. B. Addison, the Chairman of the Bench of Magistrates, however, informed the jury that he believed this evidence alone insufficient to demonstrate Abraham's participation in the burglary. Accordingly, Abraham was acquitted. A second charge of burglary was then read. William pleaded guilty, and the other two were acquitted. Found not guilty on both counts, Abraham was ordered to be liberated. Any joy he felt was to be short-lived. A sentence of ten years transportation was handed down to Simon, while William Rodgers, found guilty on both counts, aggravated by a prior conviction, received transportation for fifteen years. On hearing his brother's sentence Abraham Rodgers broke down in tears.[5]

Simon was now faced with the task of writing to his father to break the news. He entreated him to 'make yourself as happy as you can on my account . . . I do intend to refrain from all my wickedness and turn into the Lord'.[6] It was surely a cruel blow to George Taylor that two of his sons should be sentenced to transportation in the space of a single year. He kept the two letters that bore the bad news—as he kept every other letter that his sons sent on their journey to a new penal existence at the ends of the globe. This little cache of memories grew over the years to form a remarkable series of correspondence that endured nineteen years, and defied the separation of transportation.

Following sentencing Richard and Simon were held in gaol, awaiting removal to the hulks, and ultimately embarkation for Australia. This period was marked by prolific letter writing, evidence that impending transportation provoked fear and uncertainty, although the letters are also punctuated by other more mundane matters, including the necessity of settling outstanding affairs. This contradictory vortex of emotion and practicality characterises the early correspondence of both brothers. Only days after his trial, Richard wrote of his desire to see his father again before he sailed. In the process, however, he revealed an ulterior motive; no parcel was allowed into the gaol unless brought by a prisoner's friend or relation. More plainly Richard noted, 'I shall want a little money to by a few things which will be easeful to me'.[7]

Writing from gaol in Preston in August 1840, Simon displayed similar regret, whilst providing his father with a list of items to despatch, including combs, and a belt, which were to be 'as strong as you can get them for to last me til I get my liberty'.[8] Both men also asked that outstanding debts be collected, and petty property secured. From York, Richard advised his father that he should recover two silk handkerchiefs and two pairs of shoes, along with other items and three shillings in money, from Bethey Summers. He failed to make it clear whether Summers was his landlady or lover.[9]

While Richard and Simon attempted to organise their affairs, their immediate fate remained uncertain. It is evident from the letters that they did not know when or where they were to be moved or where they were to be transported to. 'I don't know how long I have to stop', Richard wrote to his father 14 April 1840. On 22 April he ventured, 'I think we are going to leave York soon . . . ye mus send me a letter as quick as posepl'.[10] Richard finally left York on 13 May, having the distinction of being in a parcel of prisoners transferred to London by steam, rather than horse-drawn van. News of his departure reached his father in a letter from 'D.P.' who wrote on his behalf.[11] Simon remarked while imprisoned at Preston, 'we expect to go off every day now', and by 16 August, both he and William Rodgers were in the *Warrior* hulk at Woolwich where they remained until Rodgers was embarked on the transport *Asia* which sailed for Van Diemen's Land on 6 April 1841.[12]

Richard was held on the hulk *Fortitude*, at Chatham docks in Kent, until 3 July 1840. During this time he was one of over five hundred prisoners held to daily labour in the dockyards, from 7 a.m. to 5.30 p.m. Among his fellow prisoners he witnessed men severely punished for misconduct, although whether he was ever among them or not remained unstated.[13] As the unscrupulous nature of some of his fellow prisoners became apparent, Richard was

Prison-ship in Portsmouth Harbour, *by Edward William Cooke,* c. *1829, shows prisoners being embarked on a hulk.*

forced to instruct his father to send him no money, as there were those who would steal the letter if he did so.[14] From the *Warrior* in February 1841 Simon explained that he was only allowed to send a letter once every two months, although he could freely receive letters from his father; parcels or money were not allowed to be sent to him.[15] Theft from mail was evidently as rife on the *Warrior* as Richard had found it on the *Fortitude*. George Taylor sent Simon a parcel and a letter, which were not delivered, but only the letter was returned.[16]

Prisoners were allowed the indulgence of parcels and letters in the final days before their departure. While lying at Sheerness on board the *Eden*, Richard wrote to his father asking for two pounds of twist tobacco, ending his letter abruptly to catch the post.[17] Simon wrote while lying off Plymouth on board the *David Clarke* in May 1841, requesting that his sister send him a pound of tobacco, two or three newspapers, and as much money as she could.[18] He also asked her to ask his uncle to send him a 'trifle of money', to buy a few items for the voyage. As if sensing that he was testing his sister's generosity, he reminded her 'this will be the last time ever I shall write or trouble you in England for any thing'. The request for newspapers is revealing. Simon's convict record reveals that he could read, although in itself this classification does not clearly demonstrate fluent reading.[19] More persuasive here are Simon's later requests in letters from Van Diemen's Land for his father to 'send me a paper as often as you can it will be a pleasure for to here all the news and particulars of what is going on at home'. Local newspapers evidently had a particular poignancy for those about to be separated by the seas, the text itself forming an important contact with home. Significantly, Simon appears to have later sent newspapers back to Burnley from Australia.[20]

Richard Taylor sailed on the *Eden* on 10 July 1840; Simon Brown left on the *David Clarke* almost a year later. The voyage to Australia abruptly curtailed both series of correspondence. Being at sea enforced a literal hiatus. Indeed, no further letter from Simon survives until one dated 1855.[21] Although, unlike his half-brother, Richard wrote to his father from Sydney within a year of his arrival, there is a thematic break between those letters written in England, and those sent from Australia. Intervening months had been spent gathering information on the colony of New South Wales, in order that his letter 'should not be altogether uninteresting'.[22] Since his arrival Richard had been employed as a cook at the General Hospital, a position he held throughout his sentence.[23] His first letter also contained a wealth of descriptive material, relating details of prices, wildlife, wages and employment, agriculture, and the character of Sydney.

Subsequent letters written by Richard from Sydney while still under sentence emphasise his contentment with his situation. In August 1842 he

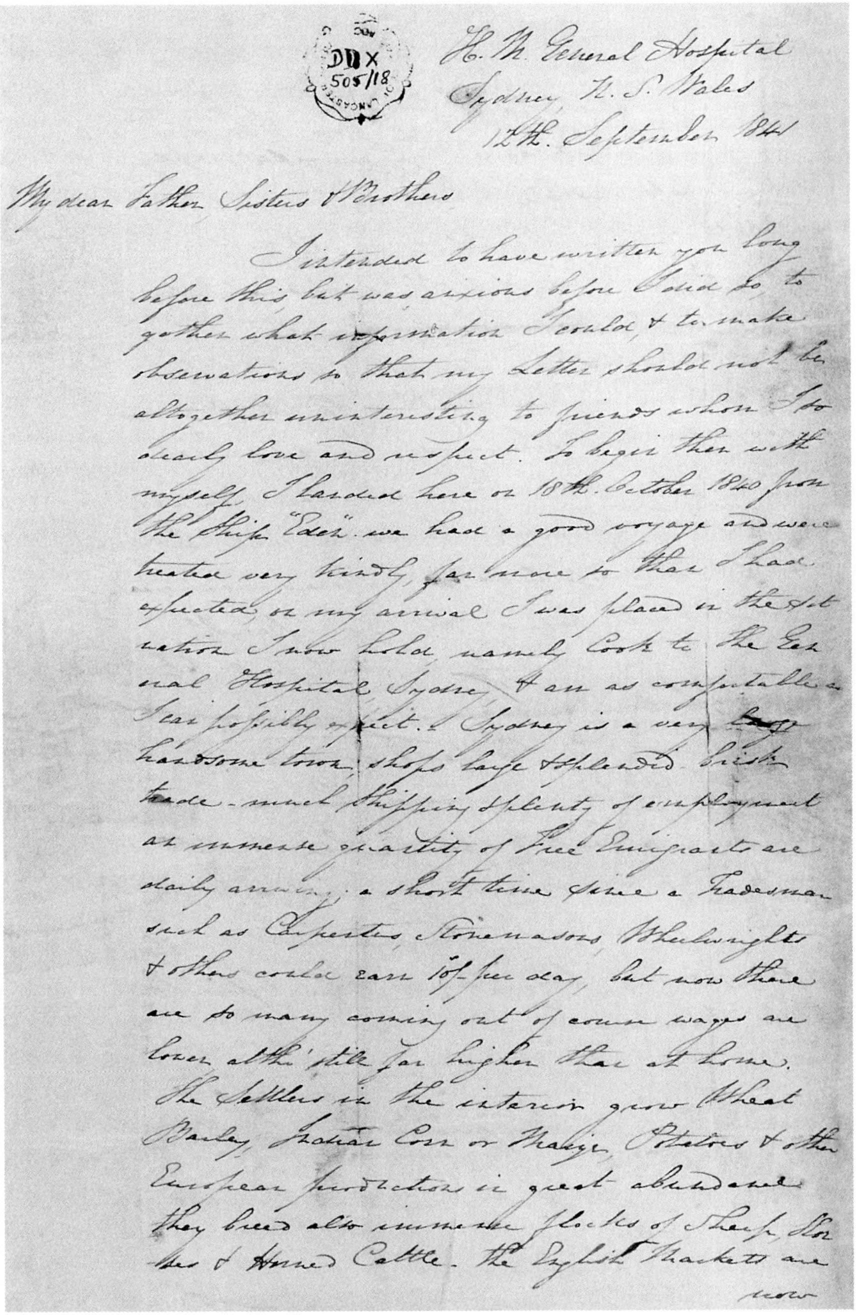

H.M. General Hospital
Sydney N.S. Wales
12th. September 1841

My dear Father Sisters & Brothers

I intended to have written you long before this but was anxious before I did so, to gather what information I could, & to make observations so that my Letter should not be altogether uninteresting to friends whom I so dearly love and respect. To begin then with myself, I landed here on 18th. October 1840 from the Ship "Eden" we had a good voyage and were treated very kindly, far more so than I had expected, on my arrival I was placed in the situation I now hold, namely Cook to the General Hospital Sydney & am as comfortable as I can possibly expect. Sydney is a very ~~large~~ handsome town, shops large & splendid - brisk trade - much shipping & plenty of employment an immense quantity of Free Emigrants are daily arriving, a short time since a Tradesman such as Carpenters, Stonemasons, Wheelwrights & others could earn 10/- per day, but now there are so many coming out of course wages are lower altho' still far higher than at home. The Settlers in the interior grow Wheat Barley, Indian Corn or Maize, Potatoes & other European productions in great abundance they breed also immense flocks of Sheep, Horses & Horned Cattle. the English Markets are now

Letter from Richard Taylor, Sydney, 12 September 1841.

informed his father, 'I have plenty of everything you can mention . . . it is a Butefull Cuntry . . . my elth is very good I ham very fat I ham Twelve Stone . . . I cept up my Birth Day and whe [had] a good cake and punch and I wish you had that'.[24] No doubt Richard's situation as cook facilitated the baking of his cake, and the acquiring of its ingredients. Richard had not, despite his glowing account of the colony, abandoned his intention to return home. His final letter before leaving Sydney with his ticket-of-leave in December 1845 was replete with assurances to his father. Immediately his freedom was restored he declared he would 'lose no time in coming home again, and I hope we never more will be separated in this life . . . Father I am longing for the day to come to behold your face once more'.[25]

Richard did not write again until 1850. In the intervening years George Taylor wrote to the Secretary of State's Office seeking information as to whether his sons were living, and their whereabouts. Replies informed him in 1849 that Richard and Simon had both been living at the time of the 1848 muster.[26] After nearly five years' silence, Richard wrote to his father in September 1850. In this letter Richard accounted for his actions in the intervening years, and revealed he had received a letter from his father in 1848, but had waited to answer until he 'was settled in [a] Place of my own, I only held a ticket of leave at the time so I thought it was best to settle myself in some sort of way before I would answer to yours'.[27] He had, he wrote, gained his liberty, and acquired a plot of land at Narellan where he was building a house. Narellan was then a small village near the thriving settlement of Camden, New South Wales.[28] Richard also informed his father that he was working as a boot- and shoemaker, a trade he had learned from another servant while employed as a cook in the hospital in Sydney.[29] He also revealed that he had been married 'this last six years' to Julia Hand, originally from Bawdon, County Cork.[30] One can imagine George Taylor's surprise to learn that he had three grandchildren, Ellen aged seven years, Anne aged four years and a twelve-month-old boy named George in honour of himself.[31]

Richard's correspondence was now marked by a distinct change in tone. No longer did he desire to return to Lancashire, and indeed he advised his brothers and sisters 'to come as they could do a great deal better here than at home'. It was, his letter informed his father, 'a fine place for a Poor man and in fact for the rich as well as the Poor'. His own sense of social elevation was suggested by his remark that the coming railway would ensure 'plenty of work for the Poorer Class, that is the labouring classes', amongst whom he evidently no longer placed himself.[32] Richard characterised New South Wales as 'the land of plenty a perpetual summer the trees never throw their leaves and are green all the year round and the farmers have sometimes three crops in one year'. As if sensing this vision might appear too good to be true, he concluded with, 'Brothers and Sisters believe us'.[33]

Fourteen years after his departure, a letter from Simon finally reached his uncle. The letter carried the news that Simon had 'no intentions of ever going home as I am married and doing well here much better than I could do in England'.[34] Simon had married Margaret Martin on 23 October 1854.[35] Margaret, a former factory girl, had arrived in the colony in 1852, aged twenty. She had been transported for stealing a watch from a man—probably a client, as her record notes that she had been '9 months on the Town', a euphemism for prostitution.[36] Margaret had been tried in Liverpool, and gave Lancashire as her native place and it may have been this local connection that first drew her and Simon together. No mention was made in his letter, however, of a prior marriage to Mary Ann Smith, on 4 March 1850.[37] Simon did relate that he had been 'all over Melbourne and Victoria and Geelong', but had heard nothing of his brother Richard.[38] Shipping records reveal that Simon had indeed sailed for the mainland on 21 February 1852, on board the *Gem*; possibly after the death of his first wife.[39]

In a fuller letter in 1856, Simon told his father that he had been 'all over Port Phillip side when I was in my wild rambling state'.[40] Simon's years on the mainland had coincided with the gold discoveries. At the diggings he claimed to have done well. He was now back in Van Diemen's Land, working as overseer to Edward Bisdee at Lovely Banks. Bisdee had employed him the past eleven years, and had kept him in his service after he gained his freedom. It was his intention, he revealed, to save and establish his own business as a fellmonger. The letter also demonstrated, that while cut off by transportation from 'home' in the wider sense of England, Simon nevertheless patriotically identified himself with Britain's trials in the Crimean War. Van Diemen's Land in general responded with zeal to this crisis, raising substantial funds. Simon noted with pride the contributions of his master and fellow workers.[41]

The first word that Simon received of Richard's whereabouts was delivered in a letter dated March 1856 from Isabella Risley, wife of Camden publican William Risley. The letter bore the news that Richard had died on 7 January 1855, leaving a widow and two children, a girl and a boy.[42] Simon duly forwarded the letter to his father.[43] Neither of the children were named, but the ages are given, and it appears that earlier misery had visited the family in the death of Anne, the second child. Expenditures on the funerals and headstones exhausted the Narellan Taylors' capital. Julia was reduced to selling provisions from a horse and cart. Her welfare was a theme in many of the later letters, although Simon ultimately concluded pragmatically, 'I wrote to my brother Richard's widow about four months ago but never got an answer from her so I expect that she has got married again and thinks no more about Richard's relations'.[44]

Just as Richard had done earlier, Simon wrote encouraging other family members to migrate to Australia. He encouraged his brother Thomas to come out to join him in the leather business, and sent him a parcel of kangaroo skins by the *Aurora Australis*.[45] Of his own situation he related, 'we are doing very well we do not know any hardships or what it is to want we have plenty to eat and drink and a house to live in rent free and plenty of wood and water gratis, no taxes or poor rates'.[46] Simon's admission that he had narrowly missed a situation in New Zealand owing to his being 'no scholar', further testified to the many opportunities awaiting those who would join him. The position was almost certainly as overseer on a sheep farm, given Simon's experience and the nature of the New Zealand economy in this period.[47] A number of gifts sent back to his family also spoke of his success, not least the ring of Port Phillip gold he sent to his sister Betty.[48] Such a gift was a clear signal of his position, and indeed of the value he continued to attach to his far-away kin. In return Simon received 'cards', the precise nature of which is uncertain. These assumed pride of place in the family home. He had a walnut frame made by a cabinet maker for the 'card' sent by his uncle.[49] When Simon and his wife received further 'cards' from his family in 1858 he noted, 'my Wife is very proud of them as a keepsake for when we look at them we shall think of you all'.[50] While such technologies were in their infancy, it seems plausible that these were in fact small photographs, again an expensive but potent reminder of family connections.[51]

Simon Brown's final surviving letter is dated 9 March 1859. Addressed from Hobart, it reveals that he and his wife had quit Lovely Banks and were about to embark on the *Tasmanian* steamship bound for Sydney.[52] The purpose of the trip was to carry out George Brown's instructions with regard to Richard's property in New South Wales. Pragmatically, Simon instructed his family not to write until he had established a contact address. As no further letters survive, Simon's narrative abruptly ends at this point.

The letters of Richard Taylor and Simon Brown are not unknown to historians. Both A.W. Baker and Robert Hughes used excerpts to illustrate their work.[53] Like other historians, however, they mined Richard and Simon's correspondence for illustrative choice pickings rather than exploring their wider nature and context.[54] Richard Taylor and Simon Brown should not be represented as writing for that essentialisation 'the convict', by proxy; their experiences cannot speak for all, but their letters, thirty-eight in all, can be read as narratives of two particular convict lives. Moreover, there is a comparative historiography which can be used to aid this task. An extensive scholarly literature exists that explores letters of free migrants, both to Australia and other areas of colonisation. While convicts are only a marginal presence in such works, they provide useful insights in the approach to the study of convict letters.[55]

This literature is of particular use in exploring the many changes in writing style characteristic of Richard and Simon's correspondence. Before their transportation both men resorted to rather hackneyed tropes to account for their situation. A letter from Richard on 14 April 1840 carried the lines, 'I wish I had taken your Advice I should not [have] been placed in this unhappy Situation but I hope god has done it for [the] best If I had kept fewer bad Company I should not have been placed in this unhappy situation'.[56] Drink was a further element in his fall into crime; Richard wrote, 'I hope this whill be a warning for all my Brothers and I hope they whill keep good company and I hope my brother Thomas whill keep Tetottle'.[57] Simon displayed a similar turn of mind, writing in May 1841, 'I will make Ammends for all my last bad conduct . . . it is praps for the Best as I now feel the effects of keeping Bad Company and I think it will be the means of making a good man of me'.[58] The emphasis on the dangers of bad company and alcohol mirrors the treatment of these themes in conventional criminal biography, fictional and non-fictional.[59]

That Richard and Simon should represent themselves in this manner can be attributed to a number of influences. While not as fully formed or finished, letters can be read as a form of autobiography in progress. Each letter offers a partial account of the life—psychologically as well as eventful—in progress, and must within that frame enforce some coherence and selection of events. That the writer should take recourse to such models through which to understand his or her situation need not diminish the writer's credibility; rather, such forms were appropriate because they had cultural meaning for both writer and reader.[60]

Religious language is a feature throughout the correspondence. Richard assured his father that 'the Prayers of a sincere heart are as acceptable to God from the dreary Prison as from the splendid Palace. What a blessing that assurance is to a poor unfortunate mortal in my hopeless situation'.[61] Further, he wrote, 'all things in this probationary world are but Vanity, and pass away as if they had never been—but Religion, my dear Father, is a continual source not only of happiness in this world, but it prepares us for an inheritance . . . in the everlasting Kingdom of God.'[62] Simon equally placed his fate in God's hands; 'With the blessing of god I hope I shall live to see you again if it please god to spare us both to live till my time is up and if not I hope whe shall meet in heaven'.[63] A religious tone also characterises sections of letters from Australia. From Sydney in 1845 Richard wrote urging his brothers and sisters in England to 'be careful how you carry yourselves through this transitory life fear God and attend Divine worship, keep good Company and take particular care of your poor Father, and nourish him in his old days then God will reward you'.[64]

There can be little doubt that these passages are standard lines inserted by professional letter writers. Baker is surely wrong to argue, however, that the amanuensis had fully obscured the sentiments of Richard Taylor and Simon

Brown.[65] Presumably Simon and Richard approved of passages selected by the letter writers they employed. It is not beyond the bounds of belief that they chose particular passages from the writer's repertoire of standard phrases. That they repeated the trick, purchasing other letters which included such formulaic passages, reinforces the point. Taken as a whole, a consistency is evident in their correspondence which denies the dismissive and reductionist argument advanced by Baker, for to adopt the approach that the sentiments expressed in the letters were purely the imposition of unknown scribes is to miss the wider point. In the culture in which Simon and Richard were brought up, fear and grief were areas of experience that were not commonly verbalised, nor written. Lacking an adequate personal vocabulary to discuss such emotions, the brothers resorted to phrases from contemporary religious discourse.[66] In itself this does not deny the genuine religious feeling of the two men, nor the importance of religion in their coming to terms with transportation. Indeed, their background in the industrial north-west of England may have exposed them to a popular culture heavily influenced by religion. Methodist faith was strong in the growing industrial towns, and its memberships predominantly working class. Lancashire and Yorkshire were notable areas of large-scale Methodist worship in the mid-nineteenth century.[67] The emphasis placed in their writing by both brothers on the next world as an ultimate reward for hardships and separation endured in this one accorded with Methodist beliefs. Whilst confined at York Castle gaol Richard wrote that he attended Chapel every day. From the *Fortitude* at Chatham he mentioned attendance at Chapel every Sunday and Thursday and that he was 'glad that we have such a privilege'; from 1812 each hulk had a Chaplain, and religious service was held in the evening following work.[68] Richard's religious observance while imprisoned may further have promoted his understanding of his circumstances though a religious framework.

Similar processes can be detected in the letters written from Australia. Both Richard and Simon portray a positive image of the Australian colonies, and the prospects for other family members who might join them. Richard's early letters from New South Wales are obviously full of generic descriptions of the colony which, like the religious passages, have all the hallmarks of the work of a paid letter-writer. The letters lack the idiosyncratic spelling of earlier examples, and phrases such as 'It is expected that very shortly something very handsome will be done for the unfortunate prisoners next year the Colony will have a House of Assembly of its own & then it will be impossible to keep Englishmen in slavery' do not sit easily alongside the style of earlier letters. [69]

By contrast, neither of the brothers has much to say about their experiences as convicts. Although Richard wrote while still under sentence, he reported nothing of the boredom, loneliness or punishment which he must have experienced and or witnessed. Simon's conduct register reveals that he was sentenced to both solitary confinement and hard labour in Van Diemen's Land. Yet, when he reopened the correspondence with his family in Britain, he was silent on both matters. It is possible that while under sentence Simon did not have access to sufficient cash to hire a letter writer, or a fixed address to ensure the safe receipt of precious replies from home. His subsequent silence about his colonial experiences suggests, however, he thought matters which would further grieve his relations were best passed over.[70] Silences in this regard are not incidental, but reflect a shaping of their accounts that mirrors those in free emigrants' letters. Migrants' letters commonly sought to persuade other family members to migrate and in a great many cases were then shaped by a desire to portray migration as a success. Consequently, failures and hardships were usually marginalised, if not excluded.[71] It is significant that the letters of Simon Brown and Richard Taylor represent their experiences in this manner; this would tend to question the division assumed between convict and free migrants.[72] More generally this approach suggests ways of understanding the positive representation of the penal colonies in convicts' letters. Perhaps ironically, such accounts caused concern in Britain where it was believed that they undermined the deterrent effect of transportation.[73]

The most important theme to emerge from the brothers' correspondence is the importance invested in writing to sustain family contacts. This is a particularly constant theme in the letters written prior to transportation. Richard assured his father that 'I will never miss an opportunity of writing to you, to inform you how I am going on, in whatever part of the world my lot may be cast'.[74] Simon equally wrote, 'dear father I hope you will not neglect writing to me at every opportunity As I do ashore you it is a great Pleasure to hear from you and as it will be the only means of keeping our respect for wone another'. In this letter Simon also referred to the practical problems of writing, requesting a sheet of blank paper be enclosed with his father's reply.[75] Studies of the letters of free migrants have shown a similar value attached to correspondence.[76] Letter writing was an essential means of maintaining the connection with home and family. Brothers, sisters, and uncles feature in the letters, not only nominally, but in such terms as to show a continued knowledge and interest in their affairs. In connecting prisoners to their life prior and exterior to their transportation, such letters also played an important role in sustaining links with an identity that transcended their convict status. The importance of these attachments has been emphasised in studies of convict love tokens and tattooing.[77] Letters can be considered alongside tattoos and love tokens as artifacts that embodied the connection, and could become the focus for the imaginative engagement with that past; a letter was more than its contents, it was also a physical tie.[78] In this respect the letters differed little from the pictures that Simon and Margaret had framed and placed on their mantlepiece.

> number to 7 [arranged as before with one dot in the centre]—but again from a similar cause reduced them to five . . . some of them also wore the impression of a moon & star the mean^{gs} of which is not accurately known except that one of [these meanings] is understood to be a connection with a profligate female companion. When a member is admitted he is presented with a badge of brotherhood which is a medal with the words engraved 'When this you see, remember me, & bear me in y^{r} mind, Let all the world say what they will, don't prove to me unkind'. Some of them have these words pricked upon their arms.[2]

There is a scattering of late Georgian and Victorian reports which lend credence to Martin's observations. These anticipate the wave of late nineteenth-century European medico-legal opinion which linked tattooing with criminal behaviour.[3] The *Hobart Town Gazette* printed a piece in June 1825 under the banner 'Bow Street–Highwaymen'. It reported that two suspicious characters had recently been arrested outside the opera house in Covent Garden. Recognised as reputed thieves they were taken into custody by a constable and searched. As the paper reported, the officer found upon 'John Starkey what must certainly be regarded as strongly indicative of his belonging to a certain profession. This was a copper medal, upon one side of which was very neatly and accurately engraved, a brace of pistols, a crow-bar, a picklock, and two skeleton keys, a dark lantern, phosphorous box and matches'. On the other side appeared the verse:

> When this you see,
> Remember me,
> When I am far away.

With approval the paper reported that when the case was brought to the magistrate he declared that 'in the whole course of his experience he had never met with a stronger proof of determined vice and profligacy as this. There could be no doubt that the prisoner regarded thieving as a regular trade and that he gloried in it.'

The 'First Report of the Inspector of Prisons' in 1836 had published evidence that prisoners in Newgate were in the habit of converting coins into 'love tokens' or 'leaden hearts' to give to their friends as memorials. Commenting on the practice later in the century Sir Arthur Griffiths thought that the criminal classes attached great value to these love tokens which they wore round their necks like amulets to protect them from future arrest and imprisonment. In the 1860s Henry Mayhew reported a conversation with the warder of Millbank penitentiary who informed him that 'many of the regular thieves have five dots between their thumb and forefinger, as a sign that they

George III cartwheel penny, 1797 (front and back), the raw material of a love token.

belong to "the forty thieves"'. The same warden also ventured that thieves were more commonly tattooed than law-abiding citizens.[4]

Martin's comments thus reflect a wider view which associated the manufacture of convict love tokens and the acquisition of tattoos with the badges of secret criminal fraternities. How much importance should we attach to these reports? Knowledge of the story of the Forty Thieves was certainly not out of the reach of nineteenth-century working-class Britons. When Roderick Ross and David Young broke into a house in Tain, Scotland, for example, they removed a number of articles including a 'volume of the Arabian Nights entertainment'.[5] There is also ample evidence that many convicts arrived in Van Diemen's Land with their skin punctured with Martin's secret system of dots. Sleuthing in the leather-bound description registers of the convict department provides examples, although these are not as common as may be expected. A survey of 6000 male convicts arriving on selected transports in the period 1817 to 1853 produced seventy-seven instances of convicts tattooed with patterns of dots between the fingers and thumb. As Martin correctly ascertained, these prisoners were on the whole young—their mean age was less than nineteen compared to twenty-six for male convicts generally. At least one of these prisoners, however, appears to have been responsible for the production of love tokens. Fifteen-year-old William Mollet arrived in Hobart on the spectacularly named transport *Prestonjee Bomanjee* in December 1845. He had been convicted in Norwich City Assizes for stealing tea and sentenced to seven years' transportation.[6] On arrival in Van Diemen's Land he was described as bearing '5 dots on left wrist 5 dots on back of left hand 8 dots between forefinger and thumb left hand'.[7] There are two tokens recorded in British collections which bear the text 'W Mollet Aged 13 Transported 7 Year 1843—For Get Me Not'.[8] Matching dates, age, sentence and name makes it almost certain that the tattooed William Mollet was also responsible for the manufacture of the two tokens.

Was Mollet a member of 'The Society of Forty Thieves'? He confessed that he had been arrested before. He had served one month for stealing a cap and three days for theft of bacon. He had also been twice arrested and discharged, once for suspicion of stealing trousers and once for money.[9] Hereafter, however, holes appear in Martin's analysis. If the two tokens which Mollet left behind in Britain were intended as badges of criminal identity, why do they refer to his arrest, conviction and impending transportation? Surely the chronology is wrong. These tokens must have been engraved after conviction, not while Mollet was roaming the streets of Norwich. As such it seems unlikely that they were badges of allegiance to an as yet unknown East Anglian juvenile criminal organisation. There are other problems. Mollet was asked to provide his trade on at least two occasions. His replies 'Tailor imperfect' and 'Tailor 3 years' suggest that he was serving an apprenticeship—

This love token (front and back) by Thomas Tilley, who was transported on the First Fleet, is illustrated with a chained bird.

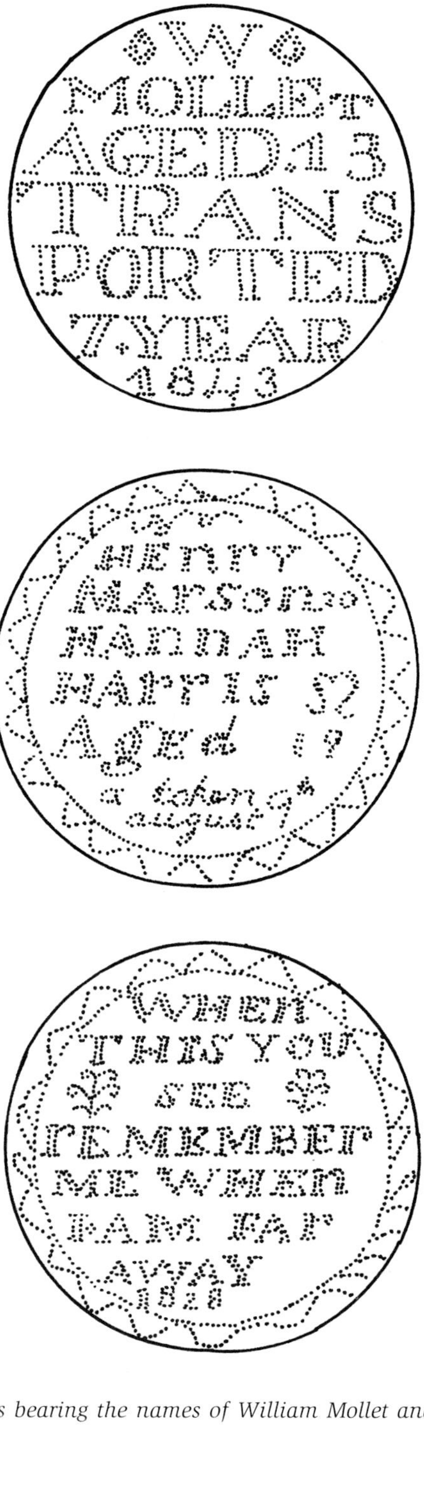

Sketches of love tokens bearing the names of William Mollet and Henry Marson, by Simon Barnard.

commonly worked in gangs employed on dock improvement schemes, and loading and unloading warships. This provided opportunities to earn cash incentives. These sums were kept by the hulk officials and handed over to the care of the surgeon on departing transports. Reference to the documentation which accompanied the *Georgina* to Hobart reveals that Marson had accumulated eight shillings, but that two had been deducted 'for letters etc'. Similar sums were deducted from the earnings of another forty-six convicts transferred from the *Retribution* to the *Georgina*.[28] This brief glimpse into the world of the hulks suggests that many prisoners sent letters in the days before they were transported (see also 'Wherever I go I whill right to you' in this volume). It is even possible that some contained objects of affection; locks of hair and possibly even tokens of love fashioned out of customised coins.

Such activities were not restricted to prisoners. Love tokens and other mementoes were commonly bestowed by members of all social classes in the late Georgian and Victorian eras. While convicts fashioned precious objects of memory from copper coins, the wealthy commissioned professionally engraved silver tokens or earrings and brooches woven out of human hair.[29] Indeed, the verse which Martin identified as a criminal badge was commonly reproduced on everyday nineteenth-century objects manufactured to supply the burgeoning trade in souvenirs. Glass rolling pins and jugs were embellished with variants of the 'when this you see' verse.[30] Other verses inscribed on convict love tokens or pecked out on arms and chests also appear on objects of popular consumption suggesting everyday preoccupations, rather than membership of a criminal fraternity. Thus, for example, transported seaman John Popjoy was tattooed with the verse:

> From rocks and sands
> And barren lands
> Kind fortune set me free
> And from roaring guns and women's tongues
> Good Lord deliver me

As it turns out this is a verse inscribed on lustreware punch bowls manufactured for sale in the British Isles.[31]

Perhaps not surprisingly, such gifts were particularly popular amongst soldiers and sailors. Before Private Henry Watts of the 4th or King's Own Regiment embarked for New South Wales, he ordered a postcard-sized portrait of himself in full dress uniform embellished with the verse:

> Dear Parents
> When this you see remember me,
> And bear me in your mind
> When I am in a Foreign Clime[32]

Lustreware jug c. *1820 and mug* c. *1796 bearing the verse 'When this you see' and the Sailor's Return.*

The *lingua franca* of convicts was also the *lingua franca* of their guards. It is possible that amongst the thirty-nine rank-and-file of the 14th and 17th Regiments who served as a guard on the *Elizabeth* transport were men who had left promises of reunion behind that were similar to those manufactured by prisoners. The same could be said of the thirty-six sailors.[33] The guards on convict transports were on the outward-bound leg of a tour of duty in Australia and India which could last as long as fourteen years. Many would never see their families again.[34] Ocean voyages were notoriously dangerous and death from disease or accident was a constant threat for deep-sea mariners. No wonder that convicts, sailors and soldiers resorted to similar strategies in order to ward against the slings of outrageous fortune. The point is illustrated by one of the few convict descriptions of on-board tattooing: 'One dark, rough, but not unpleasant-looking man, John Hill by name, a Cornish sailor, worked all and every day with his needle, and earned from the crew plenty of tobacco and other necessaries'.[35] Note that Hill, a convict, secured a stream of little luxuries by tattooing the crew. He no doubt worked on his fellow convicts as well, although this is likely to have proved less lucrative.

While the texts pecked out on convict love tokens, chests, and arms are short, these inscriptions are not short of meaning. The objects on which Henry Marson chose to record his love for Hannah form part of a wider narrative. A coin was not just a precious object, but was also stamped with the King's head. Henry and Hannah were separated by the sentence imposed by the state—he wrought his own private revenge by removing Britannia and George III so that he could record his promise to Hannah. The symbolism of the act may well have been heightened by knowledge that defacing the coin of the realm was a criminal offence.[36] A similar argument can be applied to the tattoo Marson had inked into his skin. Marson had not only been incarcerated by the state, but through the mechanism of a sentence the state had also expropriated his body. He was now an object of administration, stripped of identity, clad in slop clothing and provided with a number. Soon he would be ordered to labour for the public good, in his case in the gang at Bridgewater constructing a causeway over the Derwent River. But just as he had converted the coin to his own purpose, Henry Marson reappropriated himself, inscribing his arm with an intention to be reunited with a nineteen-year-old girl he had left behind in Birmingham.

Convict bodies occupy an uneasy and contested space at the heart of the transportation process—expropriated by the state but self-evidently owned by the individual.[37] In the museum at Port Arthur there is a poster which records this tension between object and individuality. This huge list is an inventory of missing prisoners: rank upon rank of descriptions, ordered by name and number and assembled in trim columns in a manner of which Dr Martin would have surely approved. Amongst the hundreds of descriptions is one for Henry Marson—he had absconded from the Bridgewater chain gang eight years earlier. There is a certain irony in this. Public works gangs were organised into units of forty under the charge of an overseer. Forty thieves ranked up in a line and then—'hey presto'—there were thirty-nine. Marson had stolen himself, complete with tattooed memorial to Hannah Harris, and slipped beyond the gaze of the state with its attendant surgeon superintendents and missionary auxiliaries. Presumably his intention was to work a passage back to Birmingham in order to reassemble the fragments of his scattered trans-global narrative. As Henry Marson, and thousands of other transported convicts knew, few words are needed to tell a universal story—a message which was succinctly summed up in another verse commonly inscribed on convict love tokens—'The Gift is Small—But Love is All'.

13

Alexander and the mother of invention

James Bradley and Hamish Maxwell-Stewart

The sins of the mothers

On 9 August 1852, Alexander Anderson embarked upon the convict ship *Lady Montagu* bound for Hobart. His journey had begun five years earlier with a sentence at the Perth Spring Assizes to transportation for seven years. As a 'Pentonvillian', Anderson had been sent first to a British prison to serve the majority of his sentence before being sent into exile. His trip to Van Diemen's Land was uneventful and the *Lady Montagu* made the roads south of Hobart 122 days after departing from the Thames.[1] Shortly after docking Alexander, like all other convicts, was brought forward, questioned, measured and described. His entry in the conduct register is a testament to this process. He was named Alexander Anderson or Syme or Simms (the latter two being variations of his mother's maiden name). He had been born in Aberdeen, was twenty-two years of age and a bricklayer by trade. He was able to read and write, and stated that he was convicted for stealing 'a gun and two swords'. His behaviour in prison had been 'latterly good'. Physically he was five feet six-and-a-half inches tall, and between his finger and thumb he sported a 'rather indistinct' personal mark—'anchor star, Oh my mother'.[2]

'Oh my mother'—one might expect to stumble across these melodramatic words not upon the body of a transported exile but in the pages of a nineteenth-century convict narrative, for the wayward son who disappoints his saintly mother is a standard trope of mid-nineteenth-century convict autobiography.[3] In James Connor's words, as the transport put out to sea 'the sad sound of my mother's "Dear Jamie, Jamie," died on my ear'.[4] Equally common variants suggest, however, that early separation from the parental bosom, pure neglect, and mistreatment by the mother were all factors that triggered the narrator's descent into crime. In Daniel's narrative his clergyman father died when he was young and his mother, unable to support him, despatched him to school in Northamptonshire.[5] George Palmer claimed he was sent to boarding school following the death of his mother.[6] James Porter was separated from his mother at an early age to be brought up by his grandmother.[7] John Frederick Mortlock was neglected by his mother, 'who had deprived herself of the power of rendering service to any belonging to her'.[8] Jones contrasts the fond memory he has of his real parents with the maltreatment suffered at the hands of his surrogate mother—his aunt.[9] 'Jack Bushman's' testimony is more poignant still: his mother sows the seeds of his destruction by neglecting his 'moral or religious training'.[10] Does Anderson's tattoo, with its convict narrative echoes, belong to the same tradition? A reconstruction of his story suggests it might.

Alexander's story

Although born in Aberdeen, Alexander was living in Dundee at the time of his arrest. During his youth the city was in the throes of rapid industrialisation with all that that entailed—over-population, mass immigration, dirt, disease and poverty. Indeed, the Dundee of the mid-century could almost have been created in the likeness of Dickens's grimy Coketown or Engels's Manchester.[11] Dundee's expansion had resulted from the growth of the flax industry, itself catalysed by steam power. There were those who were sanguine about the future of Dundee and its inhabitants. According to the *New Statistical Account*, the city was characterised by a 'buoyant spirit of intelligence, enterprise, assiduous labour, and successful speculation'.[12] Others were rarely so kind. In 1841 the Reverend George Lewis reported that, on a recent visit to English industrial towns like Birmingham and Manchester, he had 'looked in vain for the evidence of a deeper physical degradation than I meet daily in Dundee'.[13] 'Bonnie Dundee', commented a sardonic Reverend Samuel Green some years later, 'is not exactly the epithet one would choose'.[14]

As the city grew, so too its vices. To cope with spiralling crime the law inflated its puny apparatus: a police department was created in 1824; a new purpose-built bridewell opened for business in 1837; and, following the committal of over one hundred children to the bridewell in the mid-1840s, an industrial school was also established.[15] Alexander, it seems, never made it to the reformatory school, graduating straight to the bridewell to which he was sentenced to a ten-day stint for theft in May 1846. He returned in January 1847 to serve fifteen days for stealing a brass bracket.[16] He appears, however, to have been undeterred by short-term imprisonment. It was a minor inconvenience—an occupational hazard—that interrupted his acquisitive efforts. Indeed, if anything, he became more ambitious.[17] Between December 1846 and March 1847 Alexander engaged in a series of ventures that were to land him on the other side of the world. In all, he was tried on several counts of theft, breaking and entering, and stealing from lockfast places. While he was not the only person arrested and tried, he was the thread that, at least in the eyes of the police, bound a string of accomplices together in a common enterprise.

At the time, Alexander lived with his mother, Elizabeth Sime or Anderson, in Shepherd's Close, the Overgate, Dundee. In the detailed case compiled by the police, Mr Anderson is conspicuous by his absence and Alexander appears to have been raised by his mother. The other protagonists were five young boys: the brothers William and Peter Ritchie; James McDonald *alias* Wilson; and William Small. Between them Alexander and his young friends were accused of stealing a variety of objects. The first items to disappear were three cut-glass decanters from outside the shop of J. & W. Smith, Stoneware Merchants. These were probably cheap mould-blown decanters, cut in imitation of the top end of the trade.[18] The second theft occurred on the morning of Tuesday, 23 February 1847. William Ritchie, McDonald and Alexander broke into a garret at Thorter Row belonging to James Jack, Surveyor of Taxes. McDonald knew the area well since he used to come round the garrets 'with a couple of other lads' who kept pigeons in the vicinity. The boys forced open two trunks taking several petticoats, the property of Jack's live-in servant, and a book, *The Young Man's Best Companion*. Several books bearing this title were published in the nineteenth century, but in all probability this was the volume printed in Edinburgh in the early 1840s, *The Young Man's Best Companion: being A Regular System of Education, Without the Aid of a Tutor*. This work contained chapters on: the English language and grammar, reading and speaking; writing; arithmetic; algebra; logarithms; and much more besides including an extensive section on geography (although this lacked an entry on Australia). The chief objects of their attention, however, and the real prizes, were a rifle and three swords. If McDonald is to be believed, these items had a ready market at his workplace, a mill. A number of the hands were saving up to buy kilts and weaponry, possibly to engage in some form of Highland pageantry. The final scene of the mini crime-wave was enacted at David Johnston's shop on Barrack Street. On a night in early March, Peter Ritchie and Alexander forced open the shutter with an iron pinch while William Small kept watch. Three-quarters of an hour later the burglars emerged, each carrying an armful of footwear.

Obtaining the stolen property was one thing, disposing of it quite another. In their attempts to convert their ill-gotten gains into cash, the boys dragged a whole cast of peripheral characters into the tangled web of intrigue. David Angus, who 'wrought' at the same mill as William Ritchie, was recruited to pawn the rifle. McDonald used a friend, apprentice blacksmith Alexander Addison, to take the rust off one of the swords (presumably to increase its sale value). Small, who had been given three pairs of boots as payment for his part in the raid on the shoemaker's, disposed of his cut though Mrs

Morren, a fish-wife. Morren, like many of the other witnesses who were subsequently called to give evidence, gave no indication that she knew the property was stolen. Given the previous conviction of Small in July 1846 for housebreaking and stealing twenty-seven pieces of salt fish, some potatoes, and a small quantity of hair and wool, it might seem surprising that she was so unquestioning.[19] But then, she was hardly likely to admit to the crime of reset. Morren is just one example of the seemingly wide network of reset, only partially revealed in this case.

The bulk of the stolen property, however, was entrusted to Alexander's mother, Elizabeth Syme. She pawned the petticoats and other clothes with ease—belonging to Jack's servant, these were items of working-class consumption and, as such, raised little suspicion. Each boy paid her ninepence for her services. According to Ritchie, the remaining money was spent on a trip to the theatre where the boys feasted on 'pyes, tarts, ginger beer &c'. Turning the other objects of ill-gotten gain into currency proved more difficult. The pawnbroker's office would not take the gun. When Elizabeth attempted to pledge the decanters the clerk remarked 'they were not like her'. She told him they were a present from a sailor, but she was forced to leave the glass behind the counter while she vainly attempted to find witnesses to corroborate her story. She approached Rebecca George or Taylor, a neighbour, and asked if her brother, the sailor David George, would go to the office and claim he had brought the decanters from Newcastle (a famous centre of glass production). Rebecca refused this request, but suggested Elizabeth ask David in person. He was, however, wary and rebutted Elizabeth despite her heartfelt lamentations that not only were the decanters a genuine present but she also needed money to buy shoes for Alexander.

The quality footwear, however, proved Elizabeth's undoing. Robert Robertson, the manager of the Caledonian Loan Company, noticed that, although the soles had been rubbed in mud, they were new and had never been worn. Elizabeth doggedly argued they were her own: they had been made by a shoemaker who had subsequently moved to Monifieth (a small town some five miles from the city), and she had worn them about a dozen times. She was told that before the boots could be pledged she would have to produce the shoemaker in person. Robertson was convinced they were stolen and he sent George Thomson, one of his clerks, to follow Elizabeth and have her apprehended by the police. And so Elizabeth was arrested by David Grant of the Dundee Police Establishment's day patrol. The case did not take long to wrap up. Finlay Forbes, criminal officer, accompanied by James Smith, went to the Anderson abode, broke the door open and found much property connected with Jack's garret and Johnston's shop. Furthermore, they discovered pawn tickets for the stolen petticoats. Finally, they removed a hammer and chisel, likely candidates for the instruments used to jemmy Johnston's shop.

In the course of their inquiries it proved all too easy to connect Elizabeth to her son and the other boys. All were arrested and remitted to the Procurator Fiscal upon two charges of theft.[20] Later the police were to unpick the thread that bound the Andersons to the decanters.

On the day he was charged, Alexander appeared in front of John Irving Henderson, the Sheriff Substitute for Forfarshire. The transcript of the interview suggests it was a short encounter: 'being judicially admonished and examined . . . [and] being shown a Gun. Declares that he never saw it before, and declines to answer any further question'. Henderson met with the same response from McDonald. William Small and Anderson's mother were, however, altogether more forthcoming. Small admitted to his involvement in burgling the shoemaker's shop and his confession was corroborated by the Ritchie brothers, who themselves were charged but not tried. Elizabeth, however, was instrumental in the conviction of her son and McDonald. On the day of her arrest, she told the police that many of the items found in her house had been brought by 'her son and the laddie Ritchie & another boy'. She identified 'the other boy' as McDonald. Using the time-honoured excuse that the boys told her they had found the articles but she did not believe them, she nevertheless agreed to act as the conduit for the goods' reset. At later interviews, on 17 March and 8 April, she denied any knowledge of the crystal decanters and the shoes. The damage, however, had been done. At the ensuing trial Small was recommended to the leniency of the Court, 'but the case of the female prisoner (the mother of Anderson) was declared to be particularly aggravated'. McDonald and Small were sentenced to eighteen months' imprisonment, Alexander and his mother to seven years' transportation—'Oh my mother'.[21]

Alexander was duly sent to a convict prison for four and a half years and then forwarded to Van Diemen's Land where he was awarded a pardon in 1854.[22] Shortly afterwards he applied for permission to marry Janet Miller, a prisoner from Falkirk in Scotland who already had a small child named John.[23] The marriage certificate reveals that he again used the surname Anderson.[24] After his marriage, Alexander disappears from view. If the church registers are to be believed, he and Janet had no children of their own. Neither are there any recorded deaths in Tasmania for a Janet Miller or Anderson, or a John Miller or Anderson. A search of departure indexes for the colony proved equally unproductive.

Nine years later in May 1864 Elizabeth Drinkwater tried to cash a cheque for £7 at the Railway Hotel in Deloraine, Tasmania. The owner, Edward Spencer, realised that the cheque was made out to James Jordon of Longford and 'not liking the quarter from which the cheque came' (Drinkwater kept a local 'house of ill fame'), asked to see the man who had given it to her.[25] He was duly introduced to 'Scotty'. Scotty claimed he had received the cheque from Jordon *in lieu* of wages. Spencer relented and handed over a £1 note, a half-sovereign, and a bottle of grog, promising to pay the rest in the morning. He was probably unsurprised when neither Scotty nor Drinkwater returned to collect the additional £5. Predictably the cheque was stopped by the bank.[26] When it was shown to James Jordon he said he had received it from Richard Hood of Trafalgar, near Evandale, as payment for 'the servicing of a horse'. Although he had put the cheque in his breast pocket, Jordon had been unable to find it upon returning home. A warrant was issued for 'Scotty's' arrest. The suspect was described as about five feet six or seven inches tall, aged thirty to thirty-five years with dark brown hair and whiskers 'worn around the chin'. He was dressed in a black billy cock hat, grey tweed jumper and moleskin trousers.[27]

It took nearly two years to apprehend the elusive man with the Scottish accent.[28] When finally recognised by Detectives Lanham and White and brought in for questioning his true identity was revealed as Alexander Sims, aged thirty-five and imperfectly educated. The charge book also noted that a silver watch and guard were found on his person that were clearly not like him. Sims was remanded in custody for a week and later committed for trial for stealing a cheque from James Jordon.[29]

Although there was no material evidence to link him to the theft, it transpired in the Supreme Court that he had been working for Hood at the time of the cheque's disappearance, and this was enough to mount a case against him. Despite his claims that he had received the cheque 'from a man whose name or whereabouts he knew not', it took the jury only half an hour to convict him.[30] He was duly sentenced to two years' imprisonment. When a record was made out in the register of the convict department it included the line—'F[ormer] G[overnment] S[ervice]/ May 1854 for previous history see A. Anderson'.[31] Alexander was shipped to Port Arthur penal station where, after a short stint in the gangs, he was made an attendant in the recently constructed asylum abutting the model prison.

Making Alexander Anderson

Throughout this account, the one person whose voice remains most elusive, who hardly speaks for himself at all, is Alexander. In the official transcript his voice is muted. When interrogated by the Dundee police he famously revealed little in contrast to his blabbing mother. When paraded before the Board of Health on arrival in Van Diemen's Land his recorded replies were laconic and sometimes inaccurate. He incorrectly recalled the name of his prosecutor, referring to him as 'Jackson' rather than Jack. Asked to state his offence, he replied stealing a 'gun and two Swords'.[32] As an admission of guilt, this was somewhat partial. He failed to inform the Hobart authorities of the decanters, or the incriminating shoes which had finally led to his downfall. Curiously he also failed to recall correctly the number of swords stolen in the raid on Jack's garret. Perhaps he thought the rusty weapon, with its lower reset value, did not really count. Perhaps the passing of the years had blunted his memory. Neither does Alexander provide an explanation for why he chose to express his feelings at his mother's betrayal in such a permanent manner. Nor will we know how his tattoo was received by others—whether it was noticed by fellow immigrants and served as the launching pad for a yarn about the nature of fate.

There can be little doubt, however, that Alexander's plaintive tattoo indicates a particular construction of the self that almost certainly underwent modification as time passed. It seems the original point of the tattoo was to script himself as the central and sinned against figure in a narrative not dissimilar from *Martin Cash*.[33] Our reconstruction of the crimes for which he paid with transportation indicates that he saw himself as a victim betrayed by a heartless mother. Whether semi-literate or not, Alexander would undoubtedly have had knowledge of narratives from this tradition. His sense of betrayal is reinforced by the terse replies he gave on arrival in Hobart. When asked to name his next of kin he answered 'Uncle James near Dundee'—omitting to mention his mother at all. It will also be remembered that he used the name Anderson, although his convict record notes that his proper name was 'Simms'.[34] At the time of his marriage he continued to insist that his name was Anderson. The breach with his mother appears to have been serious enough for Alexander to wish to disown all connection with Elizabeth Syme, with the exception, of course, of the tattooed memorial to her grand act of betrayal.

At some point between his marriage in 1855 and his arrest by detectives Lanham and White, Alexander had reverted to his mother's name, suggesting a softening in his earlier determination to disown her. This change may have been linked with estrangement from his wife and stepson, who are conspicuous by their absence in the reporting of the case. It might also have marked an attempt to escape his convict past—not that he was to remain free for long. Anderson, now an itinerant labourer who often travelled the road into Launceston, appears to have once more blown the proceeds of his ill-gotten gains on a night's entertainment. This time, however, he sought the company of a prostitute rather than pies, tarts, ginger beer and the pleasures of the theatre. Of course, while his attitude to his mother may have changed, his post-betrayal narrative remained fixed—etched into his skin between thumb and forefinger, a reminder of his former life and follies, a mark of how far he had come from Dundee, and, perhaps, a sign of reconciliation with his mother's memory.

The state too created an identity for Alexander, of which the tattoo was an important component. Throughout the nineteenth century senior law enforcement officers regarded registers of tattooed offenders as one of the most important tools in the fight against crime.[35] This view was reflected in popular literature. In *A Study in Scarlet*, Sherlock Holmes was able to identify an ex-marine partly on the basis of an anchor tattooed on his hand: 'Even across the street I could see a great blue anchor tattooed on the back of the fellow's hand. That smacked of the sea.'[36] It is possible that Alexander's tattoo played a similar role in his detection.

Anderson lived at a time when official identities were fluid. Outside of the poor law, the prison, or the armed forces, the state had little need to know its subjects; state records were, therefore, less developed. Names had variant spellings because they were more things you said than words you wrote. Someone like Anderson could chose between being Anderson, Sims or Syme, by dint of his mother, who in the traditional Scottish mode, was referred to by both her maiden name (Syme or Simms) and her married name, Anderson. Physically, Anderson would have changed from the time of his sentence at age fifteen, or thereabouts, to his arrival in Australia five years later and his subsequent re-conviction in 1866. He developed in other ways too: having been illiterate in 1847, he could read and write in 1852. But at whatever point 'Oh my mother' was etched onto his hand (and we might reasonably assume that due to its emotive nature, this occurred during the aftermath of arrest and conviction), he had created a permanent, if indistinct, sign of identification. To be Alexander Anderson/Syme/Simms/Sims, 'anchor, star, Oh my mother' had to be present between the finger and thumb of one of his hands (the state allowed potential impostors the luxury of guessing which hand). In short, his tattoo was more permanent than his name, serving as confirmation for the state that police number 5645, Alexander Simms or Syme, locally convicted and working as an attendant at the Port Arthur asylum, was the same as police number 26412, Alexander Anderson, per *Lady Montagu*. It is perhaps appropriate that someone who had contrived to etch their skin with a mark of identification should be employed as a cog in a Benthamite-inspired system of surveillance.

While for the state the blue stain which spelt out 'Oh my mother' had one fixed meaning, we have suggested that Alexander's relationship with his tattoo was more fluid. When placed against the official transcript, our story makes Alexander a very different being. Where the state record is flat, our alternative reading seeks to use Alexander's tattoo literally to get underneath the skin of the convict. In our attempts to invest his story with agency, however, we are quite clearly influenced by current thinking. The tattoo as a diary of life-events is a common contemporary trope, frequently referred to by commentators and contributors to bulletin boards.[37] Thus, for example,

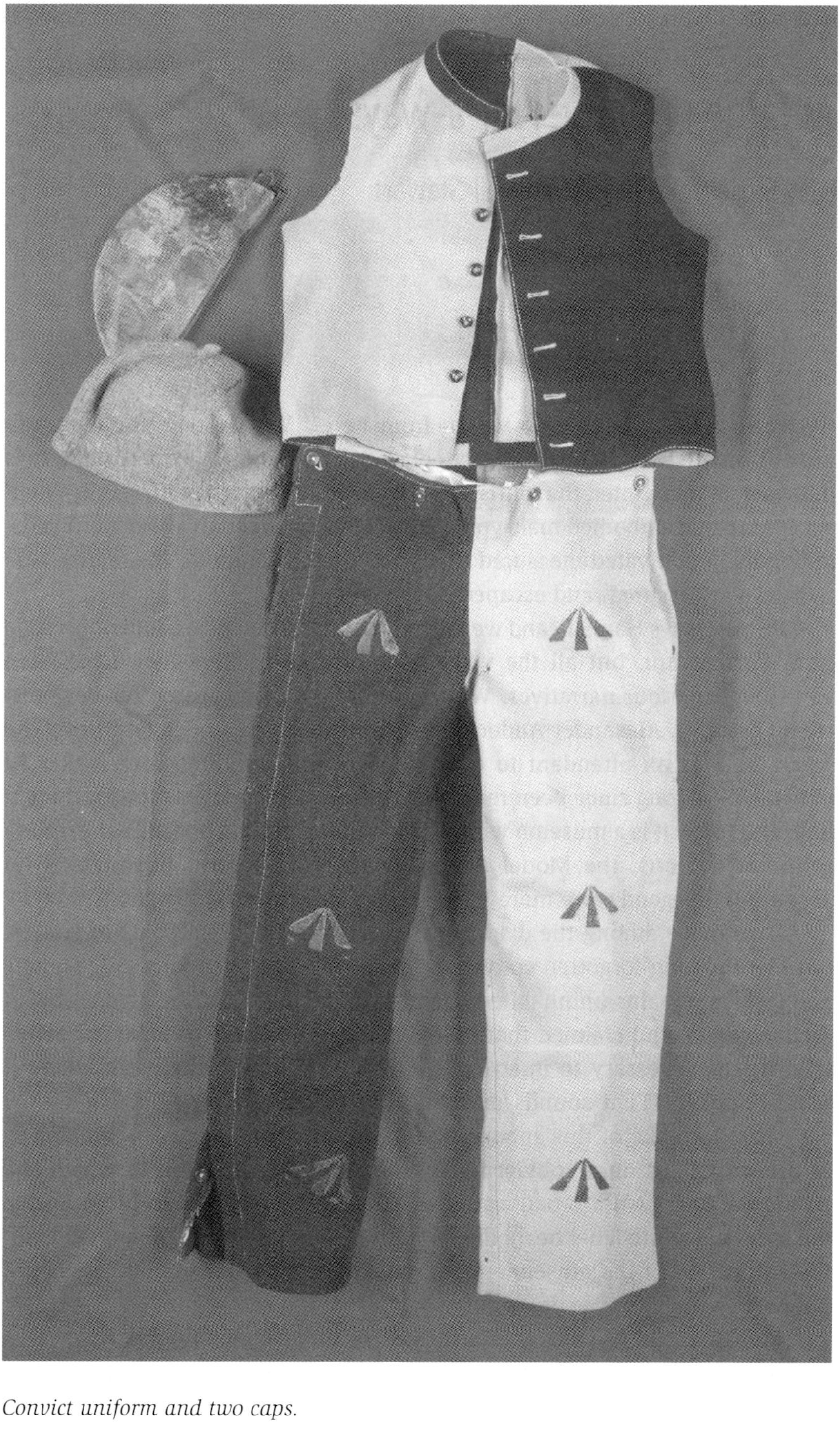

Convict uniform and two caps.

Hamish tries. '1264 could be the issue number. Each convict was given a spoon, and to keep track of every single government spoon, some clerk would record against the convict's number the number of his spoon. 33 may be a mess number. At large sites like Port Arthur convicts were routinely divided into messes of ten headed by a mess captain responsible for collecting the rations from the cookhouse and distributing them to those under his charge'.

'I'm impressed', says Lucy, 'it does make sense after all'.

'Partial sense', responds Hamish gloomily. 'We still don't have a clue about who ate from that spoon or even where. The spoon could have fed a member of a road gang from the Lovely Banks probation station, or a prisoner awaiting execution in the Hobart Town gaol. It may have nothing to do with Port Arthur'.

'Try something easier', suggests Lucy, pointing to a white metal disk inscribed with the number thirteen, and a label saying 'identity badge from the model prison'. 'This badge', says Hamish more confidently, 'hung on a hook outside cell thirteen. Each time a prisoner left his cell, he put on a hood and attached the disc to a tag on his uniform. Faceless and numbered, he marched out to walk in circles around the small exercise enclosure, or to stand locked into a chapel cubicle.[2] Number, not name, that was the idea. Become a new man by effacing the old. Number 13, unlucky indeed. And maybe untrue. This badge could be one of the theatrical ring-ins manufactured late in the nineteenth century as a prop for an ex-convict guide or gullible collector. All I'm prepared to claim for these dumb objects is that they signify an ideal, twisted though it may be. Encased behind glass and numbered, they proclaim the state as triumphant, riding the high mark uncontested in a way that we know it never could in practice'.[3]

'Ah', says Lucy, 'incarceration in perpetuity, giving a lie to what we know of the convict experience. Like death and taxes there is one thing inevitable about each convict's story—excarceration follows incarceration.[4] Every closed cell door will be reopened, whether by pardon, or by counting out the days, or by escape or execution. Ultimately, the prisoner will cease to be a prisoner'.

The room no longer seems so gloomy. Though dumb objects are confined here, the cell doors are perpetually open.

'Have a look at that', says Hamish, pointing across the room to a large poster hanging framed behind glass. 'When I was writing about Henry Marson, I said that on this poster the tension between object and individuality is manifest'.

The poster—it must be well over a metre tall—is headed 'Half Yearly Return of Run-a-way Convicts 1st of January 1851'. In columns are lists of more than 450 prisoners, and even this is not a complete itemisation of the state's lost property.[5] The names of 204 convicts who absconded before January 1830 have been struck off (like bad debts), we are told in an introduction to the

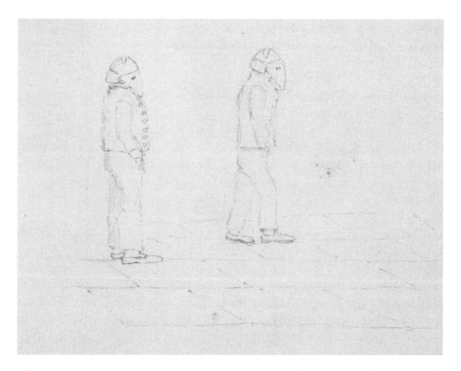

The cap worn by the separate treatment prisoners *in the exercise yard of the model prison, Port Arthur, by Frederick Mackie,* c. *1853.*

list, along with a promise that a 'Reward of £2 will be paid for the apprehension of each Convict, with the exception of Females'. Nearly one in every hundred convicts sent to Van Diemen's Land seems to have disappeared. It's ironic that this 'wanted' poster should bear testimony to the fallibility of the 'system'. In the middle of the poster is Henry Marson, with his tattoo HH HH. Unwittingly, the Comptroller General of Convicts has broadcast a message of Marson's private passion for Hannah Harris.

Our eyes search the small print for other names we might recognise, and as our fingers move over the protective glass, we begin reading aloud the brief descriptions of convict and escape. While looking for Alexander, we have stumbled upon another cache of micro-narratives. We discover that convicts ran from all over the island, and under all sorts of circumstances. John Hill absconded from the services of the Lord Bishop of Tasmania, and was presumed to have departed the colony in the *Psyche*, 'being in charge of that vessel at the time she was taken from her moorings'. Where did this lone sailor go when he slipped away from the Lord Bishop's unfree flock? Did he board a Nantucket whaler in the Derwent, or head out into the Southern Ocean and turn north for the distant mainland? How apt that he should steal the *Psyche*, brilliantly emblematic of releasing mind as well as body. Did he get the joke?

John Clarkson kept his government-issue greatcoat when he abandoned his responsibility as one of the guard detailed to search outward-bound ships for clandestine human cargo. Scrambling on board the American ship *Julia*, the gamekeeper turned poacher and stole himself. Ann Burns was 'supposed to have left with her husband and gone to Geelong'. Perhaps her husband had her carried on board in a trunk, or spoke for her as well, as he assured the Port Officer that he had come free to the colony. A housemaid named Charlotte was released from double bondage as convict and wife when she absconded from 'her husband's residence at Launceston 8 November last and is supposed to have ___ the colony'. In the tear of brittle paper, the word 'left' has made its retrospective escape, along with Charlotte's surname, her mark as wife.

Run-a-way, the poster says, and that's what these men and women did with remarkable inventiveness. The six uncaptured pirates who stole the *Frederick* and unlike James Porter, remained free are here, as is 'James Gammel', one of the unsuccessful invaders of Canada transported with Linus Miller. The clerk has recorded Gemmel's Ayrshire accent, and misspelt the name. He was a native of Kilmarnock, he informed readers of an American newspaper, the *Plebeian*, almost nine years before the poster was printed. 'I am', he wrote in June 1842, 'the first of the Canadian or American prisoners taken at Prestcott, Windsor, or the Short Hills, who has been enabled by the blessings of a kind providence to escape from the terrors of that far distant prison-house'.[6] In 1851 Gemmel was in New York, not New South Wales as the official who composed the text for the poster had speculated.

The poster also suggests that escape from the Tasman Peninsula was far from rare. William Horsely ran from the Cascade probation station, John Berriman from Coal Point, and John Jones from Port Arthur, evading the guards and dogs at Eagle Hawk and East Bay Necks. Directly above Henry Marson's entry is one for John Mitford, a stonemason from the Midlands who absconded from Coal Point, Port Arthur, in 1840. Traces of his story are recorded as identifying marks. On his left side, the red-headed Mitford bears a compulsorily acquired D for 'deserter', to which he has added a dog and a fox. As eleven years have passed since Mitford ran or swam from Port Arthur, it would seem that the fox outwitted the dog. And what about the black whaler, John Harris, from the Rhode Island port of Providence? After his escape from Port Arthur, did he make his way back to the Derwent River and secure a passage on a short-manned whaler? The possibility is alluring, however remote, that as Providence delivered Gemmel to New York, it returned Harris to that Providence from which he came.

Everywhere we turn there is another story to be told, and yet we are both aware of the inevitable inadequacy of any retrospective attempt to piece together the elements for that telling. So it is with *Chain Letters*. Our attempts to reconstruct a convict past by narrating convict lives will inevitably be attacked. We will be accused of reading too much into the evidence, for being too imaginative (or insufficiently so), for seeking alternative meanings where perhaps there are none. We face the charge of speaking for convicts in our own latter-day middle-class voices.[7] Although the objection is understandable, we would argue that no order can be imposed on the past except within the historical consciousness of the present. While our dedication of this book to a neatly ordered list of convict names makes us uneasy, we resist the temptation to go back and mess it all up. If we retreated, then what? The alternative surrounds us in this museum at Port Arthur, a collection of objects bearing cautious curatorial labels. Here the past has been pegged out to speak for itself, but of course it does not speak in a neutral voice. Others too have been angered by the near absence of convict voices in historical sites like Port Arthur; in place of the silenced convict men and women, interpretation has been handed over to custodial powers redolent of the nineteenth-century state.[8] In this museum where visitors are not encouraged to think for themselves, we share with the current staff at Port Arthur a desire to sweep away the old displays and put up something else in their place. If the new installation, whatever it might be, is criticised for representing the past not as it was (whatever that might mean) but as the design team sees it, then why not welcome a public debate? Why not encourage people to handle the shards, and risk speculating?

The research for *Chain Letters* has been an exercise in seeking fragments of text and offering interpretations which are plausible within the shape of the individual convict's life and the specifics of his or her historical circumstances. Our deliberate speculations are signalled as such. There is no intentional blurring of boundaries between history and fiction. We write, however, from within the historical specificity of our time and place, and think through the discourses available. For some of the contributors to *Chain Letters*, the motive for narrating convict lives is primarily intellectual, combining the intrigue of detective work with the satisfaction of understanding how historical moments generate historical consciousness. For others, the research helps to make sense of the places where we live. Hamish and Lucy live in Tasmania as immigrants from elsewhere, Hamish from the United Kingdom and Lucy from the United States. For us, the research into a convict past helps us imagine ourselves into a place which once was foreign but now is becoming home.

For our first contributor, Terri-ann White, the personal rewards of research are even more direct. Terri-ann became a sleuth in the archives because she knew she came from a family with secrets, and she wanted to find out what

North view of Eagle Hawk Neck, which joins Tasman's Peninsula to the main land of Van Dieman's Land, *by Charles Hutchins and Charles Staniforth Hext, showing the dog line.*

they were. The story begins with her grandmother's grandfather, Theodore Krakouer, who arrived in the Swan River Colony in the 1850s and should be among those early settlers memorialised publicly as pioneers of the West. Why was everyone so determined to forget him? Terri-ann has refused the forgetting, and has assiduously collected pieces of a convict life which began with Krakouer's birth in the Polish city of Cracow, from which he [as a Jew] may have taken his surname. In 1848, he was convicted of theft in London and, after transportation to New South Wales and Tasmania had stopped, sailed late in the convict era to Western Australia. His story ends with death in the asylum for lunatics in Fremantle, an asylum now transformed into a museum (as is the asylum at Port Arthur) and also into the Fremantle Arts Centre. Here Terri-ann as a writer of fiction taught creative writing classes, and began to ponder how the fictions within her own family were made.

Like the other contributors to *Chain Letters*, she has pursued her story by tracking through the records kept by the authorities who administered the technologies of surveillance, the usual records of trials, transportation, some newspaper reports. She learned that the convict from Poland died a lunatic, and her first remarkable find was in the records of the asylum—two letters and a certificate. She then searched assiduously through admission books, casebooks, the surgeon's day journals. Although Theodore appeared only twice, the entries for his fellow patients helped Terri-ann imagine her dislocated ancestor within a community of lunatics.

In all of these documents Theodore Krakouer was the subject of power—the object on which a reporter's, or a convict administrator's, or a doctor's attention was momentarily focused before the next case was wheeled in. These were unpromising circumstances under which to rescue for memory some vestige of Theodore. As others have discovered, it is often the history of private life which is the most difficult to write despite its self-evident importance.[9] The traces of the past, particularly the traces of the convict past, are public documents, be they registers, or prison jackets or identity numbers. They tell us little or nothing about prisoners as fathers and mothers, though the legions of convict descendants stand testimony to this other convict story. In writing Theodore's story Terri-ann has faced a complex task in bridging the gaps between the brief recorded encounters which have trapped her grandmother's grandfather in the historical record. To admit, however, to the impossibility of imagining Theodore would be to leave him incarcerated within those nineteenth-century constructs which littered the pages of the archival record: 'Jew', 'thief', 'convict', 'patient'. Under these rules, her search—like our quest for Alexander—would have proved equally futile. Where we discovered nothing of Alexander but his official routine, she would have found little of Theodore but a medical diagnosis.

We were reminded of an old conundrum about the impossibility of being able to prove that such a thing as justice exists being 'matched by an urgent need to behave as if it does'.[10] Surely the same is true of history: The impossibility of ever knowing the past is matched by an equally urgent need to do just that. This, it struck us, is little more than human nature. We could no more conceive of Terri-ann closing her eyes and imagining that she had no past beyond that penned by a clerk's terse copperplate hand on an official report, than we could conceive of societies with no concept of where they had come from. We are condemned like some runaway convict to continue the search for a Providence that we will almost certainly never reach.

Note on conversion

Currency

12d (12 pence) = 1/–, 1s (1 shilling) = 10 cents
20s (20 shillings) = £1 (1 pound) = $2.00
21s = £1.1s = 1 guinea = $2.10

Weight

1 pound = 0.4 kilograms
14 pounds = 1 stone = 6.4 kilograms
8 stone = 1 hundredweight = 50.9 kilograms
20 hundredweight = 1 ton = 1.02 tonnes

Length

1 inch = 25.4 millimetres
12 inches = 1 foot = 30.5 centimetres
3 feet = 1 yard = 91.4 centimetres
22 yards = 1 chain = 20.1 metres
10 chains = 1 furlong = 201.2 metres
8 furlongs = 1 mile = 1.6 kilometres

Area

4840 square yards = 1 acre = 0.4 hectares
640 acres = 1 square mile = 259 hectares

Volume

1 pint = 0.57 litres
8 pints = 1 gallon = 4.55 litres
8 gallons = 1 bushel = 36.4 litres

2 In search of 'Jack Bushman'

1 Bushman, 'The Lash'.
2 Bushman, 'Passages from the Life of a Lifer'.
3 Duffield, 'The Life and Death of "Black" John Goff', pp. 30–2.
4 Bushman, 'Passages', 9 April 1859.
5 Quarterly Return of Public Labour and Expenditure of Materials at Moreton Bay, 25 December 1825–24 March 1826, 4/1917.1 SRNSW; Petrie, *Tom Petrie's Reminiscences of Early Queensland*, p. 226.
6 Entries for T. Brooks, 6 December 1827–5 October 1832, *Chronological Register of Convicts in the Moreton Bay Settlement 1826–42*, Microfilm SLQ; Bushman, 'Passages', 16 and 23 April 1859.
7 4 March 1850 and 3 April 1851, Magistrates' Bench, Brisbane, Small Debts, CPS1/1 and CPS1/AT1–2 Queensland State Archives.
8 *Moreton Bay Courier*, 15 and 26 June, and 3 July 1852; Thomas Dowse, 'Diary', 27 June 1852; 'Passages', 30 April 1859.
9 Index to Convict Ships, 1819–20, CP52/106, 42/2021 SRNSW; Alexander, *Mrs Fraser on the Fatal Shore*, pp. 58–60 and 140; 'Passages', 30 April 1859; Ryan, 'The Several Fates of Eliza Fraser', pp. 101–2.
10 'Passages', 30 April 1859.
11 Duffield, 'The Life and Death of "Black" John Goff', p. 33; Committal of T. Brooks, 7 December 1825, in Return of prisoners tried and sentenced by Supreme Court, Fiche 3298, X730, p. 27.
12 'Passages', 2 April 1859.
13 'Passages', 9 April 1859; Index to convict ships: *Grenada* I, CP52/106,43/201.
14 List of Prisoners on *Elizabeth and Henrietta* for Newcastle, 10 January 1822, 4/3504A SRNSW; Hughes, *The Fatal Shore*, pp. 433–8.
15 Commandant's Daily Diary (Port Macquarie), 8 February 1825, 4/5641 SRNSW; 'Passages', 9 April 1859.
16 'Passages', 16 and 23 April 1859.
17 Raymond Evans and Bill Thorpe, 'Commanding Men', pp. 24–26.
18 'Passages', 9 and 23 April 1859.
19 'Passages', 16 April 1859.
20 Duffield, '"Jack Bushman's" Convict Narrative', p. 23.
21 Jenkins, *Rethinking History*, p. 50.
22 Somers, 'Deconstructing and Reconstructing Class Formation Theory', p. 82.
23 Spivak, 'Can the Subaltern Speak?', pp. 285, 292.
24 Moran, *Jack Bushman's Short Stories*, pp. 3–6.
25 Moran, *Jack Bushman's Short Stories*, p. 7; Wilkes, 'Henry Arrowsmith' and 'The Raid', pp. 14–15.
26 See Moran, *Jack Bushman's Short Stories*.
27 Cryle, *The Press in Colonial Queensland*, p.23, and 'Writing and Local Identity', pp. 208–9.
28 Said, *Culture and Imperialism*, pp. 121–3.
29 Bushman, 'My Siesta Disturbed by Justicia'.
30 Cryle, *The Press in Colonial Queensland*, pp. 205, 208–9.
31 Bushman, 'The Press Gang'; Jones, *Chartism and the Chartists*, pp. 21–9.
32 *ADB* Vol. 6, pp. 230–1.
33 Cryle, *The Press in Colonial Queensland*, p. 210.
34 Smith, *The Scots of Moreton Bay*, pp. 31, 49, 126, 127, 145, 155–6, 251.

[35] Smith, *The Scots of Moreton Bay* pp. 147–8, 150–1; Cameron, *A Green and Pleasant Land*, pp. 28–9; H. Fanshawe *et al*, *Country Ways to Modern Days*, pp. 6, 10.

[36] Bushman, 'My Story of Moggill', 'My Siesta Disturbed by Justicia'; Cryle, *The Press in Colonial Queensland*, pp. 23, 35; Smith, *The Scots of Moreton Bay*, pp. 31, 204, 227, 246, 251.

[37] See *ADB* Vol. 6, pp. 398–9.

[38] 'Passages', 30 April 1859.

[39] See *ADB* Vol. 6, pp. 230–1, 398–9; Bushman, 'A Romance of Separation'.

[40] Bushman, 'My Story of Moggill'.

[41] Duffield, '"Jack Bushman's" Convict Narrative', p. 25; Evans, 'Review of . . . *Representing Convicts* . . .', pp. 191–2; Gosling, 'Thomas Dowse, Brisbane's Samuel Pepys', pp. 102–9; *ADB* Vol. 5, pp. 458–9.

[42] Petition of James Hardy Vaux, 18 May 1831, 31/3648 SRNSW.

[43] Duffield, '"Jack Bushman's" Convict Narrative', pp. 25, 32.

[44] 'Passages', 30 April 1859.

[45] 'Passages', 30 April 1859.

[46] 'Passages', 30 April 1859.

[47] 'Passages', 30 April 1859.

3 The search for the invisible man

[1] Evans & Thorpe, 'Power, Punishment and Penal Labour', pp. 98–100 and Nicholas (ed.), *Convict Workers*, pp. 3, 45.

[2] Davis narrative, Evans Norfolk Island Convict Papers, MS. Q168, *c.* 1842, DL.

[3] 31 George Davis per *Almorah* and *Pilot*, List of casualties at Macquarie Harbour Van Diemen's Land from the formation of the Settlement, 3 January 1822 to 8 March 1832 inclusive, entry for 28 March 1822, add 281, DL.

[4] 292 John Davis per *Elizabeth*, List of Prisoners who have Absconded from the Penal Settlement at Macquarie Harbour since the formation of the Settlement, B706, ML.

[5] 280 Thomas Davis per *Caledonia*, Muster list of prisoners at Macquarie Harbour, Van Diemen's Land taken by Lieut. Wright 3d Regiment (or Buffs) Commandant, on the 16th day of November 1824, add 568, DL and B706, ML.

[6] 197 John Davies per *Medway* (1), Alphabetical return of male and female prisoners at Macquarie Harbour for the quarter ending 31 March 1829, CO 280/20, PRO.

[7] 388 William Davis per *Ocean*, Return of male and female prisoners and their respective sentences at Macquarie Harbour for the quarter ending 30 September 1825, add 568, DL.

[8] Robinson (ed.), *Jack Nastyface, Memoirs of a Seaman*.

[9] Evans & Thorpe, 'Power, Punishment and Penal Labour', pp. 95, 98–100; see also 'In Search of "Jack Bushman"' in this volume.

[10] 297 John/Joseph Gough per *Marquis of Wellington*, Convict Indents, SRNSW and CON 13/2, p. 405, AOT.

[11] 297 John/Joseph Gough, CON 31/13, AOT.

[12] 314 Daniel McGee per *Claudine*, Musters and Other Papers Relating to Convict Ships, reel no. 2420, SRNSW; 150 Thomas Kent, per *Caledonia*, Musters and Other Papers Relating to Convict Ships, reel no. 2418, SRNSW; 1 James Roberts per *Fanny* and *Emu*, CON 23/1, AOT; 22 Thomas Yates per *General Hewitt*, CON 23/1, AOT; 96 Peter Keefe per *Castle Forbes*, CON 13/2, p. 46, AOT and 404 John Sharp per *Lord Hungerford*, CON 23/1, AOT. See also respective CON 31 entries for 1 May 1823.

[13] Rawlings, *Drunks, Whores and Idle Apprentices*, pp. 1–18.

[14] 382 Thomas Brain per *Medway*, CON 23/1 and CON 31/1 and 26 William Yates per *Lord Hungerford*, CON 23/1 and CON 31/45, AOT.

15 382 Thomas Brain per *Medway*, CON 23/1, AOT.
16 Reel 6023; x820 p. 356 and 6019, 4/3864 pp. 352–3, SRNSW.
17 CON 148, AOT.
18 CON 13/2, AOT.
19 27 Hans Olsen per *Guildford* (4), Musters and Other Papers Relating to Convict Ships, reel no. 2422, SRNSW.
20 *Hobart Town Gazette* 24 December 1824 and CO 280/20, PRO.
21 Hughes, *The Fatal Shore*, p. 226.
22 Sprod, *Alexander Pearce*, p. 10.
23 Lempriere, *The Penal Settlements of Van Diemen's Land*, p. 35.
24 24 John Ollery per *Coromandel*, HO/10/43, PRO; CON 31/29, AOT and add 281, ML.
25 *BPP*, XXII (1837–8) Minutes of Evidence, Surgeon Barnes.
26 Duffield, 'Jack Bushman's Convict Narrative', pp. 27–9.
27 Lempriere, *The Penal Settlements of Van Diemen's Land*, p. 45.
28 150 George Wray Elderidge, arrived free per *Caroline*, *Hobart Town Gazette*, 26 November 1824, CON 23/1, AOT.
29 150 George Wray Elderidge, CON 31/9, AOT.
30 See for example Jack Bushman's narrative and the discussion on Connor's narrative in 'Seven Tales for a Man with Seven Sides' in this volume.
31 *ADB* Vol. 2, pp. 184–6.
32 Robson, *Convict Settlers of Australia*; Shaw, *Convicts and the Colonies*; Clark, 'The Origins of the Convicts Transported to Eastern Australia'; Hirst, *Convict Society and its Enemies*; Hughes, *The Fatal Shore*; Robinson, *The Women of Botany Bay*.

4 Seven tales for a man with seven sides

1 Surgeon's Report, *Sarah*, Admin 101/66 PRO.
2 Muster Roll for the *Sarah*, CSO 5/19/398 AOT.
3 Fitzsymonds (ed.), *The Capture of the Frederick*, pp. 47–9.
4 Convict Conduct Register CON 23/1 AOT, and Musters and Other Papers Relating to Convict Ships, reel 2417 SRNSW.
5 Musters and Other Papers Relating to Convict Ships, reel 2417 SRNSW; Convict Conduct Register CON 31/34 AOT.
6 Fitzsymonds (ed.), *The Capture of the Frederick*, p. 74.
7 'The Convict', *Fife Herald*, 10 October 1844, p. 136.
8 'The Convict', *Fife Herald*, 6 February 1845, p. 204.
9 *The Recollections of a James Connor a Returned Convict containing an account of his sufferings in, and ultimate escape from New South Wales.*
10 Y-Le, *Recollections of a Convict*.
11 James Porter's Narrative, Colonial Secretary's Correspondence, CSO1/700/15339 AOT.
12 Hartwell, *The Economic Development of Van Diemen's Land 1820–1840*, pp. 156–7; Maxwell-Stewart, '*Convict Workers*, "penal labour" and Sarah Island: life at Macquarie Harbour, 1822–1834', pp. 142–62.
13 'The Convict', *Fife Herald*, 17 April 1844, p. 36.
14 Duffield, '"Jack Bushman's" Convict Narrative', pp. 27–9.
15 Y-Le, *Recollections of a Convict*, introduction.
16 James Porter's Narrative, Colonial Secretary's Correspondence, CSO 1/700/15339 AOT, and Fitzsymonds, *The Capture of the Frederick*, p. 52.
17 *Colonial Times*, 26 April 1827.
18 *ADB* Vol. 1, p. 355.
19 Porter, 'A Narrative of the Sufferings and Adventure . . .' *The Hobart Town Almanack*, p. 38.

20 *Tasmanian*, 5 May 1837.
21 *Tasmanian*, 5 May 1837.
22 Fitzsymonds, *The Capture of the Frederick*, p. 74 and Outward Despatches, Colonial Secretary's Correspondence CSO 33/32, and Executive Council Minutes, EC 4/6, minute 230 AOT.
23 Fitzsymonds, *The Capture of the Frederick*, pp. 72–3.
24 James Porter's Narrative, Evans Norfolk Island Convict Papers, MS. Q168 [typed copy], p. 31, DL.
25 James Porter's Narrative, Evans Norfolk Island Convict Papers, MS. Q168, DL.
26 Clarke, *For the Term of His Natural Life*, p. 274.
27 Robson, 'The Historical Basis of *For the Term of His Natural Life*', pp. 204–11.
28 Clarke, *For the Term of His Natural Life*, p. 79.
29 Clarke, *For the Term of His Natural Life*, pp. 55, 85.
30 Clarke, *For the Term of His Natural Life*, pp. 150–5.
31 For convicts as innocent and manly see Wood, 'Convicts', pp. 177–208.
32 Clarke, *For the Term of His Natural Life*, preface.
33 Hobart Town Bench Book 1827, Case 35, Tuesday 24 July, Tas. papers 268 ML.
34 James Porter's Narrative, Evans Norfolk Island Convict Papers, DL MS. Q168, *c*. 1842.
35 On convicts and beer consumption, see Hindmarsh, 'Beer and Fighting: Some Aspects of Male Convict Leisure in Van Diemen's Land', pp. 150–6.
36 CSO 1/700/15339, p. 112 AOT.
37 Harris, *The 1811 Dictionary of the Vulgar Tongue*.

5 Eliza Churchill tells . . .

1 *Plymouth, Devonport and Stonehouse Herald*, 23 April 1840.
2 *Plymouth, Devonport and Stonehouse Herald*, 18 April 1840.
3 Walsh & Hooton, *Australian Autobiographical Narratives*.
4 Report of the Committee of Enquiry into Female Convict Prison Discipline, CSO 22/50 AOT.
5 Conditional Pardons Registered by the Colonial Secretary 1826–70 HO10/57 PRO.
6 Convict Appropriation List MM 33/7 AOT.
7 Report of the Committee of Enquiry into Female Convict Prison Discipline CSO 22/50, p. 295 AOT. See *Hobart Town Gazette*, 3 January 1818; Bartlett, 'The Launceston Female Factory', p. 115.
8 Description List of Convicts CON 19/1 AOT; Oxley, *Convict Maids*, p. 249.
9 Convict Conduct Register CON 40/2 AOT.
10 Franklin, *A Confidential Despatch*, pp. 20–1.
11 Report of the Committee of Enquiry into Female Convict Prison Discipline CSO 22/50, p. 293 AOT.
12 Report of the Committee of Enquiry into Female Convict Prison Discipline CSO 22/50, p. 294 AOT.
13 Report of the Committee of Enquiry into Female Convict Prison Discipline CSO 22/50, pp. 293–4 AOT.
14 Report of the Committee of Enquiry into Female Convict Prison Discipline CSO 22/50, p. 293 AOT.
15 See Bartlett, 'The Launceston Female Factory', p. 118.
16 Report of the Committee of Enquiry into Female Convict Prison Discipline CSO 22/50, p. 292 AOT.
17 Report of the Committee of Enquiry into Female Convict Prison Discipline CSO 22/50, p. 294 AOT.

[18] Report of the Committee of Enquiry into Female Convict Prison Discipline CSO 22/50, p. 292 AOT.
[19] Report of the Committee of Enquiry into Female Convict Prison Discipline CSO 22/50, p. 296 AOT.
[20] Convict Conduct Register 40/7 AOT, Tardif, *Notorious Strumpets and Dangerous Girls*, pp. 1176–7; Convict Conduct Register CON 46/6 AOT.
[21] Report of the Committee of Enquiry into Female Convict Prison Discipline CSO 22/50, p. 143 AOT.
[22] Report of the Committee of Enquiry into Female Convict Prison Discipline CSO 22/50, p. 387 AOT; Bartlett, 'The Launceston Female Factory', pp. 120–1; *Hobart Town Gazette* 18 March 1842.
[23] Kerr, *Design for Convicts*, p. 93.
[24] Correspondence, Colonial Secretary's Office, CSO 22/80/1750 AOT.
[25] Correspondence, Colonial Secretary's Office, CSO22/28/999, pp. 161, 174–6, 183 AOT.
[26] Correspondence, Colonial Secretary's Office, CSO 22/28/999, pp. 174–5 AOT.
[27] Correspondence, Colonial Secretary's Office, CSO 22/28/999, p. 177 AOT.
[28] Correspondence, Colonial Secretary's Office, CSO 22/28/999, p. 177 AOT.
[29] Correspondence, Colonial Secretary's Office, CSO 22/28/999, pp. 184–5 AOT.
[30] Correspondence, Colonial Secretary's Office, CSO 22/28/999, pp. 190–1 AOT.
[31] Correspondence, Colonial Secretary's Office, CSO 22/28/999, p. 187 AOT.
[32] Correspondence, Colonial Secretary's Office, CSO 22/28/999, pp. 192–3 AOT.
[33] Franklin, *A Confidential Despatch*, p. 20.
[34] Report of the Committee of Enquiry into Female Convict Prison Discipline CSO 22/50, p. 293 AOT.
[35] See Daniels, 'The Flash Mob', pp. 139–40; *Convict Women*, p. 148, 155–6, 173; Damousi, *Depraved and Disorderly*, p. 82.
[36] *Lancaster Gazette*, 21 March 1829.
[37] *Old Bailey Sessions' Papers*, 1829, p. 516.
[38] Convict Conduct Registers CON 40/9, CON 32/1, and CON 32/4 AOT.
[39] Convict Conduct Registers CON 40/9, CON 32/1 AOT.
[40] 'Female Factory', *Colonial Times* 12 May 1840.
[41] Report of the Committee of Enquiry into Female Convict Prison Discipline CSO 22/50, pp. 283–4 AOT.
[42] Report of the Committee of Enquiry into Female Convict Prison Discipline CSO 22/50, p. 382 AOT.
[43] Correspondence, Colonial Secretary's Office, CSO 22/80/1742, p. 5 AOT.
[44] Correspondence, Colonial Secretary's Office, CSO 22/28/999, p. 194 AOT.
[45] Correspondence, Colonial Secretary's Office, CSO 22/28/999, p. 194 AOT.
[46] Correspondence, Colonial Secretary's Office, CSO 22/28/999, pp. 194–6 AOT.
[47] Register of Marriages AOT.
[48] Frost, *No Place for a Nervous Lady*, 1999, pp. 196–222.
[49] Smith, *A Cargo of Women*, p. 14.

6 A Spanish convict . . .

[1] See Picton Phillipps, 'Margaret Catchpole's First Ride?', pp. 62–77.
[2] Sydney: Foster & Fairfax, General Printers, 1878. See Cameron, *My Two Servants* and *Centenary History of the Presbyterian Church in New South Wales*.
[3] Cameron, *Adelaide de la Thoreza*, pp. 5–6.
[4] Cameron, *Adelaide de la Thoreza*, p. 6.
[5] Cameron, *Adelaide de la Thoreza*, p. 7.

6 Cameron, *Adelaide de la Thoreza*, p. 8.
7 Cameron, *Adelaide de la Thoreza*, p. 8.
8 Cameron, *Adelaide de la Thoreza*, p. 10.
9 Cameron, *Adelaide de la Thoreza*, p. 11.
10 Cameron, *Adelaide de la Thoreza*, pp. 10, 11.
11 Cameron, *Adelaide de la Thoreza*, p. 14.
12 Cameron, *Adelaide de la Thoreza*, p. 15.
13 Cameron, *Adelaide de la Thoreza*, p. 16.
14 Cameron, *Adelaide de la Thoreza*, p. 17.
15 Cameron, *Adelaide de la Thoreza*, p. 18.
16 Cameron, *Adelaide de la Thoreza*, p. 19.
17 Cameron, *Adelaide de la Thoreza*, p. 21.
18 Cameron, *Adelaide de la Thoreza*, p. 22.
19 Cameron, *Adelaide de la Thoreza*, pp. 23–4.
20 Letter to Susan Ballyn.
21 Telephone communication with Susan Ballyn.
22 *Old Bailey Sessions' Papers*, 1829, p. 609.
23 *Old Bailey Sessions' Papers*, 1829, p. 609.
24 *Old Bailey Sessions' Papers*, 1829, p. 609.
25 *Old Bailey Sessions' Papers*, 1829, p. 609.
26 *Old Bailey Sessions' Papers*, 1829, p. 609.
27 Cameron, *Adelaide de la Thoreza*, p. 25.
28 Cameron, *Adelaide de la Thoreza*, p. 26.
29 Cameron, *Adelaide de la Thoreza*, pp. 26–8.
30 Cameron, *Adelaide de la Thoreza*, pp. 27–9.
31 Cameron, *Adelaide de la Thoreza*, pp. 29–30.
32 Cameron, *Adelaide de la Thoreza*, p. 31.
33 Cameron, *Adelaide de la Thoreza*, p. 32.
34 Cameron, *Adelaide de la Thoreza*, p. 35.
35 Cameron, *Adelaide de la Thoreza*, p. 35.
36 Reprinted as Alfred Smith, *Some Ups and Downs of an Old Richmondite*.
37 Smith, *Some Ups and Downs of an Old Richmondite*, p. 1.
38 Smith, *Some Ups and Downs of an Old Richmondite*, p. 145.
39 Smith, *Some Ups and Downs of an Old Richmondite*, pp. 1–2.
40 Smith, *Some Ups and Downs of an Old Richmondite*, p. 67.
41 Smith, *Some Ups and Downs of an Old Richmondite*, pp. 50–1. See Sam Broughton, Reminiscences of Richmond, MS 991.3/B, pp. 39, 26, ML.
42 Certificate of Baptism, New South Wales, 688/Vol. 49.
43 Smith, *Some Ups and Downs of an Old Richmondite*, pp. 6, 8, 11.
44 Certificate of Baptism, New South Wales, 808/Vol. 22.
45 Smith, *Some Ups and Downs of an Old Richmondite*, p. 135.
46 Smith, *Some Ups and Downs of an Old Richmondite*, p. 39.
47 Certificates of Baptism, New South Wales, 10704/Vol. 1C and 117/Vol. 15.
48 Correspondence from Individuals, New South Wales, CO 201/101 PRO, and Unregistered Original Letters, Correspondence to Colonial Secretary 1829, 4/2062 SRNSW.
49 Letter to Nicholson, 18 December 1829 and Nicholson letter to Colonial Secretary, 22 December 1829, Unregistered Original Letters, Correspondence to Colonial Secretary 1829, 4/2062 SRNSW, Convict Indent for *Lucy Davidson*.
50 Boyes, *The Diaries and Letters of G. T. W. B. Boyes*, p. 181.
51 Letter received by Sir Thomas Brisbane, quoted in Boyes, *The Diaries and Letters of G. T. W. B. Boyes*, note 19, p. 176; Cunningham, *Two Years in New South Wales*, pp. 113–

15; Macarthur Papers, Vol. 66, pp. 118–20, A 29962 ML; Marsden Papers, Vol. 1, pp. 334–7, and Piper Papers Vol. 1, pp. 487–9 ML.

52 Henry Antill as quoted in Fairfax, *Then and Now*, p. 150; Boyes, *The Diaries and Letters of G. T. W. B. Boyes*, p. 175; letter from Morton Pitt, Marsden Papers, Vol. 1, pp. 336–7 ML.

53 Certificate of Marriage, New South Wales 4235/Vol. 3; Register of Burial, New South Wales 3116/Vol. 22.

54 Antill, quoted in Fairfax, pp. 150–1.

55 *Sydney Gazette*, 31 May 1822; 15 November 1822; *Australian*, 10 February 1829.

56 Petition of Samuel McCrea, 21 December 1825, CSO 4/1791 SRNSW.

57 Marsden Papers, Vol. 1, pp. 334–7.

58 Cunningham, *Two Years in New South Wales*, pp. 113–14; Boyes, *The Diaries and Letters of G. T. W. B. Boyes*, p. 182.

59 Boyes, *The Diaries and Letters of G. T. W. B. Boyes*, p. 176.

60 Ticket of Leave Butts 36/469 and 36/948; Certificate of Freedom Butts 36/574 and 36/948 SRNSW; Smith, *A Cargo of Women*, pp. 89, 140.

61 Smith, *A Cargo of Women*, p. 124.

62 *New South Wales Government Gazette*, 14 November 1832, p. 403.

63 Certificate of Baptism, New South Wales 117/Vol. 15.

64 New South Wales Pioneer Index.

65 Certificate of Death, New South Wales.

7 'your unfortunate and undutiful wife'

1 Wylie, 'The Constitution of Archaeological Evidence: Gender Politics and Science', pp. 311–43; Kennedy & Davis, *Boots of Leather, Slippers of Gold*, pp. 15–26.

2 Letter reproduced, courtesy of Mrs Irene Hyde, Launceston, Cornwall.

3 Nicholas & Shergold, 'Human Capital and Irish Pre-Famine Emigration to England', pp. 158–77.

4 O'Grada, *Ireland*, p. 78.

5 Philips, *Crime and Authority in Victorian England*, p. 26.

6 Philips, pp. 25, 149.

7 Convict Indent for *Elizabeth and Henry* (2), CON 15/4; Convict Conduct Register CON 41/11 AOT.

8 Loudon, *The Tragedy of Childbed Fever*, p. 59.

9 Minute Book, Warwick Assizes, Midland Circuit 1846, ASSI 11/13 PRO.

10 Minute Book, Warwick Assizes, Midland Circuit 1846, ASSI 11/13 PRO.

11 *Warwick and Warwickshire Advertiser and Leamington Gazette*, 4 April 1846.

12 *Warwick and Warwickshire Advertiser and Leamington Gazette*, 4 April 1846; Convict Indent for *Elizabeth and Henry* (2) CON 15/4, Convict Conduct Register CON 41/11 AOT.

13 Prison Registers and Returns Millbank (female) 1846, HO 24/12/1 PRO.

14 Rudé, *Criminal and Victim*, p. 33.

15 Prison Registers and Returns Millbank (female) 1846, HO 24/12/1 PRO.

16 Surgeon's Report, *Elizabeth and Henry* (2), Admin 101 24/7 PRO.

17 Surgeon's Report, *Elizabeth and Henry* (2), Admin 101 24/7 PRO.

18 Surgeon's Report, *Elizabeth and Henry* (2), Admin 101 24/7 PRO.

19 Surgeon's Report, *Elizabeth and Henry* (2), Admin 101 24/7 PRO.

20 Surgeon's Report, *Elizabeth and Henry* (2), Admin 101 24/7 PRO.

21 Convict Conduct Register CON 41/11 AOT.

22 Convict Conduct Register CON 33/36; Description Lists of Convicts CON 18/34 AOT.

[23] Register of Marriage, 2 December 1850 AOT.
[24] Convict Indent for *Duchess of Northumberland* (1) CON 14/19 AOT.
[25] Convict Conduct Registers CON 33/36 and CON 41/11 AOT.
[26] Convict Conduct Register CON 41/11 AOT.
[27] Cotton, *Home Life in Van Diemen's Land*, p. 177.
[28] Cotton, *Home Life in Van Diemen's Land*, p. 177.
[29] Cotton, *Home Life in Van Diemen's Land*, p. 177.

8 'Stated This Offence'

[1] Maxwell-Stewart & Duffield, 'Skin Deep Devotions', pp. 118–21.
[2] See Anderson, 'The Genealogy of the Modern Subject', p. 176.
[3] Butlin, Cromwell & Suthern (eds), *General Return of Convicts in New South Wales 1837*, pp. 66–7.
[4] See Convict Conduct Registers CON 18/11 and CON 31/5 AOT; Convict Indent for *John*, F148 ML.
[5] Convict Conduct Registers CON 31/5 and CON 37/3 AOT.
[6] Eldershaw, *Guide to the Public Records of Tasmania, Section Three, Convict Department*, p. 7.
[7] Gates, *Recollections of a Life in Van Diemen's Land*, p. 40.
[8] Convict Conduct Register CON 31/5 AOT.
[9] Robson, *The Convict Settlers of Australia*, pp. 157–8.
[10] Convict Indent for *John*, F148 ML.
[11] Fyfe, *A History of Sierra Leone*, p. 125.
[12] Fyfe, *A History of Sierra Leone*, p. 178; Fyfe, *Sierra Leone Inheritance*, pp. 173–5.
[13] Fyfe, *A History of Sierra Leone*, p. 185.
[14] Convict Conduct Register CON 31/5 AOT; Convict Indent for *John*, F148 ML.
[15] Myers, *Reconstructing the Black Past*, ch. 7; Duffield, 'Skilled Workers or Marginalised Poor?', pp. 71–3.
[16] Fyfe, *A History of Sierra Leone*, p. 183.
[17] Fyfe, *A History of Sierra Leone*, pp. 127–31.
[18] Miller, *Way of Death*, pp. 508, 517–18, 681–2.
[19] Du Bois, *The Souls of Black Folk*.
[20] Davidoff & Hall, *Family Fortunes*, p. 25; Evans & Thorpe, 'Commanding Men', p. 19; Stepan, *The Idea of Race in Science*, p. 1.
[21] Convict Conduct Registers CON 31/5 and CON 37/3 AOT.
[22] Convict Conduct Registers CON 37/3 and CON 18/11 AOT; Convict Indent for *John* F148 ML.
[23] Bateson, *The Convict Ships*, pp. 362–3.
[24] Trial of Alexander Simpson, Slave Rebellion Trials Part IV, Portland Parish, CO 137/185, pp. 735–6; and A Return of Every Slave Tried and Convicted . . . during the Late Rebellion in Jamaica, CO 137/185, p. 716, PRO.
[25] Convict Indent for *Jupiter*, MM 33/2 AOT.
[26] Scott, 'Afro-American Sailors', pp. 37–52; Linebaugh and Rediker, 'The Many Headed Hydra', pp. 11–36; Duffield, '"I Asked How the Vessel Could Go?"', pp. 121–54.
[27] Slave Rebellion Trials, Parts I–IV, CO 137/185, PRO.
[28] Scott, *Domination and the Arts of Resistance*; O'Connor, Power and Punishment; O'Connor, 'A Zone of Silence', pp. 106–23; O'Connor, 'Buckley's Chance', pp. 115–28.
[29] Slave Rebellion Trials Part IV, Portland Parish, CO 137/185, pp. 737–9, PRO.
[30] Abstracts of Trials . . . during the Continuance of Martial Law in Jamaica, Case No. 10, Slave Rebellion Trials Part I, CO 137/185, p. 66, PRO.

[31] Evidence and cross-examination of George F. Smith . . . in General Court Martial of Alexander Simpson at . . . Port Antonio, Slave Rebellion Trials Part IV, CO 137/185, p. 737, PRO.
[32] Evidence of Alexander Ogilvy, Overseer of Fairy Hill, in Slave Rebellion Trials Part IV, CO 137/185, p. 738, PRO.
[33] Evidence and cross-examination of George F. Smith & Thomas Reilly, Slave Rebellion Trials Part IV, p. 737; and esp. evidence and cross-examination of Isaac Tomkins and William Ogilvy, p. 738, CO 137/185, PRO.
[34] Slave Rebellion Trials Part IV, CO 137/185, p. 738, PRO.
[35] Simpson, General Court Martial, Portland, 20 January 1832, in Slave Rebellion Trials Part IV, CO 137/185, p. 735, PRO.
[36] Abstract of Trials, case 10, in Slave Rebellion Trials Part 1, CO 137/185, p. 66, PRO.
[37] A Return of Every Slave Tried and Convicted . . . during the Late Rebellion in Jamaica, p. 716, and Abstracts of Trials . . . during the Continuance of Martial Law in Jamaica, Case No. 3, Slave Rebellion Trials Part I, CO 137/185, p. 64, PRO.
[38] Evidence of George Pussier . . . Portland, 20 January 1832, Slave Rebellion Trials Part IV, CO 137/185, p. 735, PRO.
[39] Evidence of Edward Francis, Slave Rebellion Trials Part IV, CO 137/185, p. 735, PRO.
[40] Convict Conduct Registers, CON 31/40 AOT.
[41] Convict Indent for *Jupiter*, MM 33/2 and Convict Conduct Register, CON 18/11 AOT.
[42] Convict Indent for *Jupiter*, MM 33/2 AOT.
[43] Convict Conduct Register, CON 31/40 AOT.
[44] See Duffield, 'Identity, Community and the Lived Experience of Black Scots', pp. 109–12; Duffield, 'From Slave Colonies to Penal Colonies', pp. 25–45.
[45] Tardif, *Notorious Strumpets and Dangerous Girls*, pp. 1442–3.
[46] Bush, *Slave Women in Caribbean Society*; Beckles, *Natural Rebels* and *Centering Women*.
[47] W. Hobhouse to R.W. Horton, 27 April 1827, CO 123/38/2499 PRO.
[48] Tardif, *Notorious Strumpets and Dangerous Girls*, p. 1442.
[49] Tardif, *Notorious Strumpets and Dangerous Girls*, pp. 1442–3.
[50] Maria sailed to England *per Arethusa*: Colonial Office Despatches, British Honduras, Superintendent Codd to Lord Goderich, Despatch 13, 1 November 1827, CO 123/38/98; Codd to Lord Goderich, Despatch 19, 1 December 1827, CO 123/38/226 PRO.
[51] Tardif, *Notorious Strumpets and Dangerous Girls*, pp. 1442–3.
[52] Compare Tardif, *Notorious Strumpets and Dangerous Girls*, with Convict Conduct Register CON 40/7 AOT.
[53] Tardif, *Notorious Strumpets and Dangerous Girls*, p. 1443.
[54] Trial of Maria Murray, Minutes of Proceedings, Hobart Quarter Sessions, Friday 13 July 1832, Lower Court 216 AOT (hereafter, LC 216 AOT).
[55] Evidence of Ann Davis, LC 216 AOT.
[56] LC 216 AOT.
[57] Reid, '"Contumacious, ungovernable and intolerable"', pp. 106–23.
[58] Reid, '"Contumacious, ungovernable and intolerable"', pp. 108, 112–13, 117–19; Daniels, *Convict Women*, chs. 5 & 6; Damousi, *Depraved and Disorderly*, pp. 59–61.
[59] Evidence of Ann Davis, LC 216 AOT.
[60] Evidence of William Peel, LC 216 AOT.
[61] Evidence of Ann Davis again called, LC 216 AOT.
[62] Evidence of Thomas Johnson, LC 216 AOT.
[63] Evidence of John Bodny and of Walter John Skey, LC 216 AOT.
[64] Register of Births RGD 32/2 AOT; *Tasmanian Pioneer Index*.
[65] Tardif, *Notorious Strumpets and Dangerous Girls*, p. 1443.

66 Ann Davis, examined by the prisoner, LC 216 AOT.
67 Reid, '"Contumacious, ungovernable and intolerable"'.
68 Register of Deaths, 26 June 1839, No. 190, RGD 35/1, AOT.
69 Convict Conduct Registers CON 23/1 and CON 18/8, AOT.
70 Convict Conduct Register CON 31/1, AOT.
71 Convict Conduct Registers CON 31/1, CON 23/1, CON 18/8, AOT.
72 Convict Conduct Register CON 31/1, AOT.
73 Dyster, *Servant and Master*, p. 1.
74 *ADB* Vol. 2, pp. 248–50; Shaw, *Sir George Arthur*, p. 5.
75 Shaw, *Sir George Arthur*, p. 111; *ADB* Vol. 2.
76 *ADB* Vol. 1, p. 343.
77 Neal, *The Rule of Law in a Penal Colony*, pp. 178–81.
78 Convict Conduct Register CON 31/1 AOT.
79 Atkinson, 'Writing about Convicts', pp. 16–28; Duffield, 'Daylight on Convict Lived Experience', p. 29.
80 See Duffield, '"I Asked How the Vessel Could Go?"'.
81 Linebaugh & Rediker, *The Many-Headed Hydra: The Hidden History of the Revolutionary Atlantic*.
82 Unpublished data from Duffield and Pybus.
83 Karl Marx, 'Digression: On Productive Labour', in *Theories of Social Value*, quoted in Francis Wheen, *Karl Marx*, pp. 308–9.

9 'These are but items in the sad ledger of despair'

1 PC 1/73 PRO and SR 4/1112.1A SRNSW.
2 Brown, *Meagre Harvest*, p. 5.
3 Hussey & Swash, *Horrid Lights*.
4 Convict Indent, *Marquis of Wellington*, SR 4/4005 SRNSW.
5 SR 4/4005 SRNSW.
6 Hansard, *Parliamentary Digest*, 1819, Part II, p. 89.
7 SR 4/4005 SRNSW.
8 Eastwood, *Government and Community in the English Provinces*, p. 92.
9 Arlott (ed.), *John Speed's England*, folios 31 and 32.
10 Page & Round (eds), *The Victoria History of the County of Essex*, vol. 2, p. 345.
11 Personal communication from Mrs Sandra Connelly.
12 SR 4/1112.1A, document 7, p. 18 SRNSW.
13 SR 4/1112.1A, document 7, p. 18 SRNSW.
14 Baxter (ed.), *General Muster and Land and Stock Muster of New South Wales, 1822*, p. 21, entry no. A00783.
15 SR 4/1112.1A, document 8, p. 1 SRNSW.
16 SR 4/1112.1A, document 7, p. 22 SRNSW.
17 Page & Round (eds), *The Victoria History of the County of Essex*, vol. 2, p. 344.
18 Mason, *Bartholomew Gazetteer of Places in Britain*.
19 SR 4/1112.1A, p. 19 SRNSW.
20 Sainty & Johnson (eds), *Census of New South Wales*, p. 40, entry no. B0263.
21 Atkinson, *Camden*, p. 30.
22 Bateson, *The Convict Ships*, p. 331.
23 Surgeon's Report, *Borneo*, Adm 101/12 PRO.
24 Register of Burials, Hobart Town, 1760/1828 AOT.
25 Register of Deaths, NSW 573/30 SRNSW.
26 PC 1/71, untitled document in the 'December' bundle for 1823 PRO.

[27] Spiers, *The Army and Society*, p. 52.
[28] *BPP*, 'Estimates and Accounts, 1821', XV, 'Army No. 3 Return of the amount of all deaths, Desertions and Discharges from the army; distinguishing Cavalry from the Infantry; from 25 December 1819 to 24 December 1820', pp. 129–30.
[29] See, for example, Petitions from Zaccariah Phillips; Gavin Thomas and the parents of 'Gaskell', PC1/67 (1819) PRO.
[30] *Statutes of United Kingdom of Great Britain and Ireland*, Vol. XI, 1827–1829, Cap IV, pp. 3–4.
[31] Kennedy, *Practical Remarks on the Proceedings of General Courts Martial*.
[32] Dinwiddy, 'The Early Nineteenth Century Campaign against flogging in the army', pp. 308–31.
[33] *Hansard*, 3rd Series, XCI, *c*. 1319.
[34] Dinwiddy, 'The Early Nineteenth Century Campaign against flogging in the army', p. 311.
[35] Foucault, *Discipline and Punish*, and Ignatieff, *A Just Measure of Pain*.
[36] Petition from John Sanderson, PC1/71 (1823) PRO.
[37] Taylor, 'General Order 18 March 1829 cited in *United Service Journal and Naval and Military Magazine*, [hereafter *USJ*] 1829, I, p. 512. Strachan, *Wellington's Legacy*, p. 46.
[38] Spiers, *The Army and Society*, p. 53.
[39] *USJ*, 1829, I, p. 512.
[40] *USJ*, 1849, pp. 349–50.
[41] *USJ*, 1829, I, p. 512.
[42] *USJ*, 1837, III, p. 324.
[43] Spiers, *The Army and Society*, p. 55.
[44] Spiers, *The Army and Society*, p. 53.
[45] PC1/71, December 1823 PRO.
[46] Douet, *British Barracks*, p. 109.
[47] *BPP Select Committee* 1836, Appendix, p. 72.
[48] Convict Indent, *Isabella*, SR 4/4004 SRNSW.
[49] Lloyd, *Australians from Wales*, 'Introduction'.
[50] SR 4/4006 SRNSW.
[51] Gray (ed.), *A History of Monmouthshire*, p. 35.
[52] Cited in Gray (ed.), *A History of Monmouthshire*, p. 37.
[53] Donovan, 'Descriptive Excursions through South Wales and Monmouthshire', p. 9.
[54] SR 4/1112.1A, document 36, p. 102 SRNSW.
[55] SR 4/1112.1A, document 36, p. 102 SRNSW.
[56] SR 4/1112.1A, document 36, p. 104 SRNSW.
[57] SR 4/1112.1A, document 36, p. 102 SRNSW.
[58] Baxter (ed.), *General Muster and Land and Stock Muster of New South Wales, 1822*, p. 174, entry no. A07587.
[59] Sainty & Johnson (eds), *Census of New South Wales*, p. 154, entry no. F1235.
[60] See for example, *Sydney Gazette*, 11 July 1822.
[61] SR 4/1112.1A, document 36, p. 102 SRNSW.
[62] SR 4/1112.1A, document 36, pp. 101–3 SRNSW.
[63] See Inga Clendinnen, 'Fellow Sufferers: History and Imagination', *Australian Humanities Review*, http://www.lib.latrobe.edu.au/AHR.
[64] Convict Marriage Banns 1826–41, SR 4/2127.2 SRNSW.
[65] *BPP* Select Committee 1831, VII, Minutes of Evidence before Select Committee on Secondary Punishments, Reply to Q. 748, p. 54.
[66] Entry for Richard Bankin, SR 4/4005 SRNSW.
[67] Carlyle, *Carlyle's Latter-Day Pamphlets*, p. 36.

10 Raising Lazurus

1 *Monitor* 7 April 1830.
2 Williams, *Pillars of Salt*, p. 9.
3 Tucker, *Ralph Rashleigh*, p. 214.
4 Faller, *Turned to Account*, p. 92.
5 Williams, *Pillars of Salt*, p. 9.
6 Williams, *Pillars of Salt*, p. 9.
7 *Monitor* 7 April 1830.
8 Faller, *Turned to Account*, p. 92.
9 *Monitor* 7 April 1830.
10 Cohen, *Pillars of Salt, Monuments of Grace*, p. 143.
11 *Monitor* 7 April 1830.
12 *Monitor* 24 September 1827, 27 March 1830; *Sydney Gazette*, 14 and 21 April 1829; *Monitor* 2 June 1830.
13 Faller, *Turned to Account*, p. 48.
14 Hughes, *Fatal Shore*, pp. 467–8; Richardson, *Death, Dissection and the Destitute*, p. 195; Gattrel, *The Hanging Tree*, pp. 84–5.
15 Malouf, 'Interview with David Malouf', p. 13.
16 *Monitor* 7 April 1830.
17 Petition of Robert Taylor, CSIL 4/1957 SRNSW.
18 Anne McMillan to Alexander Macleay, 1827, CSIL 4/1974 SRNSW.
19 Anne McMillan to Alexander Macleay, 1827, CSIL 4/1974 SRNSW.
20 Sophia Henshaw to James Henshaw, September 1826, enclosed with Petition of Sophia Henshaw, 24 February 1827, CSIL 4/1923 SRNSW.
21 John Milton, *Paradise Lost*, Book 1, Lines 73–4; Evans & Thorpe, 'Power, Punishment and Penal Labour'; O'Connor, Power and Punishment, chapter 1.
22 Petition of George Molyson, 19 November 1823, CSIL 4/1817 SRNSW.
23 Petition of George Molyson, 16 October 1827, CSIL 4/1957 SRNSW.
24 Griffin & Howell, *The Port Macquarie Winding Sheet*, p. 94.
25 Petition of James Henshaw, 10 January 1826, CSIL SRNSW.
26 Enclosed Innes to Macleay, 19 February 1827, CSIL 4/1923 SRNSW.
27 O'Connor, Power and Punishment, pp. 136–7.
28 Gatrell, *The Hanging Tree*, p. 197.
29 Petition of Elizabeth Davidson, 11 September 1828, CSIL 4/2047 SRNSW.
30 Petition of Margaret Connor, 19 November 1829, CSIL 4/2053 SRNSW.
31 Gattrel, *The Hanging Tree*, p. 197.
32 Zemon Davies, *Fiction in the Archives*, p. 64.
33 Zemon Davies, *Fiction in the Archives*, p. 64.
34 Petition of David Connor, 13 July 1831, A2.5, 146; Petition of Margaret McDermott on behalf of Margaret Connor, 6 November 1835, A2.9 222; Petition of Margaret Connor, February 1832, A.2.6, 597, Petitions Relating to Convicts at Moreton Bay, John Oxley Library.
35 Enclosed with Cross to Macleay, 17 September 1829, CSIL 4/2047 SRNSW.
36 From a selection of Port Macquarie petitions in CSIL 4/1817 SRNSW.
37 Petition of James Holland, 24 May 1830, CSIL 4/2076 SRNSW.
38 Petition of John Francis and Henry Taylor, 17 October 1827, CSIL 4/1951 SRNSW.
39 Gatrell, *The Hanging Tree*, p. 217.
40 Quoted in Zemon Davies, *Fiction in the Archives*, p. 63.
41 Petition of Warren Kerr, 24 April 1829, CSIL 4/2080 SRNSW.
42 Minutes to the Petition of Warren Kerr, 15 August 1828, CSIL 4/2080 SRNSW.

43 Scott, *Domination and the Arts of Resistance*, pp. 22–3.
44 Petition of Warren Kerr, 23 February 1822, CSIL 4/1817 SRNSW.
45 'Behind Bars', BBC Television, May 2000.
46 Petition of a Class of Prisoners at Port Macquarie Convicted by the Magistracy for Life, 9 March 1825, CSIL 4/1817 SRNSW.
47 Petition of a Class of Prisoners at Port Macquarie Convicted by the Magistracy for Life, 9 March 1825, CSIL 4/1817 SRNSW.
48 Scott, *Domination and the Arts of Resistance*, pp. x–xi; O'Connor, Power and Punishment, pp. 22–3; Said, *Culture and Imperialism*, p. 260.
49 Zemon Davies, *Fiction in the Archives*, p. 112.
50 Zemon Davies, *Fiction in the Archives*, p. 5.
51 Gatrell, *The Hanging Tree*, p. 198.
52 Extract from Police Records at Port Macquarie, November 1830, CSIL 4/2091.2 SRNSW.
53 Atkinson, *The Europeans in Australia*, p. 30.
54 Hely to Macleay, 9 September 1831, A2.6, 667–70, John Oxley Library; Ross, *The Fell Tyrant*.
55 McLiam & Wilson, *Eureka Street*, p. 314.

11 'Wherever I go I whill right to you'

1 See Convict Indent for *Eden* SRNSW.
2 Richard Taylor to George Taylor, 11 April 1840, DDX 505/1 Lancashire Record Office (hereafter, LRO), Convict Indent for *Eden* SRNSW.
3 *Preston Chronicle* and *Preston Pilot*, 4 July 1840.
4 *Preston Chronicle*, 4 July 1840. See Farnie, *The English Cotton Industry and The World Market*, pp. 83–5, Fleischmann, *Conditions of Life Among the Cotton Workers of South-eastern Lancashire, 1780–1850*, pp. 79–86; King, *Richard Marsden and the Preston Chartists 1837–1848*, pp. 1–29.
5 *Preston Chronicle* and *Preston Pilot*, 4 July 1840.
6 Simon Brown to George Taylor, 1 August 1840, DDX 505/7a LRO.
7 Richard Taylor to George Taylor, 11 April 1840, DDX 505/1 LRO.
8 Simon Brown to George Taylor, 1 August 1840, DDX 505/7a LRO.
9 Richard Taylor to George Taylor, 14 April 1840, DDX 505/2 LRO.
10 Richard Taylor to George Taylor, 14 April 1840, DDX 505/ 222 April 1840, DDX 505/3 LRO.
11 *Yorkshire Gazette*, 18 April 1840, DDX 505/5 LRO.
12 Simon Brown to Sarah Rawlinson [sister], 16 August 1840, DDX 505/8 LRO. See also Convict Conduct Register CON 33/9 AOT, Register of Deaths in the District of Longford, 1852, RGD 35/21 AOT, Inquest into the Death of William Rodgers, SC195, Number 2745 AOT.
13 Richard Taylor to George Taylor, 24 May 1840, and 1 June 1840, DDX 505/5a and DDX 505/5b LRO.
14 Richard Taylor to George Taylor, 1 June 1840, DDX 505/5b LRO.
15 Simon Brown to Sarah Rawlinson, 28 February 1841, DDX 505/14 LRO.
16 Simon Brown to George Taylor, 2 May 1841, DDX 505/6 LRO.
17 Richard Taylor to George Taylor, 3 July 1840, DDX 505/6, Richard Taylor to George Taylor, 9 July 1840, DDX 505/7 LRO.
18 Simon Brown to Sarah Rawlinson, 24 May 1841, DDX 505/16 LRO.
19 Convict Conduct Register, CON 33/13 AOT, Stephens, *Education, Literacy and Society*, pp. 266–7; Houston, *Scottish Literacy and the Scottish Identity*, pp. 162–92.
20 Simon Brown to George Taylor, 2 February 1856, DDX 505/24a and Simon Brown to George Taylor, 16 March 1856, DDX 505/25a LRO.

[21] Simon Brown to George Taylor, 8 July 1855, DDX 505/24 LRO.
[22] Richard Taylor to George Taylor, 12 September 1841, DDX 505/18 LRO.
[23] Richard Taylor to George Taylor, 12 September 1841, DDX 505/18; 22 August 1842, DDX 505/19; 8 July 1843, DDX 505/19a; 14 February 1845, DDX 505/20; 21 December 1845, DDX 505/20a LRO.
[24] Richard Taylor to George Taylor, 22 August 1842, DDX 505/19 LRO.
[25] Richard Taylor to George Taylor, 21 December 1845, DDX 505/20a LRO.
[26] 31 May 1849, DDX 505/21 and 12 November 1849, DDX 505/22 LRO.
[27] Richard Taylor to George Taylor, 30 September 1850, DDX 505/22a LRO.
[28] Atkinson, *Camden*, p. 33.
[29] Richard Taylor to George Taylor, 15 January 1851, DDX 505/23 LRO.
[30] Richard Taylor to George Taylor, 30 September 1850, DDX 505/22a; 15 January 1851, DDX 505/23 LRO.
[31] Richard Taylor to George Taylor, 30 September 1850, DDX 505/22a LRO.
[32] Richard Taylor to George Taylor, 30 September 1850, DDX 505/22a LRO.
[33] Richard Taylor to George Taylor, 15 January 1851, DDX 505/23 LRO.
[34] Simon Brown to unnamed uncle, 8 July 1855, DDX 505/24 LRO.
[35] See Register of Applications for Permission to Marry, CON 52/7; Register of Marriages, RGD 37/13, number 467; Convict Conduct Register 41/34 AOT.
[36] See Convict Conduct Register 41/34 AOT.
[37] See Register of Applications for Permission to Marry, CON 52/3, p. 26; Register of Marriages, RGD 37/9, number 81A AOT.
[38] Simon Brown to unnamed uncle, 8 July 1855, DDX 505/24 LRO.
[39] See Pol 220/1 p. 588 AOT.
[40] Simon Brown to George Taylor, 2 February 1856, DDX 505/24a LRO.
[41] Simon Brown to George Taylor, 2 February 1856, DDX 505/24a LRO; Robson, *A History of Tasmania*, pp. 526–8.
[42] See Isabella Risley to Simon Brown, 6 March 1856, DDX 505/25 LRO.
[43] See Atkinson, *Camden*, p. 146.
[44] Simon Brown to George Taylor, 2 August 1857, DDX 505/25. See also 8 March 1857, DDX 505/27; 2 May 1858, DDX 505/30a LRO.
[45] Simon Brown to George Taylor, 2 May 1858, DDX 505/30a LRO.
[46] Simon Brown to George Taylor, 2 May 1858, DDX 505/30a LRO.
[47] Simon Brown to George Taylor, 2 May 1858, DDX 505/30a LRO. Gardner, 'A Colonial Economy', pp. 57–64.
[48] Simon Brown to George Taylor, 8 March 1857, DDX 505/27 and 22 November 1857, DDX 505/30 LRO.
[49] Simon Brown to George Taylor, 8 March 1857, DDX 505/27 LRO.
[50] Simon Brown to George Taylor, 2 May 1858, DDX 505/30a LRO.
[51] Gernsheim, *The History of Photography*, pp. 224–9; Clarke, *The Photograph*, pp. 13–17.
[52] Simon Brown to George Taylor, 9 March 1859, DDX 505/28 LRO.
[53] Baker, *Death is a Good Solution*, pp. 66–8; Hughes, *The Fatal Shore*, pp. 134–5 and 143.
[54] See Hirst, *Convict Society and its Enemies*, p. 128; Kent & Townsend (eds), *Joseph Mason*, pp. 160–1; Smith, *A Cargo of Women*, pp. 151–63.
[55] O'Farrell, *Letters from Irish Australia*, and Fitzpatrick, *Oceans of Consolation*. See for comparative value, Fender, *Sea Changes*; Erickson, *Leaving England*; Erickson, *Invisible Immigrants*; Thomas & Eves, *Bad Colonists*.
[56] Richard Taylor to George Taylor, 14 April 1840, DDX 505/2 LRO.
[57] Richard Taylor to George Taylor, 1 June 1840, DDX 505/5b LRO.
[58] Simon Brown to George Taylor, 31 May 1841, DDX 505/17 LRO.
[59] Rawlings, *Drunks, Whores and Idle Apprentices*, pp. 1–18.

[60] Egan, *Patterns of Experience in Autobiography*, pp. 3–14 and 170–98; Thomas & Eves, *Bad Colonists*, pp. 83–7; Vincent, *Bread, Knowledge and Freedom*, pp. 4–7.
[61] Richard Taylor to George Taylor, 4 May 1840, DDX 505/4 LRO.
[62] Richard Taylor to George Taylor, 4 May 1840, DDX 505/4 LRO. See also DDX 505/4a and DDX 505/20a LRO.
[63] Simon Brown to Sarah Rawlinson, 6 November 1840, DDX 505/12 LRO.
[64] Richard Taylor to George Taylor, 21 December 1845, DDX 505/20a LRO.
[65] Baker, *Death is A Good Solution*, p. 68.
[66] Vincent, *Bread, Knowledge and Freedom*, pp. 40–1.
[67] McLeod, *Religion and the Working Class in Nineteenth-Century Britain*, pp. 14–36; Andrews, *Methodism and Society*, pp. 56–92.
[68] Richard Taylor to George Taylor, 22 April 1840, DDX 505/3 LRO; Richard Taylor to George Taylor, 1 June 1840, DDX 505/5b LRO. See also Branch-Johnson, *The English Prison Hulks*, pp. 125–9.
[69] See DDX 505/18 LRO.
[70] See 2874 Simon Brown, *per David Clarke*, CON 33/13 AOT.
[71] Fender, *Sea Changes*, pp. 64 and 353–6; Erickson, *Invisible Immigrants*, pp. 4–9; D. Fitzpatrick, *Oceans of Consolation*, pp. 20–30; O'Farrell, *Letters from Irish Australia*, pp. 10–18.
[72] This theme has been suggested in Haines, Kleinig, Oxley & Richards, 'Migration and Opportunity', pp. 235–63.
[73] Meredith, 'Full Circle?', pp. 20–1.
[74] Richard Taylor to George Taylor, 4 May 1840, DDX 505/4 LRO.
[75] Simon Brown to George Taylor, 13 September 1840, DDX 505/10 LRO. See also Simon Brown to Sarah Rawlinson, 4 October 1840, DDX 505/11 LRO.
[76] See O'Farrell, *Letters from Irish Australia*, p. 17; Thomas & Eves, *Bad Colonists*, pp. 1–7; Frost, *No Place for a Nervous Lady*, pp. 4–6; Fitzpatrick, *Oceans of Consolation*, p. 20.
[77] Millett, 'Leaden Hearts', pp. 5–30; Bradley & Maxwell-Stewart, 'Embodied Explorations', pp. 183–203.
[78] Parkin, 'Mementoes as Transitional Objects in Human Displacement', pp. 303–20.
[79] Richard Taylor to George Taylor, 22 August 1842, DDX 505/19 LRO.
[80] Vincent, *Literacy and Popular Culture*, pp. 34–41.
[81] Donnelly, '"When This You See Remember Me"', p. 26; *The Dillingham Convict Letters*.

12 Dr Martin and the Forty Thieves

[1] Journal of George Walker, B708–1, p. 211 ML.
[2] Journal of George Walker, B708–1, pp. 210–4 ML.
[3] Caplan, '"Speaking Scars"', pp. 109 and 121.
[4] As quoted in Bradley, 'Body Commodification? Class and Tattoos in Victorian Britain', p. 138.
[5] Precognition against David Young and Roderick Ross (Theft by Housebreaking), April 1845, AD14/45/120 SRO.
[6] Convict Conduct Register, CON 33/74 AOT.
[7] Convict Conduct Register, CON 33/74 AOT.
[8] Millett & Lane, 'Known Love Tokens', p. 107.
[9] Convict Conduct Register, CON 33/74 AOT.
[10] Convict Conduct Register, CON 33/74 AOT.
[11] Convict Conduct Registers CON 33, CON 23, CON 18 AOT.
[12] Convict Conduct Register CON 23/1 AOT.
[13] Bradley & Maxwell-Stewart, 'Embodied Explorations', p. 184.

[14] Report of the Arrival in Hobart Town of the *Elizabeth*, CSO 1/576/13043, pp. 53–5, Convict Conduct Registers CON 31/1 and CON 18/6 AOT.
[15] Maxwell-Stewart & Duffield, 'Skin Deep Devotions', p. 128.
[16] Convict Conduct Register CON 18/6 AOT.
[17] Convict Conduct Registers CON 31/26 and CON 18/6 AOT.
[18] Duffield, 'Problematic Passages', pp. 27–9.
[19] Dyster, 'Transported Workers', pp. 84–92 and Mayhew, *London Labour and the London Poor*.
[20] Bateson, *The Convict Ships*, p. 348.
[21] Surgeon's Report for the *Elizabeth* ADM 101/24 AOT.
[22] Report of the Arrival in Hobart Town of the *Elizabeth*, CSO 1/576/13043, pp. 53–5, AOT.
[23] See Daniels, *Convict Women*, p. 198.
[24] Millett & Lane, 'Known Love Tokens', p. 111.
[25] Donnelly, 'A Bracelet of Bright Haire', p. 55.
[26] Millett & Lane, 'Known Love Tokens', pp. 86–7 and Sheppard, 'Catalogue of Love Tokens', pp. 116–17.
[27] Convict Conduct Registers CON 31/29, CON 31/45 and CON 27/4 AOT.
[28] Papers accompanying the transport *Georgina* CSO 1/390/8829 AOT.
[29] Donnelly, '"When This You See Remember Me"', pp. 23–37.
[30] Coleman-Smith & Pearson, *Excavations in the Donyatt Potteries*, pp. 289–305; Sotheby's, *Early English and Continental Ceramics and Glass*, lot 385, p. 155; Towner, *Creamware*, p.129; Morris, *Victorian Table Glass and Ornaments*, p. 73.
[31] Bedford, *Old English Lustre Ware*, p. 57.
[32] Stanley, '"Huzza, My Boys, for Botany Bay!"', p. 59.
[33] Report of the Arrival in Hobart Town of the *Elizabeth*, CSO 1/576/13043, pp. 53–5, AOT.
[34] Stanley, '"Huzza, My Boys, for Botany Bay!"', p. 58.
[35] Mortlock, *Experiences of a Convict Transported for Twenty-One Years*, p. 61.
[36] Donnelly, 'A Bracelet of Bright Haire', p. 61.
[37] See also Caplan, '"Speaking Scars"', pp. 112–13, 133.

13 Alexander and the mother of invention

[1] Bateson, *The Convict Ships*, pp. 370–1, 394.
[2] Convict Conduct Register CON 33/110 AOT.
[3] See for example Anon, *A True History of Bernard Reilly*, p. 4; Baker, *Death is a Good Solution*, pp. 3–5 and Rawlings, *Drunks, Whores and Idle Apprentices*, pp. 1–18.
[4] 'The Convict', *Fife Herald*,10 October 1844, p. 136.
[5] Daniel's Narrative, Evans Norfolk Island Convict Papers, *c.* 1842–67, MS Q168, pp. 2–3, DL.
[6] George Palmer's Narrative, Evans Norfolk Island Convict Papers, p. 1.
[7] James Porter's Narrative, Evans Norfolk Island Convict Papers, p. 1.
[8] Mortlock, *Experiences of a Convict*, pp. 39–40, 180.
[9] Jones's Narrative, Evans Norfolk Island Convict Papers, pp. 2–3.
[10] Duffield, 'Problematic Passages', p. 27.
[11] Dickens, *Hard Times for These Times*; Engels, *The Condition of the Working Class*.
[12] *The New Statistical Account of Scotland*, pp. 25–6; Dawson, *An Abridged Statistical History of Scotland*, p. 462.
[13] Watley, Swinfen & Smith, *The Life and Times of Dundee*, p. 105.
[14] Green, *Scotland 100 Years Ago*, p. 162.
[15] Watley, Swinfen & Smith, *The Life and Times of Dundee*, p. 108.
[16] *Dundee, Perth and Cupar Advertiser*, 19 January 1847.

Records held by State Records New South Wales

Certificate of Freedom Butts
Commandant's Daily Diary (Port Macquarie)
Convict Indents 1788–1842
Copies of Conditional Pardons Registered by the Colonial Secretary 1826–70
Index to Certificates of Freedom 1823–69
Index to the Colonial Secretary's Office Correspondence, Convicts and Others, 1826–47
Index to the Colonial Secretary's Papers, 1788–1825
Index to Convict Ships, 1819–20
List of Prisoners on *Elizabeth and Henrietta* for Newcastle
Musters and Other Papers Concerning Convict Ships
Quarterly Returns of Public Labour and Expenditure of Materials at Moreton Bay
Registers of Births, Deaths, Burials and Marriages (collated as *New South Wales Pioneer Index*)
Registers of Convicts' Applications to Marry, 1825–51
Registers of Convict Marriage Banns, 1826–41
Return of Prisoners Tried and Sentenced by Supreme Court
Unregistered Original Letters, Correspondence to Colonial Secretary, 1826–31
Registers of Certificates of Freedom, 1810–33
Registers of Tickets-of-Leave, 1824–33
Ticket-of-Leave Butts, 1827–75
Colonial Secretary's Correspondence (and Index) 1788–1825

Records held by the Public Record Office (London)

Alphabetical Return of Male and Female Prisoners at Macquarie Harbour, 1829
Colonial Office Despatches, British Honduras
Colonial Office Despatches, Van Diemen's Land
Conditional Pardons Registered by the Colonial Secretary, 1826–70
Correspondence from Individuals, New South Wales
Muster of Convicts in Van Diemen's Land, 1823
Musters and Other Papers Relating to Convict Ships
Prison Registers and Returns, Millbank (Female), 1846
Privy Council Records
Return of Every Slave Tried and Convicted . . . During the Late Rebellion in Jamaica
Slave Rebellion Trials Parts I–IV
Surgeon Superintendents' Reports for Australia Bound Convict Transports

Records, manuscripts etc. held in other collections

Account of the Court of Special Commission at Niagara, Sheriff Alexander Hamilton Papers, National Archives of Canada
Chronological Register of Convicts in the Moreton Bay Settlement 1826–42, John Oxley Library, State Library of Queensland
Dowse, Thomas, Diary, Applied History Centre, University of Queensland
Letters 1840–58 of Step-brothers Richard Taylor and Simon Brown, Lancashire Record Office
Magistrate's Bench, Brisbane, Small Debts, Queensland State Archives
O'Connor, Tamsin, Power and Punishment the Limits of Resistance, The Moreton Bay Penal Settlement, 1824–1842, BA Hons thesis, University of Queensland, 1994
Petitions Relating to Convicts at Moreton Bay, John Oxley Library, State Library of Queensland
Precognitions, Perth Spring Circuit 1847 and Inverness Spring Circuit 1845, Scottish Record Office

Official and government sources

British Parliamentary Papers, Select Committees
British Parliamentary Papers, 1831, VII, Minutes of Evidence before Select Committee on Secondary Punishments
British Parliamentary Papers, Estimates and Accounts
Gaceta Oficial
Hansard, *Parliamentary Digest*
The New Statistical Account of Scotland
Old Bailey Sessions' Papers
Statutes of United Kingdom of Great Britain and Ireland, Vol. XI 1827–1829

Newspapers and periodicals

Australian
Colonial Times
The Colonist
Cornwall Chronicle
Dundee, Perth and Cupar Advertiser
The Fife Herald
Hobart Town Courier
Hobart Town Gazette
Lancaster Gazette
Launceston Advertiser
Launceston Examiner
Moreton Bay Courier
New South Wales Government Gazette
Northern Warder
The Plebeian
Plymouth, Devonport and Stonehouse Herald
Preston Chronicle
Preston Pilot
Scots Times
Sydney Gazette
Sydney Herald
Tasmanian
United Service Journal and Naval and Military Magazine
Warwick and Warwickshire Advertiser and Leamington Gazette
Yorkshire Gazette

Published sources

Alexander, Michael, *Mrs Fraser on the Fatal Shore*, Michael Joseph, London 1971.
Anderson, Clare, 'The Genealogy of the Modern Subject: Indian convicts in Maritius, 1814–1853', in I. Duffield & J. Bradley (eds), *Representing Convicts*, Leicester University Press, London 1997, pp. 164–82.
Andrews, Stuart, *Methodism and Society*, Longman, London 1970.
Anon., *A True History of Bernard Reilly*, National Library of Australia, Canberra 1988.
Anon., *A Description of Sydney, Parramatta, Newcastle, etc., Settlements in New South Wales, with some account of the Manners and Employment of the Convicts, in a*

Picton Phillipps, Tina, 'Margaret Catchpole's First Ride?' in I. Duffield & J. Bradley (eds), *Representing Convicts*, Leicester University Press, London 1997, pp. 62–77.

Porter, James, 'A Narrative of the Sufferings and Adventure . . .' *The Hobart Town Almanack and Van Diemen's Land Annual*, Hobart 1838.

[Porter, James], *The Recollections of a James Connor a Returned Convict containing an account of his sufferings in, and ultimate escape from New South Wales*, Cupar, Fife 1845.

Rawlings, Philip, *Drunks, Whores and Idle Apprentices: Criminal Biographies of the Eighteenth Century*, Routledge, London 1992.

Reid, Kirsty, '"Contumacious, ungovernable and intolerable"; Convict Women and Workplace Resistance, Van Diemen's Land, 1820–1839', in I. Duffield and J. Bradley (eds), *Representing Convicts*, Leicester University Press, London 1997, pp. 106–23.

Richardson, Ruth, *Death, Dissection and the Destitute*, Penguin, London 1988.

Robinson, Portia, *The Women of Botany Bay: A Reinterpretation of the Role of Women in the Origins of Australian Society*, Macquarie Library, North Ryde, NSW 1988.

Robinson, William (ed.), *Jack Nastyface, Memoirs of a Seaman*, Naval Institute Press, Annapolis, Md. 1983.

Robson, L. L., *The Convict Settlers of Australia: An Enquiry into the Origin and Character of the Convicts Transported to New South Wales and Van Diemen's Land 1787–1852*, Melbourne University Press, Carlton 1965.

——, 'The Historical Basis of *For the Term of His Natural Life*', *Australian Literary Studies*, vol. 1, 1963, pp. 204–11.

——, *A History of Tasmania*, vol. 1, Oxford University Press, Melbourne 1983.

Ross, William, *The Fell Tyrant or the Suffering Convict*, J. Ward, London 1836.

Rudé, George, *Criminal and Victim: Crime and Society in Early Nineteenth Century England*, Oxford University Press, Oxford 1985.

——, *Protest and Punishment*, Oxford University Press, Oxford 1978.

Ryan, J. S. 'The Several Fates of Eliza Fraser', *Journal of the Royal Historical Society of Queensland*, vol. 11, 1983, pp. 88–112.

Said, Edward, *Culture and Imperialism*, Vintage, London 1994.

Sainty, Malcolm R. & Johnson, Keith A. (eds), *Census of New South Wales: 1828*, Library of Australian History, Sydney 1985.

Scott, James C., *Domination and the Arts of Resistance: Hidden Transcripts*, Yale University Press, New Haven, Conn. & London 1990.

Scott, Julius S., 'Afro-American Sailors and the International Communication Network: The Case of Newport Bowers', in Colin Howell & Richard Twomey (eds), *Jack Tar in History*, Acadiensis Press, Fredericton, New Brunswick 1991.

Shaw, A. G. L., *Convicts and the Colonies: A Study of Penal Transportation from Great Britain and Ireland to Australia and other Parts of the Empire*, Faber, London 1966.

——, *Sir George Arthur*, Melbourne University Press, Melbourne 1980.

Sheppard, T., 'Catalogue of Love Tokens, and other Engraved Pieces in the Hull Museum', *Quarterly Record of Additions, Hull Museum*, no.128, 1922, pp.116–17.

Sidney, Sidney, 'Three Colonial Epochs', *Household Words*, vol. 4, 1852, pp. 433–8.

Smith, Alfred, *Some Ups and Downs of an Old Richmondite as Chronicled by Robert Farlow in the Windsor–Richmond Gazette 1909–10*, Nepean Family History Society, Emu Plains, NSW *c.* 1991.

Smith, Babette, *A Cargo of Women: Susannah Watson and the Convicts of the 'Princess Royal'* (1988), Pan Macmillan, Sydney 1992.

Smith, J. M., *The Scots of Moreton Bay, 1841–1859*, Church Archivist Press, Brisbane 2000.

Somers, M. 'Deconstructing and Reconstructing Class Formation Theory: Narrativity, Rational Analysis and Social Theory' in J.R. Hall (ed.), *Reworking Class*, Cornell University Press, New York 1997, pp. 73–105.

Sotheby's, *Early English and Continental Ceramics and Glass*, Sothebys, London 1989.

Spiers, Edward M., *The Army and Society, 1815–1914*, Longman, London 1980.

Spivak, Gayatri, 'Can the Subaltern Speak?' in C. Nelson & L. Grossberg (eds), *Marxism and the Interpretation of Culture*, University of Illinois Press, Urbana 1988, pp. 271–313.

Sprod, Dan, *Alexander Pearce of Macquarie Harbour: Convict–Bushranger–Cannibal*, Cat & Fiddle Press, Hobart 1977.

Stanley, Peter, '"Huzza, My Boys, for Botany Bay!" The Soldier's Farewell', *Wartime*, vol. 4, 1998.

Stepan, Nancy, *The Idea of Race in Science*, Macmillan, London 1982.

Stephens, William Brewer, *Education, Literacy and Society, 1830–70: The Geography of Diversity in Provincial England*, Manchester University Press, Manchester 1987.

Strachan, Hew, *Wellington's Legacy: Reform of the British Army 1830–1854*, Manchester University Press, Manchester 1984.

Tardif, Phillip, *Notorious Strumpets and Dangerous Girls*, Angus & Robertson, Sydney 1990.

Thomas, Nicholas & Eves, Robert, *Bad Colonists: The South Seas Letters of Vernon Lee Walker and Louis Becke*, Duke University Press, Durham & London 1999.

Towner, Donald, *Creamware*, Faber, London 1978.

Tucker, James, *Ralph Rashleigh*, Angus & Robertson, Sydney 1952.

Vincent, David, *Bread, Knowledge and Freedom: A Study of Nineteenth Century Working Class Autobiography*, Europa, London 1981.

——, *Literacy and Popular Culture, England 1750–1914*, Cambridge University Press, Cambridge 1989.

Wait, Benjamin, *Letters From Van Diemen's Land, Written During Four Years Imprisonment for Political Offences Committed in Upper Canada*, Buffalo 1843, republished as *The Wait Letters*, Porcepic Press, Ontario 1976.

Walsh, Kay & Hooton, Joy, *Australian Autobiographical Narratives: An Annotated Bibliography*, vol. 1, 1850, Australian Scholarly Editions Centre & National Library of Australia, Canberra 1993.

Watley, Christopher A., Swinfen, David B. & Smith, Annette M. *The Life and Times of Dundee*, John Donald, Edinburgh 1993.

Wheen, Francis, *Karl Marx*, Fourth Estate, London 1999.

Wilkes, William, 'Henry Arrowsmith', 'The Raid', *The Queensland Magazine*, 1862, reprinted in J. Campbell, *The Early Settlement of Queensland and Other Articles*, Ipswich 1875, pp. 14–15.

Williams, Daniel E., *Pillars of Salt: An Anthology of Early American Criminal Narratives*, Madison House, Madison, Wisc. 1993.

Wood, George A., 'Convicts', *Journal of the Royal Australian Historical Society*, vol. 7, 1922, pp. 177–208.

Wylie, Alison, 'The Constitution of Archaeological Evidence: Gender Politics and Science', in P. Galison & D. J. Stump (eds), *The Disunity of Science*, Stanford University Press, Stanford 1996.

Y-Le, *Recollections of a Convict and Miscellaneous Pieces by Y-Le*, Montreal 1847.

Zemon Davies, Natalie, *Fiction in the Archives: Pardon Tales and Their Tellers in Sixteenth-Century France*, Stanford University Press, Stanford 1987.